THE LONG WALK

A History of the Navajo Wars, 1846-1868

A History of the Navajo Wars, 1846-68

The Long Walk

by

Lynn R. Bailey

Westernlore Press . . . 1988 . . . Tucson, Arizona

Library of Congress No. 64-23585
ISBN 0-87026-047-2

PRINTED IN UNITED STATES OF AMERICA BY WESTERNLORE PUBLICATIONS

To My Father

INTRODUCTION

E XACTLY one hundred years ago commenced one of the
most pathetic and tragic episodes in the history of Anglo-
Indian relations. Under the ruthless direction of General
James H. Carleton and Colonel Christopher "Kit" Carson, the
Navajo Indians of New Mexico were hopelessly and relent-
lessly pursued, rounded up and driven to a wretched disease-
ridden reservation on the banks of the Rio Pecos, in east-
central New Mexico — the infamous Bosque Redondo.

No single cause can be attributed to this event in Navajo
history known as the Long Walk. The lust for wealth on the
part of these Indians, who reckoned their status in terms of
sheep and horses; the insidious slave raids, encroachment of
New Mexican sheepmen, and the stupid and careless administration of Indian and military affairs during the first two
decades of Anglo-American control of New Mexico, were all
contributing factors to putting the Navajos upon the long
road to *Hwelte* — as these people called the Bosque Redondo. And it is the portrayal of these events and factors
leading to this traumatic episode in Navajo history that this
book is devoted.

Because of the tremendous amount of erroneous information pertaining to Navajo history between inception of Anglo-
American occupation of New Mexico until the tribe's re-

lease from Bosque Redondo, this book was undertaken with the idea of providing a well documented framework upon which future ethnohistorians and anthropologists could build. No attempt, however, has been made to portray Navajo history during the Spanish and Mexican periods. Perhaps this seems neglectful, for certainly events during those years had a direct bearing upon Navajo-Anglo American relations. The task of deciphering fragmentary Spanish documents and fitting together the puzzle of Navajo history for those early years has been left for a later date. Likewise, only cursory examination has been given the four years which Navajos spent at Bosque Redondo. These were years filled with hardships and misery, during which time the tribe was but a political pawn in the hands of military and government officials. To do justice to the Fort Sumner period in the life of the Navajo, would require a volume of considerable size — a volume now in preparation by the author.

The writing of any book — either fiction or factual — is never done solely alone. Although thousands of hours are devoted by an author to research, writing, editing and proofreading, additional time is spent consulting with persons whose vital knowledge cannot be overlooked — and it is to these people that an everlasting debt of gratitude is owed. To Dr. John Alexander Carroll, of the University of Arizona, in whose courses the seeds of this study were germinated, a heart full of thanks and admiration is here expressed. To Dr. Arthur Woodward, of Patagonia, Arizona, who kept the author from "growing complacent," goes the sincerest appreciation. Without the helpful cooperation of the staff of the Navajo Tribal Land Claims Office this book would never have gotten beyond the planning stage. Tribal archaeologists, Lee Correll, David Brugge and Dr. David DeHarport, as well as Title Examiner, Roy E. Bennett, kindly furnished copies of important documents from the immense tribal historical files at Window Rock. The staff of the Army and Navy

Branch of the National Archives have been particularly helpful in ferreting-out elusive research materials, as has Dr. Edwin Carpenter of the Huntington Library, and Miss Ella L. Robinson, Librarian of the Southwest Museum. The special collections department of the University of Arizona, the University of New Mexico, and University of Southern California at Los Angeles, generously gave access to their many holdings, as did the Arizona Pioneers' Historical Society. Last but certainly not least, a debt of gratitude is owed to the staff of Westernlore Press, for their skilled work in producing this book; and to Miss Anne Cuddeback, for her gracious editorial aid.

L. R. BAILEY.

CONTENTS

ILLUSTRATIONS

THE LONG WALK

A History of the Navajo Wars, 1846-1868

I

"THE NEW MEN"

Aᴄᴄᴇᴘᴛᴇᴅ sum of $5000 from L. B. Maxwell for buildings at Fort Sumner," read the telegram in the hands of the Secretary of War. With this cryptic message, received late on October 10, 1870, a military post in east-central New Mexico — a post which had been by far the most important of its kind in the Southwest — passed into civilian hands.

For nearly five years, from 1863 to 1868, Fort Sumner had been the home of the Navajo Indians. By one of the most intensive campaigns ever conducted against Redmen by the United States Army, this tribe had been hounded and driven from their redrock haunts in what is today northwestern New Mexico and northeastern Arizona and concentrated on the Rio Pecos. There, on forty square miles the once "Lords of New Mexico" grubbed out a meager subsistence from alkali impregnated soil, or died of dysentery from saline water, and syphilis contracted from the garrison. Never in the lives of a people had a more traumatic moment existed. Even after their release from captivity, Navajos would reckon all future events from that day — as if the tribe had been reborn and all earlier happenings were of little consequence. Now, as the Secretary of War sat reading the slip of paper, this story of suffering and misery was at last drawn to a close — a story which began more than twenty years before.

✗   ✗   ✗

It was seven o'clock on the morning of August 15, 1846, when the "Army of the West" marched through the drowsy New Mexican town of Las Vegas and encamped a short distance beyond. The village populace was turned out and assembled in the plaza to the hear the words of the conqueror of New Mexico. From atop one of the flat-roofed adobe buildings surrounding the square, Brigadier General Stephen Watts Kearny explained that he and his army had come to take possession of the country, not as an enemy, but as a protector; and in the following words made known to the people that his government was aware of at least one of the many difficulties which had plagued the area for generations:

> The Apaches and the Navajos come down from the mountains and carry off your sheep and your women whenever they please. My government will correct all this. They will keep off the Indians, protect you in your persons and property.[1]

The fulfillment of General Kearny's promise of protection was not to be an easy task. For 250 years before the coming of the "Army of the West" intermittent warfare had existed between New Mexicans and the Navajos — until reciprocal raid and reprisal had become a traditional endeavor. Source of these difficulties is not easy to determine, for both peoples contributed equally to keeping animosities alive. By the late 17th century Navajos had adopted traits which would put them on the road to plunder, and throw New Mexico into the abyss of war. The Diné[2] — as the Navajos call themselves — had adopted to their economy the horse and sheep grazing complex; and had found a ready use and market for captives taken from Spanish settlements along the Rio Grande Valley. Acquirement of these possessions transformed the Navajos from a part-time agricultural-food collecting people to a tribe of raiders, who reckoned their status and wealth in terms of the number of sheep and captives they possessed.

By the time of the coming of the "Army of the West," Navajo depredations had increased to such a high pitch that these Indians had established three main arteries of approach — which in many places were well beaten trails, trampled hard by the hoofs of thousands of sheep and horses looted from New Mexican ranchos and towns. Such an avenue ran down the valley of the Rio Puerco to the east of Mount San Mateo (now called Mount Taylor), and fanned out through lateral cañons to the valleys of the Rio Grande. Another war trail existed through the mountains north of the small frontier town of Cebolleta; and still another wound its way farther west, passing through the valley of the Rio de San José.[3]

Such was the situation which immediately faced General Kearny. The commander had been in New Mexico but a short time before he was visited by numerous delegations from New Mexican communities and pueblos, all seeking protection from the menace of the Navajos, as well as other marauding Indians. In an attempt to quiet protestations, and to fulfill his promise made that day at Las Vegas, Kearny issued orders on September 16, 1846 for movement of a portion of his command to frontier points to restrict Navajo and Ute raids. Kearny instructed his subordinate, the elected colonel of the First Regiment of Missouri Mounted Volunteers, Alexander W. Doniphan, to place three companies of his regiment under command of Lieutenant Colonel Charles F. Ruff, and station them at Cebolleta, sixty miles west of Albuquerque. To erect a barrier against Ute incursions, Kearny directed another portion of the First Missouri Volunteers to proceed to Abiquiu under leadership of Major William Gilpin. The garrisoning of these frontier points, however, had little effect upon marauding Indians. The troops, few in numbers, with mounts that were fatigued by the arduous march from Fort Leavenworth, were powerless against the incursions of the swiftly moving Navajos and Utes.

Hearing of the continued depredations, General Kearny decided to take more aggressive action against the Navajos.[4] On October 11, an express rider reached Santa Fe, bringing a communication to Colonel Doniphan from Kearny — who was by now on his way to California. The sealed letter instructed the colonel to delay for a time his contemplated movement upon Chihuahua, and proceed with his regiment into Navajo country to chastise the Indians for their depredations upon the western frontiers of New Mexico.[5] Upon receipt of these orders, Doniphan plunged quickly to work organizing the expedition, for winter was fast approaching, mountain passes would soon be blocked by deep snows, and forage for regimental mounts would be difficult to procure.

Accordingly, dispatches were sent to Major Gilpin at Abiquiu, and to Lieutenant Colonel Cosgreve Jackson[6] at Cebolleta, directing both to move upon the Navajo country by different routes and "to chastise the Navajos wherever they appeared hostile." The two forces would then unite at a spring known as Ojo del Oso (Bear Springs), situated on the north slopes of the Zuñi Mountains overlooking the valley of the Rio Puerco, fifteen miles east of present-day Gallup, New Mexico. Once assembled at this point, Colonel Doniphan would join the command and enact a treaty of peace with the belligerent Navajos.

Jackson's mission was two-fold: he was to negotiate a triple league of peace between the three existing powers in New Mexico — the Navajos, New Mexicans, and the Anglo-Americans. If he could not effect these amicable relations, he carried alternative instructions to prosecute a vigorous campaign against the tribe. Hence, all the arts of diplomacy, as well as those of war would be authorized to settle these questions involving the interests of three separate peoples.

While encamped at Cebolleta, Jackson enlisted the aid of Antonio Sandoval,[7] chief of a small band of Navajos residing on the western slopes of Mount Taylor, to spread word among the headmen of his tribe to gather at Santa Fe for signing of the proposed treaty, and thus save themselves from Anglo punitive measures. Sandoval was quickly dispatched from Cebolleta to contact the principal men, and ascertain if "they were of a disposition to make an amicable arrangement of existing difficulties." The chief was absent two weeks, and upon his return he informed Jackson, "that he had seen all the headmen of his nation, and that they were chiefly disposed for peace: but . . . were unwilling to trust themselves among the New Mexicans," unless adequate protection was afforded them by the American military. The chief stated further that Navajo headmen had expressed a desire to see "some of the white men among them" before they ventured into the settlements for council.

Upon hearing that headmen were hesitant about straying from the sanctuary of their homeland, Captain Reid, of Jackson's command, suggested to his superior that a small party of troops be sent into Indian country to urge Navajo leaders to come in — and he volunteered to lead the party himself. About the 20th of October, the captain with thirty men (ten volunteers from each company) with three mules packed with fifteen days' provisions, set out on the hazardous enterprise. Guided by Sandoval and his twelve-year-old son,[8] Reid's small party marched northwestward up the narrow cañon of Cebolleta; and with great difficulty skirted Mount Taylor. The command traveled due west for nearly a hundred miles before seeing a single Indian. Finally after six exhausting days of constant travel over rough and totally unfamiliar terrain, the party reached Ojo del Oso.

The country about Ojo del Oso impressed the weary soldiers. They beheld an inviting and beautiful valley covered with grass, from which thousands of sheep were grazing. The spring, reputed to be a great council-site of the Navajos, flowed in sufficient quantity to water their animals with ease, before sinking into the porous soil of the valley.[9]

At the Oso, which in years to come would be the site of many councils between the Navajos and Anglos, Captain Reid met with a party of Indians under the leadership of an aged chief called Narbona. This venerable old man, known among his people as *Hastin Naat'aani* (Man Speaking Peace) represented Navajos residing on the eastern flanks of the Chuska-Tunicha Mountains. Although about seventy years of age, Narbona was held in great respect as a peace speaker in the councils of his people, and possessed great skills as an orator whose wisdom and experience was not to be heeded lightly.

The great Narbona, as Captain Reid beheld him, was a prostrated and emaciated old man suffering the agonies of rheumatism. Despite his infirmities, the Indian impressed Reid as a mild, amiable person, who was anxious to secure before his death, a peace between the Navajos and the "New Men" — as the chief called the Anglo-Americans. Reid had judged Narbona correctly. As soon as the interview was concluded, Narbona sent runners in every direction to summon other headmen and warriors to council. They responded to the call, and began to assemble in large numbers. By the third day thousands of Indians were encamped about the spring, the multitude feasting on mutton, racing their horses, and discussing among themselves the issues of the forthcoming council. On the third day following the Anglo-Americans' arrival, the council convened.

Narbona was borne to his place in the center of the assembly, and the other chiefs and warriors arranged themselves about him in order of tribal importance. The guns of Reid and his men were stacked just outside the circle, and the troopers stood together near them. Captain Reid opened the council, stating through Sandoval, that Anglo-Americans desired to sign a treaty of peace with the Navajos; and he requested that a general council be convened at Santa Fe for that purpose. When the captain concluded his speech, the headmen set to discussing among themselves what he had proposed. Debate went on far into the night between the party desiring peace, and the one holding out for war with the Americans. The latter pointed out that these "New Men" were no different than the Mexicans. Had not Juan José, chief of the Apaches, and his followers, been murdered in 1837 by a party of Americans under James Johnson? At long last, the eloquent oratory of Narbona induced a compromise among the headmen. A delegation would be sent to Santa Fe to conclude a treaty of peace with the Americans.[10]

Before returning to Cebolleta, Reid and his thirty men beheld a display of Navajo strength which they would not soon forget. Jacob S. Robinson, a member of the expedition painted in his journal a word-picture of the colorful scene:

> The plain was covered with . . . mounted warriors, with their feathers streaming in the wind, their arms raised as for conflict; some riding one way and some another; and in the midst of these scenes they indulged in the wild Indian yell, or shout of triumph, as they succeed in capturing their prey. It was a sight unequalled in display of horsemanship; and can be seen nowhere but in the wild mountains and plains of the west.[11]

Shortly after Reid's return to Cebolleta, Major Gilpin, at Abiquiu, received a dispatch from Doniphan on November 22 authorizing the immediate movement of troops into Navajo country.[12] Apparently Reid's mission had been a waste of time, for now troops were being sent into Indian country instead of awaiting arrival of headmen at Santa Fe. Accompanied by sixty-five New Mexicans and Pueblo Indian allies,

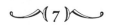

Gilpin left his encampment on the Rio Chama and executed an encircling movement of the Navajo's domain. Following the Chama northward to its source, the major crossed the continental divide to the Rio San Juan; thence by a long and arduous march over the snow-locked Tunicha Mountains. It was during this difficult passage that Gilpin received still another dispatch from his superior. The proposed meeting with the Indians at Santa Fe had been cancelled. Doniphan was now on his way into Navajo country with Lieutenant Colonel Jackson and would join Gilpin at Ojo del Oso on December 20 — there to enact the peace treaty.

By December 18, Gilpin and his men had toiled through deep snows to within a few miles of the eastern entrance of the reputed Navajo fortress — Cañon de Chelly. The major, encumbered by his command, saw that he could not possibly reach the council site in time. He therefore selected an escort of thirty troopers and started at dawn the next day for Bear Springs.[13] By the morning of December 21, Gilpin and his escort had united with the command of Doniphan and Jackson. There were present at the council site about 180 Americans and 500 Navajos, including a number of chiefs who had come in with Major Gilpin. The treaty negotiations opened with Doniphan explaining the object of his visit and the intentions of his government regarding the administration of New Mexican Indian affairs. Throughout the entire day little headway was made in negotiations, as both white and red men debated the pros and cons of the issue.

The next day treaty making continued with the "New Men" being the more aggressive participants. Arrival of Captain Waldo, with the remainder of Gilpin's command, swelled the number of soldiers to 330, and created a better bargaining position for the Anglos. With renewed vigor, Doniphan explained that the United States had taken possession of New Mexico; and was, therefore, obligated to protect its inhabitants from the incursions of Indians. He further pointed out that his government desired to live peacefully with the Navajos, and at the same time protect the Indians from the forays of New Mexicans. The Diné were at the same time warned that if they persisted in their depredations — there would be no other alternative than "to prosecute a war against them."

Many Navajos could not comprehend why this alien commander would no longer permit them to fight their sworn enemies, when they had always done so. One of the headmen, a prominent medicine man known as Zarcillas Largas (Long Earrings), stepped forward and addressed Doniphan and his staff.

"Americans! You have a strange cause of war against the Navajos. We have waged war against the New Mexicans for several years. We have plundered their villages and killed many of their people, and made many prisoners. We had just cause for all this. You have lately commenced a war against the same people. You are powerful. You have great guns and many brave soldiers. You have therefore conquered them, the very thing we have been attempting to do for so many years. You now turn upon us for attempting to do what you have done yourselves. We cannot see why you have cause of quarrel with us for fighting the New Mexicans on the west, while you do the same thing on the east."

With all the eloquence and power of a well trained orator Largas clinched his arguments. "Look how matters stand. This is *our war*. We have more right to complain of you for interfering in our war, than you have to quarrel with us for continuing a war we had begun long before you got here. If you will act justly, you will allow us to settle our own differences."[14]

In reply to Largas' words, Doniphan tried to make clear to the Navajos the reasons behind his statements. He told them that after a war was over, it was the custom of his people to treat their former enemies as friends, and extend to the conquered the rights of military protection. Doniphan then stated that if he permitted the Diné to wage war against the New Mexicans, it would not be long until they were also raiding the Anglo-Americans. In a last attempt to sway the Indians, the commander explained that it would be to the advantage of the Navajos to let the newcomers settle peacefully in New Mexico, for then trade could be established, and the Indians could obtain all their needs from the "New Men."

The wisdom of Doniphan's words and the opportunity for trade decided the issue. When next Zarcillas Largas spoke it was in a different tone: "If New Mexico be really in your possession, and it be the intention of your government to hold it, we will cease our depredations, and refrain from future war. . . . Let there be peace between us!"

With these words, both parties signed the treaty. This document was simple in its stipulations. A firm and lasting peace would hereafter exist between all the peoples residing in New Mexico. Mutual trade would be established; and the restoration of all captives and stolen property in possession of the Navajos would be forthcoming.[15]

On the morning of November 23, the Indians gradually dispersed, and the troops, in detached commands, returned to the Rio Grande Valley with utmost haste — for now they were in desperate want of provisions; and the men had suffered from extreme cold and the rigors of the march. So too, was Doniphan anxious to begin his march upon Chihuahua— where he and his Missourians would win new laurels in the war with Mexico.

When news of the treaty reached Santa Fe, its defects were immediately recognized, and a storm of criticism rained down upon its instigator:

Col. Doniphan's treaty has been discussed. It is said to be very defective, and not likely to effect any very substantial peace. Gentlemen here [in Santa Fe], well acquainted with the Nabajoes [sic], expect every day to hear of new outrages being committed by them. The achievement of this treaty does not, therefore, seem to confer many laurels; but we ought to remember that making Indian treaties is a new business to the Col., and if he has not made a very good one on the first trial, he may do infinitely better next time. But the Nabajoes, it is here thought, will continue to steal sheep and commit other outrages, until they are well whipped a few times. . . .[16]

It was true, treaty making was new business to the colonel. For if he believed that his signature and those of a few Indians would effect a cessation of hostilities, he was either sadly mistaken, or blind to the deep-seated animosities which had smoldered for generations. John Hughes, official chronicler of Doniphan's exploits, recognized the failings of the campaign and its subsequent treaty, and wrote that it must have been a "novel spectacle" to require the Navajo nation to treat with the New Mexicans, Puebloans and the Americans — the two former peoples being the Diné's perpetual and implacable enemies.[17]

It was useless, indeed, to expect the Navajos to bury their hatreds overnight, and bind themselves by treaty to abstain from war. So too, was it ridiculous to think that peace could be obtained by merely signing a document between the Indians and the American troops. Navajos had never before seen United States soldiers, and consequently had no conception of American military might. As a result, for nearly a year, the Diné persisted in pilfering livestock from the settlements of New Mexico. By the first week in September 1847, their incursions had reached such proportions that it was again deemed necessary to send a military expedition against them.

On September 10, Major W. H. T. Walker, with a battalion of Missouri volunteers, left Santa Fe to invade Navajo country. The command was well equipped with two-months' provisions and had brought along a small detachment of artillery.

These troops, determined to give the Indians a thorough chastising, apparently left town in high spirits, for as one observer commented — "nearly every man left drunk."[18]

Walker's expedition of 140 men reached the Rio Grande at Albuquerque about the 20th of the month and struck a course due west for Ojo del Oso; where they left their supply wagons, and proceeded with pack animals as far as Laguna Colorado (Red Lake). From this point, detachments were sent into the surrounding country in abortive attempts to humble the Indians. Failing to check depredations, Walker marched upon the east entrance of Cañon de Chelly — which he penetrated for six miles before realizing the impracticability and danger in proceeding farther into its labyrinth. Backtracking out of the gorge, Walker ordered his men back to Santa Fe, reaching that town by October 13.[19]

Walker had been in Santa Fe but a short time before a delegation of Navajo headmen appeared and offered to treat for peace. A council was called. The Indians again agreed to keep the peace. Throughout the remainder of the year quiet reigned.[20] By spring, however, Navajo crops had been planted, and the Indians returned to their pastime of raiding New Mexican flocks and herds. On March 27, 1848, the new commander of New Mexico (now organized as the Ninth Military Department), Colonel E. W. R. Newby, realized that the power of the army was virtually useless against these Indians; and he issued Orders No. 22 from department headquarters at Santa Fe:

> The Colonel Commanding is deeply pained at the intelligence which he daily receives of the frequent outrages, committed upon the persons and property of the peaceful inhabitants of the Territory . . . by the Navajos, Apaches and other tribes. . . .
>
> This painful feeling, not a little enhanced by the fact, that three-fourths of the force remaining in this Department are infantry, and are powerless against the rapid movements

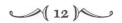

of mounted men, who are familiar with every inch of the country, and that, in consequence, his garrisons are compelled to sit still while murder and robbery is committed under their very eyes.

In consideration of the circumstances, that as the only means of protection remaining, it is ordered that the Mexican inhabitants of this Department, be authorized to arm and equip themselves — organize in parties or bands and hold themselves in readiness to repel all incursions and to recover the property that may have been taken from them by the Indians.[21]

This authorization of New Mexican irregulars to make rerisals against the Diné served only to incite the Indians to greater hostilities; and one month later, on May 1, Colonel Newby, following in the footsteps of his predecessors, left Santa Fe at the head of a column of troops bound for Navajoland. After several skirmishes Newby apparently felt confident that he had humbled the Indians — for he delivered to the head chiefs an ultimatum: they had but three days in which to assemble for the signing of a new treaty. And as before, the Diné found it convenient to comply with the white men's wishes, and another worthless piece of paper was signed[22] — which only served to increase Navajo contempt for the Anglo-American invaders.

The sustained hostilities, from 1847-1849, had a profound effect upon the attitudes of the New Mexican legislators, who clamored for the suppression of the Navajo menace. Plans were formulated, many for personal gain, ranging from total annihilation of the tribe to virtual enslavement of it. On every occasion lawmakers pressed the army to undertake the task of subduing the Indians. But regiments were few and officers lacked the knowledge of native ways — so necessary for a full understanding of New Mexico's Indian problems. The military — as well as many civilians — made the mistake of viewing the Navajos as a tribal entity with which treaties could be signed, and as a body, held responsible for the actions of all its members. In reality the tribe, at that time, was not consolidated politically. Both the army and civil authorities failed to see that the fundamental tribal unit was the clan, or natural community of related members, which usually operated independently — and often to the detriment of others. Clans close to the frontier settlements, for example, often bore the brunt of New Mexican reprisals for raids perpetrated by groups residing deep in Navajoland.[23]

✕　✕　✕

Of the many civil authorities who passed in and out of New Mexico during the first decade of the American occupation, one man tried desperately to find a solution to the mounting Indian problem. This man, a long time resident of Georgia and a veteran of the Mexican War, was James S. Calhoun.[24] He arrived in Santa Fe on July 22, 1849 to assume the duties of Indian agent for New Mexico. He was directed by Commissioner of Indian Affairs, William Medill, to gather statistical data and other information that would lead to an intelligent understanding of the Indian problems of the region.

Calhoun had been in the territory but a short time before he clearly saw one of the numerous causes of turmoil. The Indians, he discovered, had not a just conception of Anglo-American strength; and because protection had been extended to the Mexicans — for whom the Navajos harbored only enmity — the "New Men" were regarded as weaklings.[25] Faced with the task of halting hostilities, the new Indian agent attempted first to alter the opinions of the Indians respecting the power of the United States.

Working in close accord with one another, Calhoun and the Military Governor, Brevet Lieutenant Colonel John M. Washington, planned an expedition which was hoped would awe the Navajos into submission. By Order No. 32 (dated August 14, 1849), the column was organized under the command of Washington. It consisted of two companies of the

Second Artillery; four companies of the Third Infantry; a company of the Second Dragoons, and one of mounted New Mexican volunteers — in all an effective force of a 175 men.[26] On the morning of August 16 the infantry and artillery left Santa Fe, followed by the cavalry, all bound for a rendezvous three days later at the pueblo of Jemez. There the command would be joined by the volunteer company which had been stationed at the pueblo under the leadership of Captain Henry Linn Dodge.

On August 22 the elaborate expedition, guided by a pueblo chief and the now traditional go-between, Antonio Sandoval, took up the line of march for Cañon de Chelly.[27] After a rather difficult, but interesting trip through Chaco Cañon, during which the chronicler of the foray, Lieutenant James H. Simpson, meticulously recorded archaeological and geological features, the command reached the valley of Tunicha on the afternoon of August 30, and encamped. Forage for the animals had been scant along the way, and Navajo cornfields in the vicinity afforded quick relief for the exhausted animals. While recuperating from the rigors of the march, several hundred Indians appeared; and their chiefs sought a talk with Calhoun and Washington. During the ensuing council, the governor advised the Navajos that he intended to chastise them for the utter contempt they had shown for the treaties of Doniphan and Newby.

In defense, the headmen replied, that among their people were a great many *ladrones* (thieves), who were impossible to control. But for the most part the Navajos desired peace, and a restitution of stolen property would be made. Washington, believing the Indians sincere, laid before them for inspection a skeleton treaty which he hoped to enact at Cañon de Chelly with representatives of the whole tribe. After discussing the merits of the document, the chiefs agreed to summon more headmen for another council at noon the following day.

On August 31, at the designated time, three chiefs appeared — José Largo, Archuleta, and the aged Narbona who had been present at the signing of Doniphan's treaty. Through an interpreter, Washington and Calhoun proposed another treaty, to be enacted at Cañon de Chelly; and requested the Navajos assemble at that point for official acceptance of the document. Despite the chiefs' promises to comply with the white men's wishes, initial success of the first two meetings was to be marred by an unforeseen incident.[28]

Following the council, Sandoval addressed a large assemblage of Indians, to acquaint them with the terms of the forthcoming treaty. As he paraded before his brethren, a New Mexican in the command of Captain Dodge spotted a horse he thought belonged to him. Washington, being informed of the fact, immediately demanded the animal's return; and threatened to fire upon the Indians unless they at once complied. The Navajos, sensing hostile intent, reeled their horses about, and fled. In so doing, they received a volley of musket fire from the guards — not to mention a couple of round shots fired "very handsomely" by the artillery into the fleeing horde. Result of this fracas was six Indians mortally wounded, and the ancient chief Narbona left dead upon the field.[29]

Washington, blind to this incident's far-reaching effects, ordered resumption of the march to Cañon de Chelly. Six days later the troops were before the western mouth of that breathtaking cañon — chiseled by wind and water from the red sandstone of Navajoland. All was not serene, however, for wisps of smoke curled skyward as the Indians, fearing further violence, set torch to their hogans and retreated to the safety of the gorge.

Again Sandoval was used as go-between, in hopes of enticing a few headmen into Washington's camp. The chief was successful, and the following morning was back with Mariano Martinez. This headman, dressed in buckskin-leggings, a sky-

blue greatcoat of American manufacture, and a narrow brim-
med Mexican hat, informed Washington and Calhoun that
his people desired peace. He promised to pass along the word
for other chiefs to assemble at the cañon on September 9.
Since a day would elapse before the next council, an opportunity was afforded for a limited reconnaissance of the great
and mysterious chasm.

At 7:30 the next morning, Lieutenant James Simpson, with
an escort of sixty men, set out with Mariano Martinez to sur-
vey the renowned cañon. Entering the mouth of the abyss,
the party took the left-hand branch, today known as Cañon
del Muerto. For nine and a half miles they rode, looking for a
mythical "famous fort" of the Navajos.[30] During the trip the
commander of the party made some tactical observations
which in years to come would be used to great advantage by
the military:

> Should it ever be necessary to send troops into this cañon
> . . . a force should skirt the heights above to drive off assail-
> ants from that quarter, the south bank should be preferred,
> because [it is] less interrupted by lateral branch cañons.

Simpson further reported that "the mystery of the Cañon de
Chelly is now, in all probability solved. This cañon is, indeed,
a wonderful exhibition of nature, and will always command
the admiration of its votaries, as it will the attention of geolo-
gists."[31]

On September 9 Mariano Martinez and Chapitan, the latter a chief of the Navajos residing along the San Juan, met
with Washington and Calhoun. In compliance with the stipulations of Newby's treaty, and as a demonstration of their
good will, their followers drove in a small amount of stolen
sheep, and delivered four Mexican captives. The more comprehensive peace treaty proposed by Washington and the
Indian agent was then consummated. Following the signing,
the chiefs stated that they had additional stock to return, but

as it was scattered over a wide area, they requested still more time to assemble the animals. Washington consented to the Indians' request, allowing a period of thirty days to bring the flocks into Jemez.[32]

The afternoon following conclusion of the treaty a hundred Navajo warriors descended on Washington's camp to fraternize with the troopers. Trade was brisk. Blankets, dressed skins, and peaches from orchards in Cañon de Chelly, were exchanged for trinkets and accouterments from soldiers' uniforms. Thus, a seemingly happy and peaceful termination was given to the "campaign;" and the following morning, the command took up its line of march for the Rio Grande Valley, by way of Cañon Bonito (present-day site of Fort Defiance) and the pueblo of Zuñi.

Despite the outward show of Navajo friendship and goodwill, Indian Agent Calhoun was pessimistic about the faithfulness of the Diné. Although the Indians had attempted to indemnify New Mexican losses, the agent knew enough of Indian ways not to place to much reliance on their promises. He was not at all confident the Navajos would appear at Jemez.[33] There was, however, some optimism on the part of Lieutenant Simpson. He felt satisfied with the outcome of the expedition. A full and complete treaty, covering the whole range of Navajo fealty had been enacted. A portion of the stolen property and captives had been delivered to United States authorities — and restoration of the remainder had been promised within a predetermined time. Added to this, Simpson felt that the geographical knowledge which the penetration of Navajoland had given the troops would be of the highest value in any future military demonstration against the tribe.[34]

The Navajos, however, may have felt somewhat different. They had witnessed the penetration of their homeland by an alien people, who offered up an olive branch, and then picketed their horses in the Diné's fields. The Indians had attended a council of peace, during which one of their most respected headmen had promised to comply with all the terms offered by the "New Men." Then, at the conclusion of the council was shot down — over a complaint lodged against the integrity of the Navajos by one of their sworn enemies — who was just as apt to rob the Diné's herds. No wonder Indian Agent James S. Calhoun felt pessimistic regarding outcome of the newly-signed treaty, for the expedition had been one replete with mismanagement and lack of foresight.

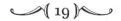

1. George R. Gibson, *Journal of a Soldier Under Kearny and Doniphan, 1846-47*, edited by Ralph P. Bieber (Glendale: Arthur H. Clark, 1935), pp. 75-76.

2. Both the Apaches and Navajos, speaking esssentially the same language (Athabascan), refer to themselves as Diné or Tineh, meaning "The People."

3. J. W. Abert, *Report of Lieut. J. W. Abert, of his Examination of New Mexico, in the Years 1846-47* (Washington: 1848), pp. 465-466; also James H. Simpson, *Journal of a Military Reconnaissance, from Santa Fe to the Navajo Country* (Philadelphia: 1852), pp. 126-127. Hereafter cited as *Simpson Journal*.

4. By now Kearny was on his way to California. These orders were issued during the march, and were forwarded to Doniphan by express rider.

5. A copy of this communique may be found in John T. Hughes, *Doniphan's Expedition; Containing an Account of the Conquest of New Mexico* (Cincinnati: 1847), p. 56. Hereafter cited as *Doniphan's Expedition*.

6. Cosgreve Jackson was originally captain of Company H, First Regiment of Missouri Mounted Volunteers. He succeeded Lieutenant Ruff, and was placed in command of the troops stationed at Cebolleta. See: William E. Connelley, *Doniphan's Expedition and the Conquest of New Mexico & California* (Topeka: 1907), p. 138. Lieutenant Colonel Jackson's force consisted of companies D, G, and F, commanded by Captain Reid, Parsons, and Hughes. This command left Santa Fe on September 18 to take up their position at Cebolleta. Hughes, *Doniphan's Expedition*, p. 61.

7. Antonio Sandoval was known among his own people as *Hastin Késhgoli* (Crooked Foot). He and his band, which has been variously estimated at from 50 to 400 members, were known as *Diné'ana'ih* or Enemy Navajos. It is generally thought by anthropologists and historians alike, that these Navajos remained in the Cebolleta-Mount Taylor area when the main

portion of the tribe pushed westward toward Cañon de Chelly. They were always held in contempt by their brethren because of their repeated alliances with the Spaniards and Mexicans against the main portion of the tribe. See Richard Van Valkenburgh, *Diné Bikéyah* (Window Rock: 1941), p. 17; and "Navajo Naataani," *The Kiva* (Vol. XIII, January 1948), p. 19.

8. The employment of Sandoval as guide produced some consternation among the New Mexicans, who feared that the chief might lure Reid and his command into an ambuscade. Jacob S. Robinson, *A Journal of the Santa Fe Expedition Under Colonel Doniphan* (Princetown University Press, 1932), pp. 39-40; also Hughes, *Doniphan's Expedition*, p. 63.

9. Connelley, *Doniphan's Expedition*, p. 294.

10. Hughes, *Doniphan's Expedition*, pp. 65-66; also *ibid.*, pp. 294-95.

11. Robinson, *Journal*, pp. 46-47.

12. The command assigned Major Gilpin consisted of two companies under Captains Waldo and Stephenson. It was originally planned that these troops would not be sent into the interior, but would operate as small detachments, making short excursions into the country surrounding Abiquiu, to clear it of marauding Indians. Hughes, *Doniphan's Expedition*, p. 67.

13. The remainder of Gilpin's command was entrusted to the leadership of Captain Waldo, who conducted it to Bear Springs with utmost haste.

Doniphan, escorted by the three companies of Lieutenant Jackson, took up the line of march from the Ojo del Oso on November 15. Leaving at Cebolleta all their wagons and other encumbrances, this command made its way to the treaty site. Hughes, *Doniphan's Expedition*, pp. 68-70.

14. Hughes, *Doniphan's Expedition*, p. 71.

15. For a facsimile of the Doniphan Treaty see *ibid.*, pp. 71-72.

16. St. Louis *Weekly Reveille*, February 22, 1847; as quoted in Marcellus B. Edwards, *Marching with the Army of the West, 1846-48*, edited by Ralph P. Bieber (Glendale: Arthur H. Clark, 1936), pp. 212-213.

17. Hughes, *Doniphan's Expedition*, pp. 62-63.

18. Santa Fe *Republican*, September 10, 1847. Also Philip G. Ferguson, *Marching with the Army of the West, 1846-48*, edited by Ralph P. Bieber (Glendale: Arthur H. Clark, 1936), pp. 320-321.

19. Santa Fe *Republican*, October 16, 1847.

20. *Ibid.*, January 15, 1848.

21. *Ibid.*, April 2, 1848.

22. Like the Doniphan Treaty and all others which would follow, this treaty demanded the restoration of livestock stolen from the New Mexicans, as well as the return of all captives. *Ibid.*, May 3, 1848, and May 21, 1848. For the official report of Newby's campaign see Newby to Brig. General R. Jones, June 17, 1848; National Archives, *Office of Adjutant General*, Record Group 94, Letters Received. Hereafter cited as *Office of Adjutant General*, LR.

23. W. W. Hill, *Some Aspects of Navajo Political Structure* (Flagstaff: Museum of Northern Arizona, n.d.), pp.1-2.

24. James S. Calhoun, the first Territorial Governor of New Mexico, was a staunch Whig, and professed a great admiration of General Zachary Taylor, which gained for him the captaincy of a regiment of Georgia volunteers during the Mexican War. He served in this capacity from June 1846 to May 1847, at which time he was commissioned a lieutenant colonel commanding a battalion of Georgia mounted volunteers. With the opening of President Taylor's administration, Calhoun received the appointment of Indian Agent at Santa Fe; and on March 3, 1851, was inaugurated as Governor and Superintendent of Indian Affairs for the Territory of New Mexico. See Annie H. Abel (comp. & ed.), *Official Correspondence of James S. Calhoun while Indian Agent at Santa Fe and Superintendent of Indian Affairs in New Mexico* (Washington: G.P.O., 1915). Hereafter cited as *Calhoun Correspondence.*

25. Calhoun to Medill, October 4, 1849; *Calhoun Correspondence,* p. 40.

26. The infantry was commanded by Brevet Colonel Alexander. The artillery, consisting of one six-pounder and three mountain howitzers, was placed under Brevet Major Henry L. Kendrick. The detachment of volunteers and Dragoons was led by captains Chapman and Kerr. See Simpson, *Journal,* p. 9.

27. *Ibid.,* p. 24.

28. Before the council ended, the venerable Narbona and José Largo, also very aged, requested that they be represented by two lesser and younger chiefs, Armijo and Pedro José; who would act on their behalf at the forthcoming council at Cañon de Chelly. Both Calhoun and Washington agreed to this.

29. Simpson, *Journal,* pp. 53-56.

30. The existence of this so-called "Navajo fort" stems from a belief on the part of Spanish soldiers, a hundred years before, that these Indians possessed a *presidio* deep in the cañon system of Chelly.

31. Simpson, *Journal,* pp. 73-77.

32. *Ibid.,* p. 80.

33. Calhoun to Medill, October 1, 1849; *Calhoun Correspondence,* p. 36.

34. Simpson, *Journal,* pp. 80-81.

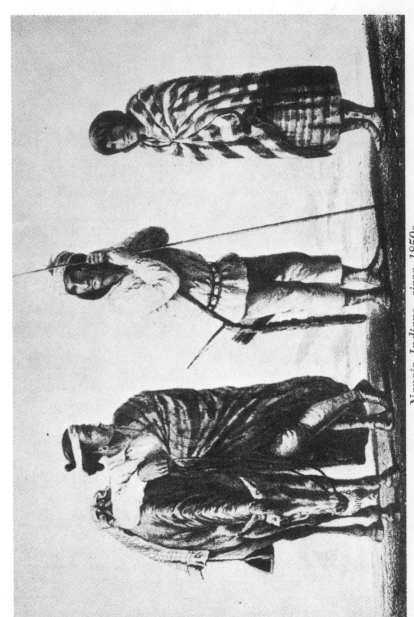

Navajo Indians, circa 1850s

II

INTIMIDATION OF THE NAVAJO

THE NAVAJOS struck before the return of Washington and Calhoun to the Rio Grande. No sooner had the troops left Zuñi than the Diné raided that pueblo's flocks and fields. Throughout October and November 1849, Navajo forays were extended to the pueblos of San Ildefonso, Santo Domingo and Santa Ana, as well as other New Mexican communities. Towns close to the Navajo-New Mexican frontier were struck at repeatedly by the illusive Indians. Cebolleta, Abiquiu, Cubero, La Pugarita and Corrales suffered heavy livestock losses, not to mention an occasional *pastore* being carried deep into Navajoland to become a slave to the Diné.

Suffering from this constant hammering, New Mexicans and Pueblo Indians approached the Indian agent for help. A deputation from Zuñi consisting of the governor, grand captain, and the captain of war, paid Calhoun a visit on October 15. Stating their grievances with great energy, and vehemently denouncing the Navajos, these puebloans requested permission to wage a war of extermination against their enemies. They proposed that the Navajos could be defeated by a coalition of puebloans, armed with weapons furnished by the United States Army.[1] The delegation informed Calhoun that more than 500 able-bodied men stood ready to march — if they could only be supplied with arms.[2] However, the coffers of the Indian Agency, as well as those of the territory as a whole, were practically empty. James S. Calhoun could only make vague promises; and then sit down and write to Commissioner of Indian Affairs, William Medill, of the woes facing New Mexico.

Blame for renewed depredations did not, however, rest solely with the Navajos. Calhoun was informed by the Zuñi, that the Diné, according to their promise, had begun to collect their stock and captives; and to prepare in every way to comply with the treaty stipulations made with the Indian agent, and Colonel John M. Washington. Their good intentions, however, were soon squelched by unscrupulous traders operating in the vicinity of Zuñi. It was alleged these traveling merchants, during mid-October, had informed Navajos that all the pueblos, the Mexicans from the neighboring villages, and the Anglo-Americans were forming a league to exterminate the tribe. Frightened at prospects of seeing their flocks raided, and their women and children carried into captivity, many Navajos promptly took to the warpath.[3]

For all Calhoun knew, this could have been just another Navajo excuse to justify their raids. Such reports were rampant and numerous in New Mexico at that time, and were usually beyond all means of verification. But the Indian agent know well the pernicious evil which existed in the form of the Indian trader. Many of these individuals would do anything to create a market for their trade; and arms, ammunition, and liquor were being traded, not only to the Navajos, but to the Apaches, Utes, Puebloans, and the Plains tribes who ranged along New Mexico's east and southern borders. From frontier towns of Abiquiu, Cebolleta and Cubero, these merchants ranged Navajoland with impunity. In an effort to restrain this illegal intercourse, Calhoun on November 2, 1849 suggested to Military Governor John Munroe — who had replaced Colonel Washington — the propriety of licensing traders, and prohibiting trade altogether with tribes at war with the United States. Three weeks later the governor authorized Calhoun to post the following notice:

> Licenses to trade with Indians, will be granted by the undersigned, upon the following conditions, provided they are approved by His Excellency, Governor Munroe, Military Commander of this Department.
>
> Applicants must be citizens of the United States, produce satisfactory testimonials of good character, and give bond in a penal sum not *exceeding* five thousand dollars, with one or more sureties, that he will faithfully observe all the laws and regulations made for the government of trade and intercourse with the Indian tribes of the United States, and in no respect violate the same, and they will not trade in fire-arms, powder, lead, or other munitions of war.
>
> Applicants will distinctly state what tribe they wish to trade with, and under a license granted, they will not be authorized to trade with others.
>
> For the present, no license will be granted authorizing trade or intercourse with the Apaches, Navajos, or Utahs.[4]

The publication of this notice served only to make the illegal trader a little more cautious. Because a profitable barter in captives had existed for generations, many of these individuals also assumed the role of slave-raider. An average Navajo boy or girl (age five to fifteen) at Calhoun's time brought as high as $200 on the auction block. So extensive had the trade become by 1850, that thousands of Indians were held in bondage as household servants and menials in the homes of New Mexico.

The traders in human flesh were anxious to keep hostilities alive between the United States and the Navajos — for then they could readily gain official sanction for their slave raids.

Not only did the New Mexicans participate in this insidious traffic, but Indians likewise took an active hand. Even among the Navajos were men seeking to gain from raiding their own brethren. The tribesmen of the *Diné'ana'ih* (Enemy Navajos) residing on the western slopes of Mount Taylor — of whom Sandoval was leader — were active participants in the slave trade. This band, and its chieftain, had long been familiar to Mexican military leaders; and as mentioned, had served well the United States military. For a number of years Sandoval had maintained friendly relations with the frontier settlements of Cubero and Cebolleta; and had used this favored position to barter Navajo prisoners captured from more recalcitrant bands. It was because of this participation in the lucrative slave trade, and his outward demonstration of friendship toward the Navajos' sworn enemies, that Sandoval was held in disrepute by his own tribesmen.[5]

Sandoval's role as a slave-raider is highlighted in many reports by military men and early-day travelers; and he was exceptionally active in the trade during the first decade of American occupation. Reverand Hiram Read, a Baptist missionary, while visiting Cebolleta, described the chief's activities in these terse words written on March 11, 1851:

A famous half-tamed Nabajo [*sic*] Chief named Sandoval who resides in this vicinity, came into town today to sell some captives of his own nation which he recently took prisoners. He sold one young man of 18 years of age for thirty (30) dollars.[6]

The great vigor with which Sandoval pursued his profession was pointed out in a letter by Calhoun to Commissioner of Indian Affairs Luke Lea:

Sandoval, our Navajo friend near Cebolleta, returned about the 20th of the mouth from a visit to his Navajo brethren with eighteen captives, a quantity of stock and several scalps.[7]

Not only did the clandestine activities of traders and slave-raiders incite Navajos throughout the remainder of the year, and into the early months of 1850, but the brutal slaying of a signer of Washington's Treaty added fuel to the fire of Navajo tempers — already burning bright from the death of Narbona. The murder of Chapiton, by New Mexicans from Cebolleta, created a state of anarchy and confusion,[8] and depredations increased as Indians sought revenge for the deaths of their leaders, and indemnification for losses inflicted by slave-raiders. Appalled at the increased raiding during spring and early summer, Indian Agent Calhoun wrote to Commissioner Orlando Brown that "these Indians [Navajos] ought, and must be, severely chastised before they will submit to a proper subjection."[9]

Throughout the remainder of 1850 Navajos struck at the herds and flocks of towns and ranchos situated on the west side of the Rio Grande. The pueblos were also kept constantly on alert and in a state of anxiety. From June through October, Zuñi sustained a number of attacks which threatened its very existence.[10] Pressure upon Zuñi, however, was alleviated when Colonel John Munroe transferred a company of dragoons from Cebolleta to the beleaguered pueblo; and a shipment of fifty obsolete muskets from army stores raised the virtual siege put upon the town by the Navajos.

Ineffectuality of the military garrisons stationed throughout New Mexico aroused contempt of civil authorities and the populace in general. When troops were ordered in pursuit of Indian marauders, they were either sent out in such small numbers as to be virtually useless, or were incapable of following a trail. Realizing it was futile to rely upon the military for protection, the New Mexicans resorted to the organization of reprisal expeditions.

✗   ✗   ✗

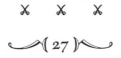

On March 3, 1851, James S. Calhoun was installed as the first civil governor of New Mexico and assumed also the duties of Superintendent of Indian Affairs for the territory.[11] His appointment by President Zachary Taylor was considered a great boon by those men attempting to raise volunteer companies to campaign against the Navajos. Two weeks later (on March 18), Governor Calhoun was presented with a proposal drawn up by a Manuel Chavez requesting authorization for the raising of six companies of militia, 100 men strong, to undertake a campaign against the Navajos. These volunteers, according to Chavez, would be furnished by the government with 100 mules, 600 rifles, and ammunition in sufficient quantity to enable them to conduct the war to successful termination. These New Mexicans would not ask remuneration for services rendered. The only recompense they desired was to have "the disposal of the interests of the country they are to conquer, such as the disposal of captives, animals, cattle, etc." In conclusion, Chavez promised to pursue the Navajos to their extermination or complete surrender, providing his volunteers would not be subject to the ineffectual command of any officer of the regular army. They would instead, "always be ready to obey the orders of the Civil Government of the Territory of New Mexico."[12]

Governor Calhoun, seeking regress from Navajo raids, fully sanctioned Manuel Chavez' proposal. He could, however, only authorize recruitment of volunteers, for the commander of the Ninth Military Department had sole control over issuance of any weapons.[13] To augment the militia, and to effect some measure of security for the Pueblo Indians, Calhoun, the day after assuming governorship, issued the following proclamation:

To the Caciques, Governors and Principals of—[all the Pueblos of New Mexico]:
The savage Indians who are daily murdering and robbing the people of New Mexico, in which I include your Pueblo,

must be exterminated or so chastised as to prevent their coming into or near your Pueblo. For this purpose you are directed to abstain from all friendly intercourse with the Navajo Indians and should they dare to come into your neighborhood, you are authorized to make war upon them, and to take their animals and such property as they may have with them, and to make divisions of the same according to your laws and customs.[14]

Meanwhile, in Washington, Secretary of War C. M. Conrad was seeking means to strengthen frontier defenses, and drastic plans were being drawn up for the reorganization of the Ninth Military Department. First step in that direction was taken when Colonel Munroe was replaced by a soldier of considerable frontier experience — Colonel Edwin Vose Sumner.[15] The instructions which were issued (on April 1, 1851) to this new commander were designed to revolutionize the efficiency of the regular army in New Mexico:

It is believed that material changes ought to be made in that department, both with view to a more efficient protection of the country, and to a diminution of expense.

You will, therefore, immediately on assuming the command, revise the whole system of defense; you will examine practically whether the posts now occupied by the troops are the most suitable, and if not, will make such changes as you may deem advisable.

In the selection of posts you will be governed mainly by the following considerations, *viz*:

1. The protection of New Mexico.
2. The defense of the Mexican Territory, which we are bound to protect against the Indians within our borders.
3. Economy and facility in supporting the troops, particularly in regard to forage, fuel, and adaptation of the surrounding country to cultivation.

The Department is induced to believe, that both economy and efficiency of the service would be promoted by removing the troops out of the towns where they are now stationed and stationing them more towards the frontier and nearer the Indians.

From all the information that has reached the Department, it is induced to believe that no permanent peace can exist with the Indians, and no treaty will be regarded by them until they have been made to feel the power of our arms. You will, therefore, as early as practicable, make an expedition against the Navajos, and also one against the Utahs and Apaches, and inflict upon them a severe chastisement.

In all negotiations and pacific arrangements with the Indians, you will act in concert with the Superintendent of Indian Affairs in New Mexico, whom you will allow to accompany you in the expeditions into Indian territory....[16]

Colonel Sumner with a detachment of dragoons and infantry recruits reached Santa Fe on July 19, 1851, after a fatiguing march from Fort Leavenworth.[17] Upon assuming command, Sumner's first step was to withdraw the garrisons from Las Vegas, Rayado, Albuquerque, Cebolleta, Socorro, Doña Ana, San Elizario, El Paso — and from "that sink of vice and of extravagance" — Santa Fe. In compliance with Secretary of War C. M. Conrad's instructions, these troops were stationed closer to the frontier. At Cottonwood, midway between El Paso and Doña Ana, Fort Fillmore was established to restrict the Apaches and south Plains tribes from making their frequent forays into Mexico. Fillmore was garrisoned with one company of the First Dragoons and two companies of the Third Infantry, under the command of Lieutenant Colonel Dixon Miles. At Valverde, long a target of Indian aggression, Sumner erected another post, naming it Fort Conrad, in honor of the Secretary of War. To this point were detailed one company of First Dragoons, and two of the Third Infantry commanded by Major Howe. In the north-eastern part of the territory, near Mora, another post was erected to protect the overland traffic between Missouri and New Mexico. This post, known as Fort Union, would serve as departmental headquarters, replacing Fort Marcy at Santa Fe.[18]

Sumner was in New Mexico but one month before he took steps to comply with Conrad's instructions to initiate a campaign against the Navajos. By mid-August, the colonel was far advanced in his preparations to humble the Diné. At Santo Domingo he assembled four companies of cavalry, one of artillery, and two of infantry, as well as a van of forty wagons to carry the column's subsistence, ammunition and camp equipage.[19] Leaving Santo Domingo on August 17, the column marched for Laguna and Zuñi, where it halted long enough to confirm the friendship of those pueblos; and then continued toward its destination — Navajoland.

The troops saw no Indians until they reached a point known to the New Mexicans as Cañon Bonito (Good-looking Cañon). This rincón, nestling between red sandstone mesas, is situated about thirty miles west of present-day Gallup, New Mexico, and six miles north of Window Rock, Arizona. The site known to Navajos as *Tsehotsohih* (Meadows between the Rocks), was a favorite rendezvous for Indians in the pre-American era. Around the bubbling springs in the cañon, Navajos had erected shrines; and into the flowing waters were thrown shells and turquoise as payment and pleas for further blessings.[20]

It was while the command rested at this picturesque spot that a lone Indian rode into camp. Immediately he was utilized by Sumner as a messenger to inform Navajo headmen to assemble for council. Navajo leaders, however, refused, and Sumner gave orders for a movement upon Cañon de Chelly.

Leaving Major Electus Backus[21] at Cañon Bonito with the infantry, part of the artillery, and the wagon train, Sumner proceeded toward the heart of Navajoland with the cavalry and two mountain howitzers. As the column penetrated deeper into redrock country, the Indians began to hover about the command's flanks in ever increasing numbers, firing occasional shots into the ranks — usually without effect.[22] By August 28 Sumner was at the west entrance of the imposing cañon. Before entering its depths, the colonel heeded the advice which Lieutenant James H. Simpson had written two years previous. To cover the movements of the troops below, a small detachment of dismounted dragoons was sent along the south rim of the gorge.[23]

As the dragoons moved cautiously, ever deeper into the colossal cañon, Indians began to appear on their left, far above in the ledges and rocks of the red sandstone walls. Out of range of soldiers' guns, the Navajos shouted insults and taunts, in Spanish and their native language, at the the passing column. Unable to get at the Indians annoying its flanks, the command moved on, halting now and then to destroy an occasional field of corn, or an orchard of peach trees — from which the troops filled their pockets and haversacks. With coming of nightfall the dragoons encamped and began preparations for what promised to be a sleepless night, for as one trooper wrote: "Over our heads and around us were to be seen at least 1,000 little fires. The dark forms of the savages were seen moving about them."

As the troopers rested uneasily, Sumner held council with his staff. It was decided not to risk safety of the command by penetrating further into unfamiliar country. The troops would therefore retrace their steps under cloak of darkness. At ten o'clock, on the night of August 29, the dragoons re-saddled their mounts and started back toward Cañon Bonito — after a rigorous march of fifteen miles through the reputed stronghold of the Diné.[24]

A day later Sumner rejoined Major Backus at Cañon Bonito; and the troops were given a slight respite to recuperate from the march. From what he had thus far observed, Sumner was convinced that a garrison must be established in the heart of Navajo country; and on September 18, 1851 he issued

Special Order Number 29, officially authorizing the construction of a post at Cañon Bonito, to be called appropriately — Fort Defiance.[25] The colonel hoped that by placing a strong military force at this point a barrier to Navajo incursions would be created, and at the same time the post would serve to enforce the conditions of Washington's treaty.

Fort Defiance, as established by Sumner, was designed for five companies, and because of nearby water and fertile meadows the proposed location was one of the most eligible in Navajo country. It was, however, isolated by difficult terrain, and its infestation with hostile Indians made travel extremely dangerous. The post, situated 70 miles northwest of Zuñi and 210 miles west of the Rio Grande at Albuquerque, was believed to be the most distant from Washington, in point of time, of any in the the army. Fort Defiance would always present a stupendous logistic problem; and to the officers and men stationed there in years to come, it would be considered the worst type of frontier garrison duty.[26]

To partially alleviate supply difficulties, Sumner put the forty quartermaster wagons, which had accompanied the command, to good use transporting supplies and materiel between Albuquerque and Cañon Bonito.[27] It was not long until a parade ground 300 by 200 feet had been surveyed, around which log and sod quarters began to take shape. Ten sets of officers' quarters, each eighteen feet square, were laid off to the north of the quadrangle. Around the other three sides, additional buildings and quarters would be erected. Five barracks, each 100 by 20 feet, with accompanying kitchens, messrooms and company storerooms, were laid out. Soon too, a hospital, of the same dimensions as the barracks, with a kitchen ten feet to its rear, was in the planning stage. A combination guard-house, office and smoke house; quarters for laundresses, and miscellaneous storerooms were immediately projected.[28]

Sumner selected Major Electus Backus as commander of Fort Defiance, and placed under the latter's charge the post's garrison consisting of Company G, First Dragoons; K, Second Dragoons; B, of the Second Artillery; and companies F, and I of the Third Infantry.[29] Before returning to Santa Fe, Sumner instructed Backus to treat the Navajos "with the utmost rigor, till they show a desire to be at peace, and . . . pledge themselves to abstain from all depredations upon the Mexicans."[30] The new post did not, however, have the immediate quieting effect upon the Indians that Sumner hoped for. New Mexican settlements still were harassed by the Diné. In fact, even as Sumner and his command were advancing into Navajoland, raids had been conducted against the herds, flocks and fields of the upper Rio Grande country, known as the Rio Arriba; and the Navajos had perpetrated a raid within eighteen miles of Santa Fe shortly after the troop's return to the capital.[31]

X   X   X

With Sumner's return to the Rio Grande, and subsequent news that the expedition had not been successful in checking the Navajo menace, the rift widened between the governor and the military. Disharmony had already existed between Sumner and Calhoun over the latter's authorization (March 18, 1851) of volunteer companies. Now, from over the length and breadth of the territory came a flood of applications to raise and arm militiamen to war against the Navajos.[32] The military commander, however, was firmly opposed to the organization of any private expeditions against the Navajos, or for that matter, any other Indians. Sumner desperately fought Calhoun and the legislature's proposals at every turn.

Despairing over the lack of cooperation between civil and military authorities, the inadequacies of the regular army, and the meagerness of treasury funds with which to equip his militia, the governor wrote to Daniel Webster, Secretary of State, on October 1, 1851: "It is folly to suppose, that *less than two mounted regiments* . . . can preserve the quiet of this territory." Calhoun informed Webster of his belief that the executive branch of the territorial government should have at its command munitions of war, and authority to call out militia at any time danger threatened. Calhoun closed his letter with postscript that if the military and civil authorities could not work in harmony, then "one, or both should be relieved from duty."[33]

Adding to the breach between Calhoun and Sumner was the colonel's apparent total disregard for one of the instructions he had received from the Secretary of War:

> In all negotiations and pacific arrangements with the Indians, you will act in concert with the Superintendent of Indian Affairs in New Mexico, whom you will allow to accompany you in the expeditions into Indian territory. . . .

As *ex-officio* Superintendent of Indian Affairs, Calhoun's hands had been completely bound by the non-compliance of this order. Colonel Sumner had denied the governor's requests for escorts into Navajo country for the purpose of parleying with Indians upon their home-ground. Calhoun was now entirely dependent upon Indians coming to Santa Fe — a thing which the Navajos would never do as long as open hostilities continued.[34]

On November 9, Calhoun was again presented with a request for arms from Preston Beck, Jr., commander of an itinerant militia company being organized in Santa Fe. The governor immediately endorsed the petition and forwarded it to Sumner. Calhoun must have been surprised when the colonel informed First Lieutenant J. C. McFerran, Assistant Adjutant General, to furnish seventy-five flintlock muskets, cartridge boxes, bayonet scabbards, belts and plates from military stores at Fort Union. Sumner, before turning the weapons over to the company, however, affixed several conditions limiting their use. The muskets were to be returned to the army upon immediate orders of the department commander; and they were never to be used in forays into Indian country, unless the volunteers were acting in conjunction with regular troops. Upon receipt of these terms, Beck and his subordinates declined acceptance of the arms. To comply with Sumner's restrictions, Beck felt, would so limit his activities, that the organization would cease to be an "independent company." They also felt that the commander of the Ninth Military Department had no authority over the movement of civilian companies; but that they would gladly comply with the will of Governor Calhoun.[35]

Sumner's reasons for thwarting the plans of Calhoun and others were not without justifiable basis. On November 20, 1851, he penned his motives to the Adjutant General of the Army, Brevet Major General R. Jones:

> This predatory war has been carried on for two hundred years, between the Mexicans and Indians, quite time enough to prove, that unless some change is made the war will be interminable. They steal women and children, and cattle, from each other, and in fact carry on the war, in all respects, like two Indian nations.
>
> This system of warfare will interfere very much with my measures, and indeed do away with all the advantages, that I confidently expect to reap from the establishment of Fort Defiance. This large post in the very midst of the Indian cannot fail to cramp them in all their movements, and it will harass them so much, that they will gladly make peace ..., provided, they find that the post can protect, as well as punish.[36]

X　X　X

By the closing months of 1851 Fort Defiance was beginning to have the desired effect upon the Navajos. For several months following Sumner's return to Santa Fe Navajos sent in delegations requesting peace. It was then that the colonel relinquished his stand against prohibiting an agent of the

Indian Department to journey among the Navajos. Comply-ing with Calhoun's frantic requests, Sumner personally ac-companied the governor to Jemez, where on December 25, 1851, a parley was held with the Diné.

At this council the Indians were severely reprimanded for their raiding; and the department commander tried firmly to impress upon the headmen "that the troops at Fort Defiance could and would prevent them from raising a single field of grain, unless they remained at peace." Aware of the severe consequences which would befall the tribe if they failed to conduct themselves according to the stipulations of the late treaty, Navajos pledged once again to keep the peace. To consummate the agreement made that day, Calhoun — against the wishes of Sumner — distributed several thou-sand dollars worth of gifts to the headmen.[37] Thus with the presentation of an assortment of agricultural implements, calico, bayeta, and brass wire, the meeting with Navajo head-men drew to a close. For the first time in decades the Diné appeared to have been subdued — at least momentarily. The erection of Fort Defiance in the heart of Navajoland had at one stroke accomplished what the respective armies of Spain, Mexico, and a series of abortive Anglo-American expeditions had tried so vainly to do. For nearly fifty years the Diné had harassed New Mexican settlements with impunity. So inten-sive had their forays become, that an impenetrable barrier had been erected against westward expansion by the settlers residing in the river valleys of New Mexico.

X X X

1. *Calhoun Correspondence*, pp. 50-51.
2. According to the report of these Zuñi Indians, the total armament of the pueblo consisted of only thirty-two guns, with less than twenty rounds of ammunition per weapon.
3. Calhoun had no way of knowing how reliable this report was. The Zuñi delegation received the story from the Navajo chief, Chapiton, who had been trading at the small village of La Pugarita, close to the Pueblo of Laguna. Calhoun to Medill, October 15, 1949; *Calhoun Correspondence*, p. 49.

4. *Ibid.*, pp. 105-106.

5. The dislike which the Navajos harbored for Sandoval and his band is illustrated in many letters and reports by military officers and early-day travelers. On June 10, 1850, Lieutenant John Buford, commanding the garrison of Dragoons at Cebolleta, reported having talked with a member of Sandoval's band. This Indian, according to Buford, reported that the Navajos were organizing into war parties of two, three to five members for the purpose of stealing stock. Sandoval at that time had charge of some stock belonging to a resident of Cebolleta, but the chief was afraid to care for the animals, as his tribesmen had threatened to "kill him and his." Buford to Lt. L. McLaws, June 10, 1850; National Archives, Records of United States Army Commands, Record Group 98, *Department of New Mexico,* Letters Received. Hereafter cited as *Department of New Mexico,* LR.

6. Lancing P. Bloom (ed.), "The Rev. Hiram Read, Baptist Missionary to New Mexico," *New Mexico Historical Review* (Vol. XVII, April 1942), p. 133.

7. Calhoun to Lea, March 31, 1851; National Archives, Records of the Office of Indian Affairs, Record Group 75, *New Mexico Superintendency Papers,* Letters Received. Hereafter cited as *Superintendency Papers,* LR. See also *Calhoun Correspondence,* p. 307.

8. Electus Backus, "An Account of the Navajoes of New Mexico," in *Indian Tribes of the United States,* edited by Henry R. Schoolcraft (Philadelphia: 1856), Vol. IV, p. 210.

9. Calhoun to Brown, June 12, 1850; *Superintendency Papers,* LR.

10. The desperate straits in which Zuñi found itself was illustrated by a letter written by Calhoun to Commissioner Orlando Brown, in which the agent stated: "The Navajos a few days since made another attack upon Zuñi, with a force, it is apprehended, that will [*sic*] have proved disastrous to the Pueblo, by the destruction of their crops." Calhoun to Brown, October 12, 1850; *Calhoun Correspondence,* p. 263.

11. See Special Orders No. 12 (March 2, 1851), reprinted in *ibid.,* p. 296.

12. Chavez to Calhoun, March 18, 1851; *ibid.,* pp. 302-303.

13. See Proclamation of James S. Calhoun, March 19, 1851; *ibid.,* p. 302.

14. *Ibid.*

15. Although not a West Point graduate, Edwin Vose Sumner was an eminent officer. He entered the service on March 3, 1818 as a second lieutenant of infantry, and served throughout the Black Hawk War. In 1833 he was transferred to the Second Dragoons, and began his service on the frontier with the rank of captain. Sumner served with General Scott throughout the Mexican War, and was commissioned lieutenant colonel of the First Dragoons. From 1851 until 1853, he acted as commander of the Ninth Military Department, as well as serving a short term as civil governor of New Mexico. See R. E. Twitchell, *Leading Facts of New Mexican History* (Cedar Rapids: 1912), Vol. II, p. 286.

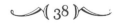

16. 32nd Congress, 1st Session, *Senate Executive Document No. 1,* pp. 125-126.

17. Sumner left Fort Leavenworth, Kansas on May 26, 1851.

18. Fort Marcy was not abandoned altogether. Sumner left at that post one company of the Second Artillery, consisting of sixty-two men under the command of Brevet Lieutenant Colonel T. H. Brooks. See 32nd Congress, 1st Session, *Senate Executive Document No. 1,* p. 204.

19. Orders No. 23 (August 4, 1851); *Department of New Mexico,* LR.

20. Richard Van Valkenburgh, *Diné Bikéyah,* p. 57.

21. Electus Backus was born and raised in New York and graduated from West Point in July of 1820. He was assigned to the First Infantry but was transferred to the Third Infantry in 1850. His service during the Mexican War was conspicuous, and he was breveted major on September 23, 1846 for gallant and meritorious conduct at the Battle of Monterey. In 1851 Backus was assigned the command of the newly erected post in the Navajo country — Fort Defiance; and in 1852 was transferred to Fort Fillmore.

22. The annoyance created by the Navajos is demonstrated by the words of Dragoon James A. Bennett, penned on August 27, 1851: "The Indians still keep with us by day. At night we can occasionally see their fires. A little after dark last night, the enemy fired several shots into our camp. Wounded one man in the leg." James A. Bennett, *Forts and Forays or A Dragoon in New Mexico, 1850-1856,* edited by Clinton Brooks and Frank D. Reeves (Albuquerque: 1948), p. 30

23 Sumner to Brevet General R. Jones, October 24, 1851; *Office of Adjutant General,* LR.

24. Bennett, *op. cit.,* pp. 30-31; also *ibid.*

25. Department Order No. 29 (September 18, 1851); National Archives, Records of U. S. Army Commands, Record Group 98; *Fort Defiance Post Returns.* Hereafter cited as *Fort Defiance Post Returns.*

26. A letter written by the post commander Captain H. L. Kendrick, a year after Fort Defiance was founded, demonstrates a few of the many bad conditions endured at that bleak outpost: "The uncertainties and difficulties attendant upon our mails, to and from the States, are among the most annoying, through by no means the worst evils of being stationed in this country. Our letters, public and private, often miss their destination; military orders from the states frequently fail to reach us; and our newspapers and public documents in many cases do not come to hand." H. L. Kendirck to Thomas L. Jesup, G.M.G., U.S.A., September 30, 1852; National Archives, *Records of the Office of the Quartermaster General,* Record Group 92; Consolidated Correspondence File, Fort Defiance.

27. W. W. H. Davis, *El Gringo or New Mexico and Her People* (Santa Fe: 1938), pp. 229-30.

28. Report of Secretary of War in 32nd Congress, 2nd Session, *House Executive Document,* No. I, Part II, pp. 75-76; also Davis, *ibid.,* p. 230;

and Electus Backus to Assistant Adjutant General, November 5, 1851; *Department of New Mexico,* LR.

29. *Fort Defiance Post Returns,* September-October, 1851.

30. Sumner to R. Jones, October 24, 1851; *Calhoun Correspondence,* p. 418.

31. Calhoun to Sumner, November 10, 1851; *Department of New Mexico,* LR.

32. The pressure put upon Governor Calhoun by the Territorial Assembly was enormous. The representatives from the northern and most exposed counties of Taos and Rio Arriba threw their weight behind a move to enlist militia companies in mid-September 1851. On the 20th of that month, Theodore D. Wheaton, Speaker of the House of Representatives presented a petition to Calhoun signed by residents of those counties:
"Sir: I write at the request of some hundreds of the citizens of the counties of Taos and Rio Arriba, who are anxious to make a campaign against the Navajo Indians who have done . . . infinite injury to the property and persons of the inhabitants of this Territory.
"The citizens to whom I refer labour under much difficulty for the want of arms as most of them have but their bows and quivers of arrows and in this respect possess no advantage over the Indians; but unarmed as they are [*sic*] only waiting authority from your excellency to organize and do all in their power to repeal these ruthless invaders. . . .
"I am well satisfied that could arsenals and arms be distributed through this country, so that these people could be furnished with arms and ammunition . . ., they could do more in one year to protect not only this but the Mexican frontier from the ravages of the different nations of Indians which surround us, than the regular army could do in three.
"My reason for believing this is derived from the fact that these people are well aware of the mountain fastnesses to which the Indians retreat and which perfectly secure them from the approach of the regular troops — and being mostly mountaineers and beaver and buffalo hunters, they have become accustomed to the mode of life necessary and best adopted to hunt out the Indians. . . ." Wheaton to Calhoun, September 20, 1851; *Calhoun Correspondence,* pp. 427-428.

33. Calhoun to Webster, October 1, 1851; *ibid.,* pp. 430-431. Calhoun again wrote to Webster on October 29, expressing his disgust with the defense situation of New Mexico. "Col. Sumner's expedition to the Navajo country has been productive of no good, as yet, and if an effort I am now making fails, the people of the Territory, to some extent, will be forced to take care of themselves, or consent to lie down quietly, and be plundered and butchered." *Ibid.,* pp. 440-441.

34. Calhoun to Luke Lea, October 31, 1851; *Superintendency Papers,* LR.

35. Beck to Calhoun, November 9, 1851; J. C. McFerran to W. R. Shoemaker, November 10, 1851; Sumner to Calhoun, November 10; and Beck to Calhoun, November 11, 1851; all in *Calhoun Correspondence,* pp. 445-454.

36. Sumner to R. Jones, November 20, 1851; *Office of Adjutant General, LR.*

37. Because Navajos had violated every treaty that had been signed, Sumner was against the distribution of annuities and presents until such time as these Indians demonstrated a sincere desire to remain at peace. He wanted to first place the tribe on a six months probation period before distributing annuities. Sumner to Jones, Jaunary 1, 1852; *Calhoun Correspondence*, pp. 433-434.

Fort Defiance 1852

III

THE INTERLUDE

THROUGHOUT the winter of 1851-52 the Navajos remained quiet. At Fort Defiance they began to drift in — first in small curious groups, then in ever-increasing numbers — as they learned that the *Belaganas,* as they called the Anglo-Americans, were extending the hand of friendship. That winter had been extremely severe and the Indians suffered greatly. Major Backus, sensing the magnitude of the situation, issued to many destitute tribesmen all the cast-off clothing procurable. To help with Indian planting, which would commence in mid-February, the post commander also distributed a few hoes and spades, after demonstrating their use. For the first time in many years the lean, dignified Diné could also be seen in the frontier towns and in Santa Fe, as they came into the settlements to trade or confer with the superintendent of Indian Affairs or one of the lesser agents. At long last the Territory of New Mexico could breathe a sigh of relief. The Navajos were quiet.

On January 27, 1852, a large Navajo delegation rode into the capital. The headmen among the party, Armijo, Raffaille

Chavez, Luke Lea, Black Eagle, Barbon, and Hosea Miguel visited the office of Indian Agent John Greiner. Since the *Belaganas* had always put strong emphasis upon the return of captives, the Indians delivered to the agent three Mexicans as a demonstration of good will. Armijo, the principal speaker of the party, informed Greiner of the great change which had taken place among his people: "We like the Americans. We have eaten their bread and meat, smoked their tobacco. The clothing they have given us has kept us warm in the cold winter. . . . With the hoes they have given us we will cultivate our lands — We are struck dead with gratitude!"

Greiner doubted the sincerity of Armijo and confronted the chief with reports from people living in the Rio Abajo or lower Rio Grande Valley, who claimed to have suffered livestock losses, and several women and children carried off by Navajos. These accusations bewildered the Indian. Not only his band, but many others of his tribe had suffered at the hands of New Mexicans. How could this agent fail to see that there were two sides to this story? Armijo responded eloquently:

"My people are all crying in the same way. Three of our chiefs now sitting before you mourn for their children, who have been taken from their homes by the Mexicans. More than 200 of our children have been carried off and we know not where they are. The Mexicans have lost but few children in comparison with what they have stolen from us. . . . From the time of Colonel Newby we have been trying to get our children back. . . . Eleven times have we given up our captives, only once have they given us ours. My people are yet crying for the children they have lost. Is it American justice that we must give up everything and receive nothing?"

At a loss as to explain "American justice," Agent Greiner feebly promised to inform the "Great Father" of what Armijo said; and then cautioned the Indians, that hereafter, all captives and livestock taken by both the Navajos and New Mexicans must be given up, and the thieves turned over to either the Indian Department or the Military for punishment.[1]

As soon as Governor Calhoun saw that Navajo depredations had ceased, he took steps to select a competent person to administer tribal affairs and adjudicate any differences that might arise between Navajos and the New Mexicans. On February 1, 1852, Samuel M. Baird received the appointment as Special Agent to the Navajos and took up his agency headquarters at Jemez.[2] The restrictions which had been placed on commercial intercourse with the Navajos were lifted, and traders began in February to ply their trade.[3] The peaceful attitude of these Indians, as might be expected, continued into spring as Navajos planted their crops. Withholding judgment that this interlude would be permanent,[4] Colonel Edwin V. Sumner took the opportunity to do what he could to cement friendly relations with the tribe. He directed the distribution from quartermaster stores, of 500 sheep, seeds of various types, and agricultural implements.[5]

Not only did this peaceful interlude extend to the Indians and the population of New Mexico in general, but also to the civil and military authorities of the territory as well. With the suspension of hostilities came a reconciliation of differences between Calhoun and Sumner; and an attempt was made by the two to work in closer accord in the administration of Indian affairs. The governor, however, was hopelessly ill. Each day his strength waned, and it became imperative for him to delegate the supervision of Indian matters to another person. On April 1, John Greiner was appointed Acting Superintendent of Indian Affairs.[6] Shortly thereafter Calhoun left for the states — which he never reached, for he died upon the Plains in June.

As Acting Superintendent, John Greiner soon had his hands full. Coffers of the superintendency were empty, and appropriations from Washington were non-existent. Each day the number of Indians seeking advice and help in straightening out their difficulties increased. On April 13, the familiar figure of Antonio Sandoval, with forty-five of his followers, appeared in Santa Fe to lodge complaints against the New Mexicans and Laguna Indians. These Navajos — in an almost fighting spirit — alleged that a portion of their lands situated at La Cienega de San José, about five leagues from the Pueblo of Laguna, had recently been taken over by the puebloans, who commenced to cut off the water to Sandoval's wheat fields, thus forcing the Navajos to abandon the land and lose a year's crop. Superintendent Greiner although sympathic, could offer no immediate help. The matter was referred to Agent Baird at Jemez for investigation.[7]

Special Agent Baird was in the meantime attempting to eliminate the potential threat to peace with the Navajos which existed in the form of those traders who paid little heed to Indian intercourse laws. In late February the agent apprehended a Vincente Romero, who had long been suspected of trading in contraband livestock and captives. Caught with liquor, powder and lead in his possession, the trader's license was immediately revoked.[8] Not only did trouble exist with unscrupulous traders, who persisted in carrying liquor to the Indians and plying their trade in captives, but also with other New Mexicans who jeopardized the shaky peace by stealing Navajo livestock. During the second week of May, Armijo and Black Eagle were again in Santa Fe lodging complaints against New Mexicans — just as John Greiner had advised them to do at the January meeting. These Navajos, who had apparently been trading at several pueblos, stated they had lost seven head of horses (four at Jemez, and three at Santa Ana) at the hands of New Mexicans.[9] Despite these incidents, the threats passed, and there were few depredations committed during that spring and summer.

✖   ✖   ✖

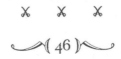

On July 17, 1852, President Millard Fillmore appointed a new territorial governor to the office left vacant by the death of James S. Calhoun. Two months later William Carr Lane, of Missouri,[10] was inaugurated in Santa Fe and officially assumed the dual role of governor and *ex-officio* Superintendent of Indian Affairs. Lane was a firm advocate of the maxim: "that it is better to feed the Indians, than fight them;" and he evolved a policy of attempting to keep the tribes quiet by the issuance of rations. He made several treaties with the Apaches in the southwest and northwest, as well as inducing a large number of Jicarilla Apaches to settle on farms west of the Rio Grande on the Rio Puerco.[11]

Although there were no major Navajo raids perpetrated during the fall of 1852, Sandoval was suspected of formenting trouble. The chief, perhaps still smarting from what he considered unjust treatment over his "water rights," was thought to be spreading a rumor among his people that the Anglos were no friends of the Diné; and that Colonel Sumner was planning a campaign of extermination. The governor, fearful that these reports would create bad feelings among the Indians, immediately dispatched orders to Agent Baird to proceed forthwith to the Navajo country with presents for the headmen and the annuities which had been scheduled for distribution in early October. Lane instructed Baird to investigate the facts connected with these reports, and endeavor to dismiss any bad feelings which might have arisen due to Sandoval's treacherous actions. Lane also wrote to Sumner late in October requesting that action be taken against the chief.[12]

Due to Lane's speedy efforts the trouble occasioned by Sandoval subsided for the moment; and the governor reported to Commissioner Luke Lea on March 4, that "this tribe is now at profound peace." Lane tried hard during the initial months of 1853 to apply his policy of appeasement to the Navajos. He hoped that, with due attention to their wants, this tribe could be settled upon a reservation where they would peacefully follow their agricultural and pastoral pursuits. In an effort to attain these ends, Baird was authorized in early March to expend $2237.65 for the purchase of "an outfit of hoes, spades, knives, axes and other necessities for the Navajos."[13]

Despite the gifts and annuities which Lane and his agent distributed to the Diné, the Indian Department was destined never to have the control over the tribe it wished. As long as the agent resided in comparative comfort at the Pueblo of Jemez the department would be virtually blind to the true conditions existing in the heart of Indian country. Soo too, did the lack of political solidarity among the Navajo cause trouble. The majority of the tribe, no doubt, enjoyed the peace. But among the estimated 8,000 to 10,000 Diné, were many bands seeking to enrich themselves at the expense of their own people. These *pobres* and *ladrones* would seek all means possible to raise their status and wealth — and New Mexican flocks and herds offered the one solution. Another source of conflict existed along the eastern border of Navajoland, skirting the Tunicha-Chuska and Zuñi Mountains, which formed the Navajo-New Mexican frontier. The bands residing within this area were openly exposed to the machinations of those New Mexicans and Anglos who had always been covetous of the Indian's large flocks and herds — including their comely women.

Spring of 1853 opened with renewed Navajo forays which threatened to explode into open hostility. The incident which dwarfed all others[14] occurred on the night of May 3. About eight o'clock that evening sheep owner Ramon Martín, his two sons, María and Librado, and four *pastores* were watching over their flock near the town of Chamas. From behind a brush pen a gun suddenly fired, bringing down Señor Martín, mortally wounded. María, seeing his father shot, ran for cover and hid until daybreak. From his place of concealment, the boy saw four Navajos approach the sheep pen and round up his brother and the four shepherds, as another Indian secured the horses of the New Mexicans. Each youth was then roped about the neck and led away to a watering place, about a quarter mile distant. Three of the captives were then released and told in broken Spanish to return and inform their people — "that when a paint horse and a mule, stolen from the Navajos, were given up, then the two boys would be delivered." With these words, the Navajos rode off with Librado and the other herder.[15]

Informed by the alcalde of Chamas of the murder of Martín and the kidnappings, Governor William Carr Lane immediately saw the danger inherent in this situation. On May 9 he ordered Donaciaro Vigil, Territorial Secretary, and a man thoroughly familiar with the Navajos, to ascertain the identity of the murderers, and proclaim to the tribe that a failure to relinquish the culprits and captives would be "considered a justifiable cause of war," and reprisals against the Indians would invariably result.[16] Governor Lane also instructed Vigil to investigate livestock losses which had occurred since March in the Las Lunas and Pena Blanca areas.

In compliance with the orders, Vigil left Santa Fe on May 10, and proceeded to Jemez. He halted at the pueblo long enough to ascertain the identity of the murderers. The puebloans told him that the malefactors were Navajos, and well known to them — most prominent of whom was a petty chieftain named Jasin, who resided in the vicinity of Tunicha.[17] Thus informed, Vigil once again set out in company with nine Jemez Indians bound for the valley of Tunicha. Four days later the secretary held council with the Navajo headmen, Armijo and Aguila Negra. At the parley, Vigil demanded the return of Librado and his companion — to which the Indians complied. He next demanded the restitution of 400 sheep belonging to a Tomas Baca of Pena Blanca, allegedly stolen by the brother of Aguila Negra. But the Indians were reluctant to comply with this demand. They denied that so many animals had been taken, and stated that they would return only what had actually been stolen.[18]

Vigil next informed the Navajos of the governor's demands for the murderer of Martín. This filled the Indians with consternation. Although Jasin and the other culprits were present, Armijo and Aguila Negra refused to give them up. Among the Navajos the powers of headmen reached only to a limited number of individuals constituting their immediate band or clan. Apparently Jasin and his accomplices were of another band, over which Armijo and Aguila Negra had no control, for the headmen told Vigil that they "had not sufficient power" to force their surrender — and to attempt to do so would result in civil war.[19] However, before leaving the council-site, Vigil succeeded in persuading the chiefs to journey to Santa Fe and confer with the governor about this touchy matter.

Vigil arrived in the capital with the two liberated youths on the forenoon of May 24. Shortly thereafter, Aguila Negra rode in, accompanied by six other Navajos and ten puebloans from Jemez. Upon their arrival at the governor's office, Lane fed the Indians well and distributed clothing before commencing the talk. In the ensuing parley Aguila Negra again explained — this time to the governor — the hazards of attempting to apprehend the culprits. Lane, however, was unrelenting in his demands. He was in the midst of a political campaign for the office of cangressional delegate from New Mexico, and felt he could increase his popularity among the native born by imposing rigorous demands upon the Navajos. The governor therefore gave the Indians to understand "that the murderers and the stock, stolen by the Navajos, had to be given up, otherwise he would declare war against them."[20] Try as they might, the Indians could not convince the governor that the return of Jasin was beyond their power. Before leaving the *Palacio,* Negra feebly promised to do all he could to arrest the murderers.

A week passed without that word from the headmen — upon which Lane had pinned his political future. By June 1, the governor had lost faith in the Indians and was consulting with Colonel Sumner. At this conference Lane and Sumner agreed that a failure to turn over the malefactors would be deemed a connivance on the part of the chiefs — and they would be considered as accessories after the fact. Should the Navajos fail in their promises, a campaign would be organized by the army and the militia, against the whole tribe. Colonel Sumner, however, could not help but express an unwillingness to cooperate with the governor in declaring war against the Navajos. He questioned the propriety of holding a tribe of ten to twelve thousand souls responsible for the acts of five marauding and ungovernable Indians. Sumner felt that a war upon these illusive tribesmen would be a futile and costly undertaking. According to the colonel, it was impossible to draw the Navajos into decisive battles; and all the army could hope to accomplish would be to lay waste to Navajoland by destroying crops and flocks.[21] But Lane urged the imperative need for the protection of life and property, and at last Sumner agreed to instruct the commander of Fort Defiance to press the demands — with force if necessary.

Complying with Sumner's orders, the new commander of Fort Defiance, Captain Henry L. Kendrick,[22] took prompt measures to investigate the trouble. On the morning of June 7, in company with Captain Richard Ewell and Henry Linn Dodge, he set out on a tour of the eastern portion of Navajoland. They proceeded in the direction of Cienega Grande; crossed the mountains to the north of Washington Pass, and returned to Fort Defiance by way of Ojo Caliente, Tunicha and Chuska. During this excursion, Kendrick met, at various points, large numbers of Indians, whom he emphatically warned "that war would result unless satisfaction was given" to all the demands of the governor. Kendrick minced no words in impressing the Navajos that, should hostilities commence, that

> this war would be the last one which it would be necessary . . . to have; that the Mexicans, the Pueblos, Sandoval's people and the Americans would be let loose upon them, their flocks seized, their men killed; their women and children taken prisoners, and ultimately the mountains made their eastern limits.

Despite his attempt to strike the one note that might bring fear to the Navajos, Kendrick was also of the opinion that depredations had been committed "by a few bad and irresponsible men" living near the Mesa de Chaco, Bear Springs, and in the valley of Chuska. He was convinced beyond a doubt that the majority of Navajos did not want war. Kendrick had found, during his tour, that those Indians residing to the west of the Chuska and Tunicha Mountains were quite adverse to war — this reluctance due in part to the "natural effect" of Fort Defiance. Those Navajos to the west — and for the most part isolated from New Mexican contact — disclaimed all responsibility for the acts of their brethren to the east.

However, Lane's designs to punish the Navajos for their transgressions were brought to a sudden halt when he was defeated as congressional delegate by José Manuel Gallegos. The governor, disappointed over the election outcome, turned over the remainder of his term to the new Territorial Secretary, William Messervy, and departed for the States. Secretary Messervy was replaced on August 8 with the arrival in Sant Fe of the new appointee to the office of governor. The man whom President Franklin Pierce had chosen was no stranger to the people of this isolated territory. David Meriwether[24] had been an Indian trader by profession, and had visited Santa Fe as early as 1819. Upon taking office he at first espoused the policies of his predecessor. But as he became more and more aware of the sources of trouble with the Indians, his opinions changed. Governor Meriwether saw that pressure was being exerted on the eastern boundary of New Mexico by Plains tribes which were being pushed westward by the movement and settlement of eastern Indians upon the central grasslands. He also saw the difficulty resulting from contact between the settlements and Indians along the territory's western frontier; and sought means to end the conflicts. On August 31, the new governor submitted his views on the management of New Mexican Indian affairs:

> ... there is but one alternative left to the government by which peace and protection can be afforded to the people of New Mexico ..., that the government must either feed and clothe these Indians to a certain extent, or chastise them in a decisive manner. The former has been the policy of my predecessor ..., and the latter has not been effectually tried. If the pacific policy be resorted to, it should be carried out upon a large and liberal scale, such as to embrace the entire Indian population.... Then, if the more stringent and vigorous policy be adopted, it should in my opinion be persisted in and carried to an extent which would leave a lasting impression upon their [the Indians'] minds as to the power of the government. Neither policy will be found to be effectual if partially carried out.[25]

Meriwether sought no half-way solution. He suggested, as wisdom, the enactment of treaties whereby title could be gained to Indian lands lying contiguous to white settlements. In compensation, the red men would receive annuities, out of which would be deducted the value of all property stolen during their forays. Meriwether hoped that by establishing such a "buffer zone" between the settlements and the Indians it would make it easier for agents and the military to enforce intercourse laws.[26]

To help execute his plans among the Navajos, Meriwether was fortunate in having an agent both capable and well-liked

by the Indians — Captain Henry Linn Dodge.[27] A seasoned soldier and frontiersman, Dodge immediately repaired to the Navajo country. Unlike other agents, who resided in the security of Santa Fe or frontier communities, this new appointee established his residence among the Navajos near the eastern approach to Washington Pass, above Sheep Springs. Dodge's guiding principle, while pursuing his duties, was basic. He believed that an agent could have little influence over his charges unless he was actually among the Indians and had daily contact with their headmen.

Upon his arrival in Navajoland, Dodge traveled virtually alone among the tribesmen, without showing the least sign of fear. The Indians were surprised at these actions, and thought it unusual when so many other Anglos had come only under military escort. The agent explained that he had not the least fear — as his intensions were good. The President had sent him among the Diné to keep the peace. They might kill him, if he gave bad advice, or injured them or their country. He further explained that he would tear up his commission as their agent rather than live like his predecessors, in the settlements. The Indians readily accepted this man — calling him "Red Sleeves" — and the headmen promised him protection from the more unruly elements of the tribe.

No sooner had Dodge set up his agency headquarters than he was off on a tour of Navajoland. In August he passed through Cañon de Chelly, following the Rio Chelly to its confluence with the San Juan — the zone of conflict between the Navajos and the Utes to the north. Dodge then proceeded to the valleys of Chuska and Tunicha. Everywhere the new agent went, he found the Indians in a prosperous state. In Cañon de Chelly he beheld orchards of peach trees and extensive fields of corn. He saw vast tracts of prime grazing land, and estimated Diné livestock at 250,000 head of sheep and horses. By August 31, Dodge had completed his tour and journeyed to Santa Fe, bringing with him a deputation of 100 Navajos.[29]

Two days later the delegation met with the governor. The Navajos must indeed have been surprised when David Meriwether spoke: for this man also talked in a far different vein. He told the Indians that he intended to keep the peace between them and the New Mexicans by hearing "the complaints of the white man with one ear and the red man with the other;" weigh both, and then give his decision with impartiality — and such decision would be "irrevocable and *must be obeyed.*" Meriwether concluded the parley by passing out medals to the headmen of the delegation. With a medallion possessing a larger ribbon, the governor appointment Zarcillas Largas (Long Earrings) as head chief of the "Navajo Nation;" and vested him with authority to speak for the tribe as a whole.[30]

❌   ❌   ❌

Except for an occasional incident, peace reigned in Navajoland for the next year and a half. Prospects of friendly relations with the New Mexicans and the Diné were bright. But isolated incidents marred the harmony. On February 10, Captain Kendrick, at Fort Defiance, reported that New Mexicans were herding in country considered traditionally Navajo. Sheep were now being grazed far to the west of Zuñi, and more than 100 miles beyond the most extreme frontier town. There were also flocks ranging the Sierra de Zuñi, between Gallina and Inscription Park.[31] How could peace be maintained when New Mexican herds were grazing on Navajo land that already was threatened with over-grazing by the tribe's 200,000 sheep and up to 60,000 horses?[32] Kendrick was at a loss for explanation to this problem — a problem which could very well disturb all the efforts expended during the past year:

. . . I know not what explanation to make of such criminal recklessness, unless I am furnished the key to it in the remarks made to me by one who seemed more anxious to protect his two or three mules than to recover his large flock of sheep, which had been stolen — *viz.*: "if I lose my sheep the Government will pay for *them*."

Now that our peaceful relations with the Navajos have a fair prospect of becoming consolidated, it is to be regretted that owners of flocks, instead of allowing us time necessary for such a result, are placing an almost irresistible temptation to robbery before a people, under whose exactions New Mexico has groaned for a third of a century.[33]

The source of this trouble, however, lay in the political machinations of the territory. Pressure was being exerted by stockmen upon members of the Legislative Assembly for passage of bills which would permit them to expand their interests into Indian country. In Santa Fe, during the winter of 1853-54, the district court ruled that under the laws of Congress there was no Indian country in New Mexico. Thus, with one stroke, by the arm of justice, Navajoland was laid open to the encroachments of stock raisers, and the illegal and insidious commerce of Indian traders. These men would have normally been restricted by the Indian Department. But now, Meriwether, as both governor and superintendent, could only inform Commissioner G. W. Manypenny that: "I have no legal power to prevent the abuses complained of [by the Navajos and Captain Kendrick]."[34]

Regardless of the temptations present, relations with the Navajos continued to improve. The mysterious, quiet Diné came in ever-increasing number to the settlements to trade. Lounging about Fort Defiance were seen Navajo *ricos* dressed in their half Spanish, half aboriginal costumes of short breeches of buckskin or baize, buttoned at the knee, with a woven blanket slung about their shoulders. Comely Navajo women in their traditional blanket skirts, fastened at the shoulders and drawn tight at the waist by a sash, attracted the roving eyes of the troops at that bleak post on the rim of the frontier.[35]

Agent Dodge had penetrated the silent exterior that is so characteristic of the Diné and everlastingly gained their confidence and respect. To his agency (which by now had been moved to Fort Defiance) he brought a blacksmith, George Carter, to instruct the Indians in the fundamentals of iron forging. As an assistant to Carter, Dodge hired Juan Anea, a Mexican silversmith. It was perhaps the latter who planted the seeds of an art which today stereotype the Navajo as an Indian bedecked with silver jewelry. Navajo crops were bountiful during 1854. The annuities of seeds, spades, hoes, and a few plows had added to the agricultural success of the Diné. Careful instructions from Dodge and the officers at Fort Defiance augmented the innate skills of these Indians.

With the removal of the constant danger that existed from New Mexican slave-raiders, Navajo women and children watched in peace and security over their flocks. Yes, it was quiet[37] in Navajoland; and despite what the district count ruled, this country was still Indian country.

1. In his report of this meeting, John Greiner confided to Governor Calhoun that it was no wonder that the Navajos had reasons to complain. These Indians were, in his estimation, very industrious; having large herds of sheep and horses, and manufactured a superior type of blanket — all of which attracted the marauding expeditions of the New Mexicans, whose constant plunderings served only to bring on the retaliation of the Navajos. Greiner to Calhoun, January 31, 1852; *Superintendency Papers,* LR.

2. The choice of Jemez as the location of the agency was deemed at that time a wise decision. The pueblo had long been a center for illegal trading activities. By placing Baird at that point, Calhoun hoped to suppress any future trouble which might erupt due to traders. Calhoun to Lea, February 29, 1852; *Calhoun Correspondence,* p. 488.

3. With the establishment of Fort Defiance, traders flocked into Navajoland. Even S. M. Baird contemplated establishing a trading post. On December 18, 1851, he requested permission of Colonel Sumner to erect a trading

post in Cañon Bonito, preferably at Fort Defiance. Baird to Sumner, December 18, 1851; *Department of New Mexico,* LR.

4. Sumner apparently expected depredations to continue, for he wrote on March 27, 1852 to the Secretary of War that: "It was too much, however, to expect that an entire stop, can be put at once, to all Indian depredations. They are educated to believe that the stealing of horses, is an act of prowess, and a few young men may occasionally band together for this purpose, but the propensity will soon wear out." Sumner to Conrad, March 27, 1852; *Calhoun Correspondence,* p. 516.

5. On May 3 Sumner directed Assistant Quartermaster, Major H. H. Sibley, to send out hoes and spades for the Navajos at Fort Defiance, and to inform Major Backus to present the gifts to the Indians in the name of the governor of the territory. Sumner to Sibley, May 3, 1852; *Department of New Mexico,* LR.

6. Annie H. Abel (ed.), "The Journal of John Greiner," *Old Santa Fe* (Vol. XVI, April 1941), p. 191.

7. Sandoval also lodged complaints against a party of New Mexicans from Cubero, who attacked a portion of the chief's band in June 1851 and drove off the Indians' stock. The Navajos, not wishing to fight, sent word to the New Mexicans that they were at peace and wished their stock back. The New Mexicans, however, shot at the messenger and ran him off before he had chance to deliver his message. Abel, "Journal of John Greiner," *op. cit.,* pp. 196-98.

8. Baird to Romero, February 23, 1852; Baird to Calhoun, February 23, 1852; *Superintendency Papers,* LR.

9. Abel, "Journal of John Greiner," *op. cit.,* pp. 207-208.

10. William Carr Lane was not a Missourian by birth. He was born in Fayette County, Pennsylvania, on December 1, 1789. Educated at Jefferson and Dickinson colleges, he took up the profession of surgery in the Army of the United States. About 1818 he resigned his commission and went to St. Louis, where he served as the first quartermaster of that state, as well as the first mayor of St. Louis. See Ralph E. Twitchell, *The Leading Facts of New Mexican History* (Cedar Rapids: 1912), Vol. II, p. 293.

11. Governor Lane expended about $20,000 in the execution of this policy; and when his treaties were not approved by Congress and the food supply could no longer be maintained, the Apaches became worse than ever in their depredations. *Ibid.,* p. 295.

12. Sandoval's treacherous actions were communicated to Governor Lane by Reverend Read, a Baptist missionary, who had returned that fall from a visit with Fort Defiance post chaplain, Reverend Shaw. Annie H. Abel (ed.), "Indian Affairs in New Mexico Under the Administration of William Carr Lane. From the Journal of John Ward," *New Mexico Historical Review* (Vol. XVI, April 1941), pp. 219-220. Hereafter cited as "Journal of John Ward."

13. Lane to Lea, March 4, 1853; *Superintendency Papers,* L.R.

14. Losses of sheep, attributed to marauding Navajos, were reported from Peña Blanca and the Los Lunas areas beginning in March.

15. Librado, the son of Ramon Martín was eight years old. The other captive, José Claudio Martín, was the first cousin of Librado. John Greiner to W. C. Lane (n.d.), *Superintendency Papers, LR.*

16. Two days previous to Vigil assignment, John Greiner was sent out by Lane to conduct a preliminary investigation of Martín's death. Lane to Vigil, May 9, 1853; *ibid.*

17. Abel (ed.), "Journal of John Ward," (Vol. XVI, July 1941), pp. 328-359.

18. According to Vigil, Aguila Negra claimed that Baca had padded his losses, for his brother had stolen only ninety sheep. As soon as the chief learned of what Baca was stating, he called upon the Prefect of Santa Ana County (from which the sheep were taken) for the purpose of satisfying himself that not more than ninety animals had been driven away. But the Prefect upheld Baca's claim. Vigil to Lane, May 25, 1853; *Superintendency Papers, LR.*

19. *Ibid.*

20. Abel (ed.), "Journal of John Ward," (Vol. XVI, July 1941), pp. 341-342.

21. Here Sumner revealed the basic inadequacy of the regular army in New Mexico. A year previous John Greiner expressed the same sentiments in a little different words: "There are 92,000 Indians . . . in this Territoiry. Many of them at war. We have not 1,000 troops here under Colonel Sumner to manage them. Our troops are of no earthly account. They cannot catch a single Indian. A dragoon mounted will weigh 225 pounds. Their horses are all as poor as carrion. The Indians have nothing but their bows and arrows and their ponies are as fleet as deer. Cipher it up. Heavy dragoons on poor horses, who know nothing of the country, sent after Indians who are at home anywhere and who always have some hours start, how long will it take to catch them?" John Greiner, "Private letters of a Government Official in the Southwest," *The Journal of American History,* (Vol. III, 1919), p. 549.

22. Henry Lane Kendrick, of New Hampshire, graduated from West Point in July 1835, and was assigned to the Second Infantry. A year later he was transferred to the Second Artillery; and remained with that regiment throughout the Mexican War. Kendrick began his duty in New Mexico in 1849; and was with Colonel John M. Washington's expedition into Navajoland. Two years later he participated in Colonel Edwin Sumner's campaign against the tribe; and assumed command of newly established Fort Defiance a year later. For additional details see: Marvin Vincent and Samuel Tillman, *Col. Henry L. Kendrick, U.S.A.* (New York: Dutton, 1892).

23. To keep the Navajos in check, Kendrick felt that some sort of pressure should be brought to bear upon them: "I feel constrained to say that the most efficient rod in terrorem [*sic*] to be held over these people is the fear of

a permission being given to the Mexicans to make captives of Navajos and to retain them, a permission at once wise and philanthropic and one which would at an early date settle the question." Kendrick to S. D. Sturgis, A.A.G., June 11, 1853; *Department of New Mexico,* LR.

24. A Virginian by birth and a Kentuckian by residence, David Meriwether was at an early date filled with the desire for adventure which bespoke of his heritage. His education was that of the frontier; and he entered the employment of the American Fur Company, spending three years trapping and hunting upon the plains and in the mountains of the far west. In 1819, in company with a party of Pawnee Indians, he was sent to open trade with New Mexico. Upon crossing the Spanish frontier, he was captured by Spanish troops and carried to Santa Fe and imprisoned as a United States spy. After a month, Meriwether was released for lack of evidence and returned to United States' soil. See Twitchell, *Leading Facts of New Mexican History,* II, pp. 295-296.

25. Annual Report of Commission of Indian Affairs, 1853; in 33rd Congress, 1st Session, *House Executive Document,* Vol. I, p. 430.

26. To illustrate the point he was trying to make to the commissioner, Meriwether quoted from the report of a tour of the Navajo country, by Captain H. L. Kendrick: "Major Kendrick . . . describes a portion of this tribe as being successfully engaged in the cutivation of the soil, and it is his opinion that those bands, far removed from the white settlements will raise more than enough grain for their own subsistence, and from this information, I am of the opinion that these Indians inhabit the most desirable lands of the Territory. That portion of this tribe thus described rarely engage in predatory excursions within the white settlements, but the other portion residing near our border, rob, steal, and murder on all occasions." Meriwether to Manypenny, August 31, 1853; *Superintendency Papers,* LR.

27. Henry Linn Dodge was the youngest son of Senator Henry Dodge of Wisconsin and brother of Augustus Caesar Dodge, Senator from Missouri. The new agent received his appointment from President Pierce in August 1853, and replaced Samuel Baird. By natural aptitude and experience, Dodge was an excellent choice. He was a soldier of considerable experience, a veteran of Rocky Mountain exploration and Santa Fe trail escort, and was with Colonel Washington and Calhoun on their 1849 expedition into Navajo country. From 1850-51, Dodge served as commissary agent for the garrison of troops stationed at Cebolleta. At the same time he engaged in trading ventures with the Navajos and Puebloans living in the vicinity of that frontier community. For additional information on the life of Dodge see: Biographical File of Henry L. Dodge, *Arizona Pioneers' Historical Society,* Tucson; also *Department of War,* Service Record of Henry L. Dodge; and J. Buford to L. McLaws, June 1, 1850; *Department of New Mexico,* LR.

28. Letters from Dodge to the editor, November 16, 1853, January 7, 1854; Santa Fe *Weekly Gazette.*

Dodge attributed much of the Navajo prosperity to the agricultural implements which had been distributed to the Indians. He also estimated that the Diné's livestock amounted to 250,000 head of sheep and horses.

29. Santa Fe *Weekly Gazette,* September 10, 1853. Meriwether to Many-penny, September 19, 1853; *New Mexico Superintendency Papers,* LR.

30. Meriwether to Manypenny, *ibid.*

31. Kendrick to Meriwether, February 10, 1854; *Department of New Mexico,* LR.

32. The surgeon at Fort Defiance, Jonathan Letterman, reported at this time that if the number of sheep owned by the Navajos were doubled, their country could not possibly sustain them. Jonathan Letterman, "Sketch of the Navajo Tribe of Indians," *Smithsonian Report, 1855* (Washington: 1855), p. 285.

33. Kendrick to Meriwether, February 10, 1854; *op. cit.*

34. Meriwether to Manypenny, February 27, 1854; *Superintendency Papers,* LR.

35. Letterman, *op. cit.,* p. 290.

36. For additional information on the Navajo art of silversmithing, see Arthur Woodward's very excellent book, *A Brief History of Navajo Silver-smithing* (Flagstaff: Museum of Northern Arizona, 1946).

37. As was to be expected, the peace was disrupted from time to time. In late October, a soldier was killed at Fort Defiance, and Dodge quickly demanded the murderer. On November 5, Armijo and Zarcillas Largas pre-sented the accused Indian to the agent. After the murderer's identity was definitely established, he was, in the words of Dodge, "hung until he was dead, dead, dead." Meriwether to Manypenny, October 29, 1854, Novem-ber 30, 1854; Dodge to Meriwether, November 13, 1854; *Superintendency Papers,* LR.

Washington Pass

IV

THE PRELUDE

THE YEAR 1855 opened with pressure upon the Navajos. But it came not from New Mexicans on the east, but from Capote Utes residing north of the Rio San Juan. Having been at war for the past year with the white men, these Indians were now trying their best to induce the Navajos to join them in an alliance. The Utes from mountains to the north boasted of their great success in past battles. They claimed to have killed "no less than eight hundred men, women, and children;" and to have driven away vast herds of horses, mules and cattle, a portion of which were offered to the Navajos. In councils, the Utes begged their southern neighbors not to plant that coming spring, but to join with them in driving the Anglos from the territory while the latter were still weak.[1] However, only a few Navajos joined the Ute scheme. As with all peoples, the Diné had within their number a poorer element who lacked those essentials of wealth deemed so important among these Indians — sheep, horses and captives; and the Utes were able to entice a few *pobres* and *ladrones* to join their alliance. However, the greater portion of the Navajos were engaged in breaking ground for spring crops. From Fort Defiance, Agent Dodge wrote in his annual report "that the condition of the Navajo tribe of Indians during this spring . . . is prosperous in a degree heretofore unknown to them."[2]

In an effort to dissuade The People from joining the plunder trail of the Utes, Dodge had scoured Fort Defiance for all the hoes and spades he could find for distribution. On May 2, he handed out to Indians residing at Tunicha and Cañon Blanco, 150 agricultural implements. Both the agent and military personnel at that isolated post reported favorably on the conduct of the Navajos. The tribe appeared to be planting more extensively that spring than they ever had since commencement of the Anglo-American occupation. March and April had been unusually wet months, and estimates of land under cultivation ran as high as 4,000 acres. Armijo, the chief from Tunicha, whom Dodge labeled "the greatest farmer in the Nation," observed the ease with which the soldiers cultivated their kitchen gardens. He felt that he too, could be as successful if furnished with the same type of tools possessed by the Americans; and he applied to Captain Kendrick for the loan of a plow and three yokes of oxen. The commanding officer would have been more than happy to comply with the chief's request, if such agricultural tools could have been spared. But Kendrick had none.[3]

The Navajos were also making rapid headway in the art of metal working — thanks to the tutelage of George Carter and Juan Anea. On April 30, Dodge reported: "they have eighteen native blacksmiths who work with hand bellows and the primitive tools used by the Mexicans with which they make all of the bridles, rings, buckles, etc."[4] The People, enjoying their prosperity could not be persuaded to join the Utes. Try as they might, the Capotes offered inducements of cattle, sheep, and horses as rewards if the tribe would rise up against the Americans. In every instance, Ute words were met with stern rebuffs: "The Diné would buy all the livestock they needed." The people to the north had deceived the Navajos in the past, and the headmen of the Diné were fearful that this was but another deception. They would not have any part of the proposals; and they replied that the Anglos were "the best friends they . . . ever had."[5]

✗   ✗   ✗

That spring David Meriwether, as *ex-officio* Superintendent of Indian Affairs, was at last furnished with means to put into effect his Indian policy. On July 31, 1854, the United States Congress approved an Indian Appropriation Act which allowed the New Mexico Superintendency $30,000 to negotiate treaties with the more troublesome tribes under its jurisdiction.[6] Eight months later, on March 16, 1855, Commissioner George W. Manypenny informed Meriwether that he had been "designated by the President" to enact articles of convention with the Apaches, Navajos and Utes. For the first time in the history of New Mexico these tribes would be guaranteed the rights of occupancy to their lands:

> You will make such arrangements as will provide for the Indians, within the country which they may respectively reside and the possession of which they claim, a suitable tract or tracts, limited in extent, for their future permanent home; and will guarantee to them the possession and enjoyment of the reserve assigned them, with provisions that hereafter the President may cause the land reserved to be surveyed, and to assign to each single person over twenty-one years of age, or head of family, a farm containing from, say, twenty to sixty acres, according to the number of persons in such family.[7]

The appropriations allowed for the treaty making were slow arriving in New Mexico. Finally, by the first week of July 1855, the governor had received the annuities, and had put his affairs in order for the scheduled trip into Navajo

country. On July 5, David Meriwether, his son Raymond, W. W. H. Davis, secretary to the governor, and two servants left Santa Fe bound for Fort Defiance, where they would meet the commander of the Ninth Department, General John Garland.[8]

The governor reached Fort Defiance on July 13 and on the following day he and Davis rode to the council site to ascertain from Agent Dodge when the Navajos would be assembled in sufficient numbers for treaty negotiations.[9]

Fourteen miles north of Fort Defiance, at the west entrance to Washington Pass, lay Laguna Negra (Black Lake). Here on a low, red, sandy ridge overlooking the dark waters of the lake, Agent Henry Linn Dodge had pitched his tent and began assembling the tribesmen. Meriwether spent the morning conferring with the agent and what headmen were already there, and set July 16 as the date for the proposed treaty signing. Upon their return that afternoon to Fort Defiance, Meriwether's party witnessed the arrival of General Garland with Captain Ewell's company of dragoons amid a thunderous salute from the post's field battery. The next day passed with a review and inspection of the garrison. On the following morning — July 16 — the governor, W. W. H. Davis, and General Garland proceeded to Laguna Negra under escort of Captain Ewell's dragoons. As the party rode along, Navajos attached themselves to the column — the throng increasing in numbers as the destination was neared.

Once at Laguna Negra, Meriwether directed that his tent be pitched near the shore of the lake; and the dragoons were encamped close by. At one o'clock the council was opened in a ramada constructed of cedar boughs. This enclosure, originally intended for the negotiators, was quickly filled to overflowing by a wave of Indians who crowded in, threatening to destroy the flimsy structure.[10] Every band (except Sandoval's[11]) that the Anglos had ever had contact with, was represented at this meeting — 1,500-2,000 buckskinned, mounted and armed warriors waited silently to hear the words of the governor.

Before the talk opened, tobacco was passed around to the assembled headmen, who quickly made *cigarritos,* which they smoked with "great gravity and gusto." Following the smoke the council commenced, with the governor speaking through two interpreters to the Indians:

"I have come here to meet the Navajos, and I am glad to see so many present. I am glad the Navajos and the whites have been at peace so long a time and hope they will remain at peace. I have come to see you and agree upon a country the Navajos and whites may each have; that they may not pasture their flocks on each other's lands. If we have a dividing line so that we know what each other's country is, it will keep us at peace. I will explain the kind of a treaty I desire to make with you; and when I am through I want you to counsel with each other whether you will agree to such a treaty, and grant an answer in the morning."

Meriwether explained fully the terms of the proposed treaty, carefully pointing out what the Indians would gain by signing such an agreement — a reservation designated by the President of the United States, annuities, and the protection by the government from New Mexican encroachments. Upon completion of the governor's speech, the council disbanded, and the remainder of the day was devoted to trading, horse racing, and gambling.

The following morning the Indians again gathered in great numbers, many of whom sat, as recorded by Secretary Davis, "so immovable upon their horses that man and beast seemed but one animal." During the morning the chiefs considered the propositions made the day before. Having determined to accept the terms, twenty of them came to Meriwether and announced the fact, and the council again opened. Before the business of treaty making could be taken up, however, the council had to pause long enough to select a new spokesman.

Zarcillas Largas had tendered his resignation to Governor Meriwether. Turning over his official staff of office and medal, the chief informed the governor that he was too old to govern his people. Meriwether, accepting the resignation, requested the assembly to select a man to fill Largas' place. The choice fell upon a war chief known as *Hastin Chilhajin* (Man of Blackweed). In the years to come, this headman would be called Holy Boy or more commonly Manuelito; and would lead his people through many troublous times. Manuelito, however, would not accept the staff of his predecessor. Nor would he allow the medal to be suspended from his neck by the same string which Zarcillas Largas had used. To do so, he insisted, would render his influence over his people ineffectual. Therefore, Meriwether presented his own steel cane to the chief, and had the medal restrung.[12] The council then resumed, with Manuelito acting as spokesman for the Navajos. Governor Meriwether opened the talk by reminding the Indians of the propositions of the day before:

"Yesterday I made known the terms of the proposed treaty and I now want to know whether you all agree to said terms." In response, Manuelito answered the governor, "We are content with what you have proposed, and will agree to the terms you have mentioned."

"I will now have the terms of the treaty reduced to writing so that we can not forget what it contains," informed the governor. "My clerk will now go to work to reduce the treaty to writing, and we will sit here and smoke until it is finished."

"It is all good," said Manuelito in agreement with the governor's actions. The Indian, showing pangs of remorse for the actions of his people when they crowded into the ramada the day before, added, "We are sorry our people treated you badly yesterday, and I am ashamed to show myself. I am now appointed in place of Zarcillas Largas, and conditions will be different."

"The boys only behave badly," said Meriwether, acknowledging Manuelito's apologies. The governor, turning to one of the interpreters, instructed him to ask the assembled headmen if they were willing to follow the decisions of Manuelito, and to signify their approval of the new chief by raising their hands. All the headmen unanimously sustained the choice of Manuelito as their spokesman in all future negotiations.[13]

The treaty having been "reduced" to writing, the governor proceeded to read it — the interpreters translating the document article by article into Navajo. After each major point, the Indians were asked if they understood and agreed to its contents. The Navajos answered in the affirmative until the fourth article was reached. This portion of the treaty set forth the country assigned to the tribe. Although it officially assigned to the Diné their traditional country, it specified exact boundaries. The western limits were defined as a line running approximately from the present location of the San Juan River (north of present-day Kayenta), to the confluence of Chevalon Creek and the Little Colorado between present-day Holbrook and Winslow. The eastern boundary, and by far the most important, was set off by a line following the San Juan from the "Four Corners area" to Cañon Largo, thence southwesterly to the Zuñi River at a point just east of the Pueblo of Zuñi.[14]

The Meriwether Treaty stipulated that the Navajos would give up their claim and title to all lands east of Chaco Cañon in the north, and Agua Azul (Blue Water) in the center, and to the south of Zuñi. After listening intently to the interpreter's explanation of the new boundaries, Manuelito stood and explained that his people claimed a much larger country than that set forth in the treaty. The chief was reluctant to give up this land, for it possessed many spots sacred to his people. The four mountains which marked the traditional limits of Navajoland were within the restricted area. As long as he and his people could remember, they had journeyed to the salina near Zuñi to gather salt. This precious substance would now be restricted to them. Meriwether, attempting to soothe the worries of Manuelito and the other headmen, traced the new tribal boundaries upon a map prepared by Lieutenant Parke of the Topographical Engineers. With the use of this map — incomprehensible as it might be to the Navajos — he pointed out that many of the Indian's sacred areas were still within the reservation. He pointed to a peak situated close to the Rio San Juan, which was held in great reverence by the Indians. Mount Polonia, he explained, was within the limits of the reserve; and he "hoped that this one sacred mountain would be sufficient." Furthermore, the tribe would be granted the privilege of gathering salt near Zuñi.[15] The lands which the Diné had previously claimed, and which now would be ceded to the United States, would be paid for by the government in the form of yearly annuities, valued at $10,000. After some consultation with the headmen, Manuelito agreed to accept the boundary. The governor then continued reading and explaining the remaining portions of the treaty; the Indians voicing their assent to each article until the ninth was reached. Here, Manuelito again interrupted the governor. Calling for the surrender by the tribe of all Indians committing depredations, this article was very offensive to the assembled headmen. Manuelito explained that although the tribesmen had turned over malefactors before, it was all "very unpleasant to them." For any Navajo to attempt to force the surrender of another tribesman, would be to risk his own life, explained Manuelito. The Diné much preferred that the Americans come and claim such men, as this would not conflict with the social and ethical values of the tribe. In reply, Meriwether stated that if the Americans went into Indian country to arrest the malefactors, they would not know the guilty from the innocent, and many would suffer needlessly. Therefore, he must insist upon this provision. After much deliberation, the chiefs also agreed to this article, and the following day, July 18, was appointed for the official treaty signing.[16]

Thus the Diné received the first in a series of reservations which would gradually reduce their lands to but a fraction of what was traditionally theirs, in a premeditated effort to move the tribesmen westward. Meriwether, estimating tribal strength at eight to ten thousand souls, was of the opinion that the new limits was adequate to sustain them. The new reservation consisted of 7,000 square miles and held, in Meriwether's opinion, all the planting grounds of the Navajos.[17] The annuities which the Navajos would receive were not as large in proportion to tribal population as the amount alloted for other tribes. But Meriwether believed that they would be sufficient, for as he wrote to the commissioner:

> . . . the necessities of these Indians does not require the payment of a large sum annually to enable them to live in comfort and improve their condition. Indeed, these Indians may now be considered in a prosperous condition; they have a large number of horses and sheep, together with their domestic animals; have planted some four thousand acres of grain this season, and by another year will be able to raise a sufficient amount to feed the whole tribe plentifully, after which time I hope that they will have a surplus sufficient to supply the wants of Fort Defiance, which now has to be hauled over one hundred miles at great cost to the government.[18]

Concluding the Treaty of Laguna Negra, Meriwether promptly returned to Santa Fe. After a few days of rest in the capital, the governor left again to enact another treaty involving the interests of the Navajos. Ute Agent Lorenzo Labadie had assembled at Abiquiu the principal men of the Capote Utes and Navajos residing along the San Juan. Governor Meriwether would meet with these headmen on August 8 in an attempt to settle difficulties existing between the two tribes.[19]

Hostilities between these two people had commenced that spring — shortly after Navajos refused to join the Utes in their fight against the white men. In June Capote Utes laid waste to Navajo rancherías along the south bank of the San Juan and carried away a number of children and livestock belonging to a few prominent *ricos*. These raids produced panic among the Diné residing within easy reach of their northern neighbors. Abandoning their crops, many Navajos moved southward to the sanctuary of Fort Defiance or concentrated in large numbers for mutual protection. Agent Dodge, receiving news of Ute incursions, expressed grave concern to the Commissioner of Indian Affairs over outcome of the threatening hostilities.

> It is impossible to say what will be the result of this war. The Utahs have fine rifles, live by the chase and are the most war-like tribe in New Mexico.
> The Navajos have but few guns of inferior quality, live by the cultivation of the soil and the produce of their flocks and herds and are not war like. And if this war is persisted in without prompt and efficient aid is [*sic*] received by them from our Government, [*sic*] must fall an easy prey to the Utahs.[20]

Dodge's concern, however, was alleviated momentarily by a series of campaigns conducted by General Garland against the Utes; and comparative peace and quiet returned to New Mexico during the fall of 1855.

During the winter of 1855-56 a far worse peril to Navajo-white relations struck. Extremely severe weather commenced in November and continued through March. The Rio Grande at Albuquerque was reported frozen over so solidly that a horse and *carreta* could be driven over it. On December 25, the thermometer at the Fort Defiance hos-

pital gave a reading of thirty-two degrees below zero.[21] This severe weather continued for the next two months. Blizzards, accompanied by deep snow drifts, forced Navajos residing in the highlands north of Fort Defiance to move south to lower elevations in quest of forage. Many of the Indians coming into the post expressed the opinion that they had not seen a winter of such severity for many years. Certainly the United States troops had not felt one like it since commencement of their occupation of the territory.

Devastation of their flocks and herds by extreme cold caused many Navajos to take to the plunder trail. In late February, members of Manuelito's band drove off a number of horses and mules from the valley of the Rio Puerco.[22] New Mexican flocks, grazing for the past year within country claimed by the Navajos, were also attacked — just as Kendrick predicted. On March 27, an estimated 11,000 sheep, belonging to Antonio José Otero, Antonio Parea, and the Rameros, were run off by Indians who left three herders dead. Major Kendrick and Agent Dodge were directed to inquire into the depredations.[28] Carrying out the orders, Kendrick and Dodge discovered that the perpetrators of the offense were influential members of the Navajo tribe — the son of Narbona, two sons of Archuleta, and two sons-in-law of Cayatano. According to the Navajo agent, these Indians were living "as outcasts" among the Capote Utes north of the Rio San Juan. They had instigated the raids on New Mexicans to revenge a loss of eight horses stolen from their Ute friends by other Navajos — who had not forgotten their losses a few months previous at the hands of their northern neighbors.

Demands by Dodge and Kendrick for the return of the murderers were met by stern refusals from the headmen. As Manuelito had previously explained to Governor Meriwether, for the tribe to hunt down and relinquish any member "was very unpleasant," if not impossible. The headmen stated that to attempt to force the delivery of the malefactors would likely produce civil war among the Navajos in which the Utes would side with the guilty. Desiring to prevent hostilities, the headmen at last promised to return all the sheep; and "give three servants in place of the herders killed, as had been the custom among them and the Mexicans."[24] However, as in past demands for indemnification, the chiefs denied that so many sheep had been stolen. They insisted that no more than 4,000 animals had been driven off. Nevertheless, the headmen would gather together the sheep and turn them over to the New Mexicans. In fact, they claimed that Armijo and Many Horses had already taken one-half of the animals from the thieves. These, however, could not be returned as it was lambing season.[25] Allowing time for the sheep to produce their young, Dodge and Kendrick set the 31st day of May as the time to receive the animals. Laguna Negra was chosen as the meeting place in hopes that the site would impress upon the minds of the Indians the necessity for a strict conformity to the terms of Meriwether's Treaty.[26] At this meeting the Indians returned in all 1,400 sheep and 30 horses, which were immediately forwarded to Señor Otero. But the Navajos still clung to their stand regarding the restoration of the malefactors — they would pay any amount of sheep requested by the governor but they could not give up the murderers.[27]

Two weeks later a complete reversal occurred in the attitudes of the Navajos. They reported that two tribesmen had recently been killed by New Mexicans, and no more sheep or horses would be surrendered.[28] To make matters worse, a full investigation of New Mexican losses, conducted by Governor Meriwether, revealed that the portion of sheep claimed to have belonged to the Pareas was "entirely without foundation." When forced to give strict account of his losses, Señor Parea finally conceded that he had not lost a single animal on March 27. Again fuel was added to the fire of Navajo tempers, which by mid-June were on the verge of explosion. The "Head Chief," Manuelito, heretofore quiet, was becoming belligerent. He had insisted upon grazing his livestock upon the haying grounds of Fort Defiance, located at Ewell's Camp. On June 13, Kendrick talked with the chief, asking him if he intended to respect the treaty signed at Laguna Negra last August, by keeping his animals off those lands reserved for use by the military. Manuelito hotly replied, "that he wouldn't: that the land was his when a boy, and would remain his until his death." The chief further asserted that Kendrick had wagons, soldiers and mules, and could get his hay at other haying grounds, thirty miles distant. Manuelito then flung the gauntlet of war at the post commander, informing Kendrick that he could order him off if he desired, but it would be to no avail. Manuelito could call forth 1,000 warriors; "and from what he had seen, he had more warriors than the governor and general of the Americans." Showing his disrespect still further, Manuelito informed Kendrick that "the Americans were too fond of *sleeping, eating, drinking* and had white eyes and could not see how to catch them [Navajos] when they chose to keep out of their way."[29]

Informed of the head chief's action, Agent Henry Linn Dodge attributed the belligerence to several causes. First, the killings of two Navajos by New Mexicans over loss of the sheep in March had caused feelings of revenge on the part of the Indians. Secondly, Zarcillas Largas had been spreading rumors since December 1855, that Fort Defiance, being too expensive to maintain, was going to be abandoned. It was true that the post was extremely costly to maintain, situated as it was far from supply depots. Troops had been withdrawn, leaving a skeleton garrison to keep the peace.

On December 11, Company B of the Third Infantry had been detailed to duty in Albuquerque, leaving only Company H of that regiment, and Company B of the Second Artillery — a total of 165 men.[30] Dodge, knowing intimately the nature of the Indians, informed Governor Meriwether that

> they [the Navajos] are no fools and see at a glance . . . that the troops at this place [Fort Defiance] are too few to prevent them killing and stealing and that they [the soldiers] are barely able to protect themselves and herds which are kept at a distance from the post without attempting an offensive movement against them.

Dodge's letter could not have been more opportune, for when finished he was informed that a large war party, headed by the son of José Largo, a Navajo headman living near Ojo Caliente, was on its way "to steal and kill all persons that may be so unfortunate as to fall in to their hands."[31]

Throughout the remainder of June, civil and military authorities received numerous reports of alleged thefts committed by Navajos. In consequence of the threatened hostilities, that June the Regiment of Mounted Rifles was ordered to duty in New Mexico from Texas.[32] Despite the prospects of a full scale Indian war, New Mexicans still persisted in grazing their sheep within Navajo country. For the most part, popular opinion within those counties adjacent to Navajoland sustained the actions of these herders; and by fall 1856, a movement was underway to re-define the reservation boundaries so that the economic interests of the Indians and the New Mexicans would not clash. On October 18, the Santa Fe *Weekly Gazette* published an editorial outlining drastic changes which should be made in the administration of territorial Indian affairs — and those affecting the Navajos were not slighted:

> New limits should be established for the Navajos, so as to give more room for our citizens to graze their stock. There is no necessity for these Indians to have grazing grounds east of their settlements, for they have far better pasture lands west of them, and where there will be no interference from any quarter.[33]

With this play of words the encroachments of sheep raisers had been justified, and the stage set for a new land grab. Events in the next few months would, in large measure, determine the course pursued in reaching these ends.

The first event — which together with others — would unleash a holocast upon the territory occurred on November 19, 1856. On that day Navajo Agent Henry Linn Dodge, while hunting some thirty-five miles south of Zuñi, was ambushed by a party of Coyotero and Mogollon Apaches, who had ridden north from their haunts along the upper reaches of the Gila River to wage war upon the Navajos. Believing that the agent had been kidnapped and would be held for ransom by the Apaches, Captain Kendrick quickly dispatched letters to department commander, Colonel B. L. E. Bonneville, Governor Meriwether, and Apache Agent Michael Steck, requesting a full and quick investigation of the abduction. When news of the attack upon Dodge reached Santa Fe, Colonel Bonneville rapidly geared for full scale operations against the Apaches. On November 29, he proclaimed to the Assistant Adjutant General of the Army, Colonel Lorenzo Thomas, what the consequence would be if harm befell the Navajo agent:

> I can only promise that in case any harm is done him, if necessary the whole strength of the Department shall be used to punish and break up these people.[35]

At the Apache Agency, located at Fort Thorn, Michael Steck endeavored to learn the fate of Dodge from the Apaches themselves. Upon questioning Mangus Coloradas, the agent definitely substantiated the report of a league between the Coyoteros and Mogollones. As this headman had been in the settlements of Limitar and Socorro at the time of the raid, his knowledge of the war party's activities was scant. But Mangus promised to send out his brother, José Mangus, to investigate the alleged kidnapping; and to determine if Dodge's release could be attained.

The fate of Henry Linn Dodge was finally determined on January 2, 1858. Late that day, José Mangus returned from his mission into Apache country. He reported to Steck, that Dodge, while hunting alone, was surprised by the warriors and "shot with a carbine on the spot." José also reported that after killing the Navajo agent, the Apaches, led by Cautivo and Tsna, continued to Laguna, where they seized a flock of sheep. Leaving that pueblo, they struck across the valley of the Puerco, and stole another flock before descending the Rio San Francisco and striking a southerly course for the Gila.[36]

The word of Dodge's death left no other course open but to chastise the Apaches. From May until September 1857, three powerful columns of dragoons and infantry operated against these Indians. The campaign was little more than a fiasco, in which thirty-two Apaches were killed and forty-five captured. The more recalcitrant members of the tribe merely slipped across the border to prey upon the frontier towns of northern Mexico.[37]

Meanwhile, Captain H. L. Kendrick — filling temporarily the vacancy of Navajo agent — was faced with the almost overwhelming task of keeping the peace between New Mexicans and the Indians. That winter and early spring occasional Navajo thefts from flocks grazing far to the west of frontier towns incited the New Mexicans. Sheep owners, despite their encroachments upon traditional grazing lands of the Diné, pressured military and civil authorities to organize reprisal expeditions.[38] Kendrick was aware of hostilities that the Indians rightfully harbored over usurpation of their lands. He knew also that Navajos had observed recent troop reductions at Fort Defiance, which only confirmed the tribe's innate feelings of superiority.

Indians to the north of the Rio San Juan were also making inroads into Navajoland. In early February, Utes raided the area between the northern point of the Tunicha Mountains and the eastern mouth of Cañon de Chelly. Eight Navajos were killed in these forays; and the tribe retaliated by slaying five Utes. Sensing the far-reaching effects which a Ute-Navajo war would likely have, Kendrick wrote a word of warning to the Assistant Adjutant General of the Department:

> Under the supposition that we are to have difficulties with other Indians, it would be well if the Mexicans were induced to keep their flocks out of the way of the Navajos, at least until those difficulties are over; this is the more important from the reduced state in which this garrison will be in soon.[39]

Kendrick had also received intelligence that the Navajos were planning further reprisals against the Utes, which might indirectly affect the New Mexicans. Although he knew that the political disunity of the tribe did not permit warfare in the sense of well organized campaigns involving great numbers of warriors, still Kendrick could not help but feel uneasy about the outcome of Navajo plans; and he added the following postscript to his letter:

> I am further informed, but doubt it, that the Navajos intend a campaign against the Utahs. Should they be successful, it will all be *very well*, but otherwise they *may* make up their losses from the Mexicans — another reason for these people being on their guard.[40]

Preparation for the campaign against the Apaches in retaliation for the death of Dodge had also threatened the peace. Bonneville had requested Navajos to participate in the expedition. Only Sandoval, of the "Enemy Navajos," accepted the offer — no doubt hoping to gain a share of whatever spoils might be taken. This reluctance on the part of other headmen was deemed by the military as indicating that plans were afoot to strike at New Mexicans as soon as military forces were tied up in the Gila country. To avoid clashes from that direction, Captain Kendrick issued still stronger

warning. In April he advised stockmen to move their flocks "well in towards the Rio Grande, or even to the east of that river."[41]

Not enough that New Mexican encroachments and Ute raids would incite the Navajos; still another factor was added — that of the weather. Extreme drought that spring and summer had brought ruin to tribal crops. With the chief source of Navajo subsistence considerably reduced, tensions increased that fall and winter. The stage now was set for the eruption of hostilities. No one knew exactly from what quarter would come the final contributing factor that would set it all off. New Mexicans on the east, and the Utes to the north, were naturally the first choice of the more perceptive officials. But then, there was always the chance that some blunder arising out of the chaotic administration of military and Indian affairs of the territory would touch off an Indian war.

✕ ✕ ✕

1. Captain Kendrick reported that Tomache's band of 200 Capote Utes, together with a few Jicarilla Apaches, had met with Navajos in council at Ojo del Gallo. H. L. Kendrick to A.A.G., February 25, 1855; *Department of New Mexico,* LR.

2. Dodge to Meriwether, April 17 and 30, 1855; *Superintendency Papers,* LR.

3. Dodge to Meriwether, April 17, May 2, 1855; *ibid.*

4. Dodge to Meriwether, April 30, 1855; *ibid.*

5. Dodge to Meriwether, April 17, 1855; *ibid.*

6. Manypenny to Meriwether, August 7, 1854; National Archives, *Records of the New Mexico Superintendency,* Record Group 75, Letters Received from Commissioners, 1854. Hereafter cited as *Superintendency Records.* See also: 34th Congress, 1st Session, *House Executive Documents,* Nos. 7-12.

7. Manypenny to Meriwether, March 16, 1855; 34th Congress, 1ts Session, *House Executive Document,* Vol. I, Part I, pp. 526-528.

8. Department Commander, John Garland, had planned to accompany the party with an escort of troops. He was, however, detained by official business, and arrived a day or so later.

9. As early as May 24, 1855, Meriwether had issued orders to Henry Linn Dodge, directing the agent to assemble as many Navajos as he could at or near Fort Defiance, for a council which would convene about July 10. Meri-

wether to Dodge, May 24, 1855; *Superintendency Records,* Letters received from agencies, 1855.

10. W. W. H. Davis, *El Gringo,* pp. 231-232.

11. Sandoval's absence was attributed to his reluctance to make an appearance among his own people. His fellow tribesmen held he and his band in disrepute over the treacherous actions they had shown, by siding in the past with the Navajo's mortal enemies, the New Mexicans.

12. Davis, *op. cit.,* pp. 232-234; see also "Notes of a Talk between Meriwether and the Navajos, July 16-17, 1855;" *Superintendency Papers,* LR. These notes were probably transcribed by W. W. H. Davis.

13. The dialogue herein presented, was set forth by W. W. H. Davis, in "Notes of a talk . . .," *ibid.*

14. Charles C. Royce (comp.), "Indian Land Cessions in the United States," *18th Annual Report of the Bureau of American Ethnology, 1897,* Vol. II, pp. 849-850.

15. Meriwether granted the Navajo permission to gather salt from the salina near Zuñi because it would not interfere with any vested rights. The lake was not within the grant claimed by the Pueblo of Zuñi; and by the laws of Spain and Mexico, all salt lakes in New Mexico were the common property of all inhabitants thereof. Meriwether to Manypenny, July 27, 1855; *Superintendency Papers,* LR.

16. Davis, "Notes of a Talk . . .," *op. cit.*

17. Despite the fact that Navajos were receiving 7,000 square miles of land, Meriwether estimated that the entire area did not contain over 125-130 square miles suitable for cultivation; and that this land was in small detached portions situated on cañon floors and along streams which afforded water for irrigation. Meriwether to Manypenny, July 27, 1855; *ibid.*

18. *Ibid.*

19. 34th Congress, 1st Session, *House Executive Document,* Vol. I, Part I, pp. 510-511.

20. Dodge to Meriwether, June 30, 1855; *Superintendency Papers,* LR.

21. Assistant Surgeon Jonathan Letterman wrote that "two hundred yards distant the mercury, in January 1856, ranged from four to eight degrees below that at the hospital, and there was not the slightest doubt of the freezing of the mercury had the instrument been placed in the more exposed situation on the morning of December 25, 1855." Letterman, *Smithsonian Report, 1855,* p. 287.

22. J. H. Carleton to Kendrick, February 1, 1856; *Department of New Mexico,* LR.

23. W. W. H. Davis, acting as governor in Meriwether's absence (the latter being in Washington endeavoring to get the treaties ratified), requested Dodge to inform Navajos that loss of these animals would be considered a grave offense. The acting governor desired the Indians to surrender both the animals and the thieves, "or suffer the consequences." Davis to Dodge, April

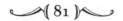

8, 1856; *Superintendency Records,* Miscellaneous correspondence, 1854-56.

24. Dodge to Davis, April 19, 1856; *ibid.*

25. *Ibid.;* also Meriwether to Manypenny, April 20, 1856; *ibid.*

26. Dodge to Meriwether, May 16, 1856; *ibid.*

27. As early as May 3, Dodge had anticipated the Navajo refusal to turn over the culprits. On that day he wrote to W. W. H. Davis: "The delivery of the murderer is out of the question until they are severely whipped which is no easy matter as their number have always been under estimated. And they have facilities for running not possessed by any tribe on the continent of America." Dodge to Davis, May 3, 1856; *Superintendency Records,* letters received from agencies, 1856; also see Dodge to Meriwether, June 2, 1856; *Superintendency Papers,* LR.

28. Dodge to Meriwether, June 13, 1856; *Superintendency Papers,* LR.

29. *Ibid.*

30. From December 1855 to July 1856, the garrison at Fort Defiance consisted of only 160 effectives. On July 16, Company B, Third Infantry, again joined the garrison, raising its strength to an aggregate of 228 men. *Fort Defiance Post Returns, 1855-56.*

31. Dodge to Meriwether, June 13, 1856; *Superintendency Papers,* LR.

32. Report of Secretary of War; 34th Congress, 3rd Session, *House Executive Document,* Vol. I, Parts II & III, p. 3.

33. Santa Fe *Weekly Gazette,* October 18, 1856.

34. Kendrick's letters were forwarded through Major J. Van Horne, commanding garrison at Albuquerque. Kendrick to Van Horne, November 22, 1856; *Department of New Mexico,* LR.

35. Bonneville to Thomas, November 29, 1856; *Superintendency Papers,* LR.

36. Capt. Thomas Claiborne to Maj. William A. Nichols, January 2, 1857; *Department of New Mexico,* LR. Steck to Meriwether, January 3, 1857; *Superintendency Papers,* LR.

37. For additional information on Bonneville's Apache campaign see: 35th Congress, 1st Session, *House Executive Document,* Vol. II, Part I, pp. 561-593; 35th Congress, 2nd Session, *House Executive Document,* Vol. II, Part I, pp. 536-560; and Vol. II, Part II, pp. 279-281.

38. J. Van Horne to Meriwether, January 21, 1857; *Superintendency Records, Miscellaneous Correspondence,* 1857.

39. Kendrick to William A. Nichols, February 11, 1857; *Department of New Mexico,* LR.

40. *Ibid.*

41. Kendrick to Nichols, April 11, 1857; *ibid.*

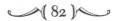

V

THE DINE ARE CHASTISED

THE PRECARIOUS peace was broken on several occasions during the early months of 1858. On February 5 two Mexicans followed a small party of Navajos from Albuquerque
and attacked them upon the road. A Navajo man was
wounded and a woman killed in that sudden ambush. In mid-
March another such incident occurred. A party of New Mexicans and Utes from Abiquiu took the trail of some animals
allegedly stolen by Navajo raiders. Instead of following the
marauders, the group struck due west into Indian country
and made reprisals upon the first Indians encountered. Five
more Navajos paid with their lives, and three captives were
brought back to the settlements, placed upon the auction
block and sold as menials to New Mexican householders.[1]
These wanton actions of the New Mexicans greatly exasperated the Indians; and reprisals were soon launched against
frontier towns, the Utes, and the pueblos throughout late
winter and early spring.

Navajos near Fort Defiance were also demonstrating a
restlessness which put the whole garrison on edge.[2] Sensing

this anxiety, the new commanding officer, Major Thomas H. Brooks became alarmed over the inadequate strength of the post. Feeling he could not possibly forestall trouble with only three companies, the commander requested additional troops. Department strength, however, had been jeopardized by the transfer of soldiers to California, and the request was denied.[3]

As Brooks had anticipated, trouble occurred at Fort Defiance — this time over a long recognized source of irritation — the post's grazing grounds located at Ewell's Camp, twelve miles to the north. Little rain had fallen, and grass had been sparse. Navajo herds and flocks had suffered greatly. Manuelito, who claimed much of the pasturage upon which post herds were grazing, turned his horses and cattle onto the nearby pasture in mid-March.[4] Informed of this apparent total disregard of military rights, Major Brooks ordered a detachment of troops out to chastise the belligerent Indian. On May 29, the soldiers mercilessly slaughtered nearly sixty head of livestock as a warning against further encroachments upon Fort Defiance's grazing grounds.[5]

On July 7 Brooks established another hay camp at the opposite end of Cañon Bonito, and detailed a squad of soldiers to harvest the grass at that location. During the evening a number of Indians stole within range of the sleeping men. The barrage of arrows shot into camp accomplished nothing more than to frighten the soldiers and kill a dog. The commander lodged a complaint with Zarcillas Largas and other headmen without delay warning them "that it might be a dangerous experiment to try again." Tension increased during the next few days. Finally on July 12, 1858, the shaky peace was broken altogether. The Territory of New Mexico was thrown into the abyss of war.

On that day a Navajo buck came into Fort Defiance, to all intent and purpose to sell a couple of blankets. After about three or four hours he succeeded in disposing of one blanket to a camp woman. He no sooner had concluded the bargain than he observed Jim, the Negro servant of Major Brooks approaching. As the colored boy was about to pass, the Indian jumped upon his horse; and as soon as the Negro's back was to him, let fly an arrow which passed under the boy's shoulder blade and penetrated the lung. The buck immediately put whip to his pony and raced out of the post, leaving the Negro wounded.[6]

The following morning, Major Brooks sent for Zarcillas Largas. In fury he demanded the culprit. Largas' reply was cool and calculated. It had been six weeks since Manuelito's cattle had been killed. The army had done nothing toward paying for them! But, the chief did tell Brooks that he was on his way to Zuñi, and would look into the affair upon his return. The major, demonstrating intense dissatisfaction at this indifference and impertenance, stated that the Navajos would suffer drastic consequences if his words were not obeyed. Regardless of Brooks' threats, the die already was cast. Jim lingered between life and death for two days, and finally expired on the morning of July 15.[7]

When Largas returned from his "trip to Zuñi" he was again summoned to the post. On July 21, the headman was informed of the Negro's death and given twenty days to produce the murderer. Brooks, however, was in no mood to idly wait for Largas to comply with the demand. The major began taking immediate steps to organize an expedition against the Indians. Rapidly he gathered intelligence of Indian concentrations, location of planting and grazing grounds. Orders were dispatched to sound all Indians venturing into Defiance as to the attitudes of the tribe as a whole. Juan Lucero, a Navajo interpreter, conveyed to Major Brooks the news that the killer of Jim belonged to a band of *"ricos"* residing in the Tunicha Mountains. But, Lucero added, this band would die to a man, rather than surrender any of its members — "as was their custom." Further, it was learned that the murder of the servant boy stemmed from a marital misunderstanding between the killer and one of his women some days before. It was alleged he wished her to go some place with him, but she refused; and at a dance he tore off her clothing in a fit of anger. Still she refused, whereupon he started out to kill someone outside the tribe to appease his wrath. This he succeeded in doing and he returned to his woman and proceeded with her to the destination he originally had planned to go.[8]

The death of Jim was a terrific affront to the ideals and pride of the army in New Mexico, staffed as it was with officers from the south. War seemed inevitable. On July 22, Major Brooks wrote to the Adjutant General of the Army suggesting that a large force of troops take the field not later than early September. He further urged that permission be granted the Utes to raid the Navajos; and he also suggested that Mexicans be employed as guides.[9] By the first of August, department commander Brevet Brigadier General John Garland had concurred wholeheartedly with the plans; and he proclaimed that the Navajos had assumed a boldness in their forays "which forces upon me the necessity of opening a campaign against them with not less than one thousand men."[10] Lieutenant Colonel Dixon S. Miles was directed to proceed to Fort Defiance to organize the forthcoming operations. He arrived at that post on the afternoon of September 2, bringing with him Company A of the Regiment of Mounted Rifles, and Company C, Fifth Infantry — a total of 124 rank and file.[11] Two days later Miles summoned Sandoval and instructed the chief to notify as many headmen as he could, that the tribe had until eight o'clock on the morning of September 9 to deliver the killer of Jim. Sandoval showed much concern over the prospect of war. During the days that followed, he would show up at Fort Defiance and say that the murderer had been seen at Bear Springs. Another time, the chief reported the culprit's location as being in a cave near

Laguna Negra. Finally, on September 6 Sandoval rushed into the garrison and stated in great haste that the murderer had been caught near Chuska after a terrific struggle. The chief promised to return the next day with the man. On September 7, Sandoval again reappeared bearing sad tidings. The murderer had died from wounds sustained during his capture; and the chief asked for a wagon with which to bring the body in. Miles refused this request, but furnished a blanket instead which Sandoval accepted with the promise to return next morning with the corpse.

September 8 opened with Navajos congregating at the post in such numbers, that by mid-morning there was an estimated 300 to 500 mounted and armed warriors present. At eleven o'clock Sandoval, accompanied by a delegation of headmen, arrived with the body. Suspecting Navajo treachery, Colonel Miles immediately ordered a careful medical examination of the corpse.[12] The post mortem examination conducted by Assistant Surgeon J. Cooper McKee substantiated Miles' suspicions. His report revealed that the corpse was that of a man

> . . . about five feet, two or three inches high, and not over eighteen years old. The body was perfectly fresh and pliant as in life. There was no rigor mortus anywhere except some little in the left elbow. The face and hair was daubed and smeared with mud and dirt. After washing, and examination I found the following wounds: The most marked was one immediately over the left eye, involving the eye as well as the ridge above it. The integraments were much lacerated and the bone extensively shattered. The weapon must have been very close, and the ball a very irregular one to have made such a wound. The ball did not pass out. Another bullet wound — very regular — was over the region of the stomach, running upwards. Another, very irregular through the right shoulder blade into the cavity of the chest. This bled freely. Another regular wound, just above the left collar bone. Upon opening the cavity of the chest

and abdomen, I found the ball which entered the region of the stomach had passed upwards, wounding in its course the left lobe of the liver, passing through the diaphragm into and through the right lung, going out through the ribs and shoulder blade. There was a quantity of *uncoagulated blood* in the cavity of the chest, and *very considerable heat in the intestines.* This wound could not have been immediately a fatal one. The ball above the left collar bone had penetrated into the integraments of that region, and was not a wound of much import. Upon opening the cavity of the cranium, I found a battered and flattened slug lying in the brain near the wall of the skull opposite to where it had entered, having passed directly through the brain.... This wound was an immediately fatal one.

The wounds were all fresh — there being not the least suppniation [*sic*]. The blood was uncoagulated — the skin perfectly natural. The uninjured eye still preserved its natural appearance. All the organs and tissues were healthy. The blood had not gravitated or settled in any part of the body. From these evidences I am certain that the man had not been dead over eight hours. I am of the opinion that he was first shot through the liver and lungs by a rifle ball while he was in a reclining position — probably asleep. This not being fatal, he was dispatched by a pistol held near his head. This was the immediately fatal wound.

The Indians asserted that he had been badly shot some days ago, and had died last night, after lingering with his wounds. The anatomical evidence — which never deceives — prove positively to the contrary. They also assert that he died some forty miles from the post. The evidence indicates that the boy was murdered in the neighborhood. The man who shot the Negro boy was known from appearance to be at least forty years of age. This man was not over eighteen....

They have thus added another murder to their long account, not saying anything of the falsehood and deception attempted to be practiced upon the government.[13]

McKee's findings justified the opening of actual war against the Navajos. A general council was called with all headmen. The newly appointed Indian Agent, Samuel M. Yost,[14] told the Indians "frankly and plainly" that his function as their agent had ceased. He then turned the council over to the commanding officer of Fort Defiance. Major Brooks, speaking for Colonel Miles — who refused to see or speak with the Indians — informed the Navajos that their falsehood had been exposed and that further talks were useless; and from that time on a state of war would exist between the United States and the tribe.[15]

In preparation to taking the field against the Navajos, Colonel Miles penned a formal declaration of war on September 8 through issuance of Order Number 4:

I. Since the arrival of the commanding officer at this Post ... sufficient time has been given the Navajo tribe ... to seek, secure and deliver up the murderer of Major Brooks' Negro; to atone for the insult to our flag, and the many outrages committed on our citizens. They have failed to do so; our duty remains to chastise them into obedience to the observances of our land, and after tomorrow morning war is declared against them.

II. At 8 o'clock tomorrow morning the column designated by Order No. 2 will be in readiness to march with 12 days' rations to fight these Indians wherever found.[16]

The colonel, in addition, requested of Assistant Adjutant General, Major William A. Nichols, that proper measures be taken to keep his command at full strength and supplied with the necessary requisitions of mules, horses, mule shoes, clothing, and especially shoes for his troops as to enable them to keep the field constantly. Miles had seen too much of frontier duty to be under any illusions about this campaign. He felt "confident no one, two, or three scouts, with as many battles, would end this war." However, he believed that all means at the disposal of the army should be utilized against these Indians — "all the surrounding tribes and inhabitants"—particularly the Utes and New Mexicans should be let loose upon the Navajos.[17]

Miles would be laboring under an extraordinary handicap in his military movements. The previous commander of Fort Defiance, Captain Henry L. Kendrick, had been transferred to the Military Academy at West Point, where he assumed the professorship of chemistry, mineralogy and geology.[18] He had vacated the post, leaving not a single map or sketch of his many reconnaissances and explorations of Navajoland. Nor was there anyone at Fort Defiance who knew the country further than Laguna Negra, fifteen miles to the north. There is little doubting the words of Miles' when he wrote: "My march will be like an exploration of an unknown region."[19] Having received intelligence that the Navajos collected in great numbers at Cañon de Chelly during that time of year, the commander determined to direct his initial movements toward that reputed citadel of the Diné.

On the morning of September 9, Miles marched from Fort Defiance with companies A, I, and F of the Mounted Rifles, and a contingent of the Third Infantry, consisting of companies B and C. Acting as guides for the column were Captain Blas Lucero's "New Mexican Spies" recruited from the vicinity of Albuquerque.[20] First day's march was directed toward "Ewell's Camp," twelve miles northwest of Fort Defiance. The meadows at this point afforded ample grass for the horses and mules, while the troops made camp for the night. By 6:30 next morning the column was again underway, moving in a westward direction. After a two hour march the guides apprehended a mounted, well dressed, and fully armed Navajo, who had been observing the movements of the troops. Upon questioning the warrior, Miles confirmed his previous intelligence of a large concentration of

Indians at Cañon de Chelly. Pace of the march was increased until late afternoon, at which time the column again encamped. This bivouac, however, was annoyed throughout the night by sporadic sniping by the Indians.

On September 11, after traveling about fourteen miles, the column reached Cañon de Chelly. A Zuñi guide, assigned to the company of Blas Lucero, pointed out an obscure trail into the gorge by way of present-day Monument Cañon. Following this narrow path, the command slowly made its way down the precipitous rocky walls, descending 1,200 to 1,500 feet into the cañon below. After a short rest, Captain Elliott was detached in command of his and Captain Hatch's companies of Mounted Rifles to sweep down the cañon, and if possible reach its mouth near Chinle before dark. In the meantime, Miles would press forward with the infantry. As the columns moved on, Indians gathered on the heights above. They shouted taunts at the passing troops, rolled rocks off the cliffs, and occasionally fired upon the command, all without effect. At five o'clock Captain Elliott returned, not having reached the mouth of the cañon. He reported having had a fight with a party of ten Navajos, of whom at least one was killed. The troops once again reunited, a wide area on the cañon floor was chosen as a bivouac for the night. As the soldiers unsaddled their horses and prepared their mess, the Indians gathered on the heights "as crows to a feast;" and, throughout the night, fires twinkled nerve-wrackingly a thousand feet or more above the weary troopers.

At dawn the next day the march was resumed. After five or six miles of plodding through deep red sand, the command succeeded in reaching the cañon mouth near present-day Chinle, Arizona. There, the men encamped amid extensive fields, and feasted on green corn and peaches — "glad enough to get rid of that remarkable hole in the earth."[21] The Navajos, however, continued to hover about, which gave the soldiers that afternoon "the opportunity of practicing at long ranges with their rifles," while the officers planned the next movement.

A Navajo, captured during the passage of the cañon, informed the officers that about twelve miles to the south were several large lakes[22] where many Indians had taken refuge with their flocks. Again Captain Elliott and the Mounted Rifles were detached in a midnight attempt to get through the Indians without being detected; while the infantry followed with the first rays of dawn. The movements of the cavalry, however, were discovered, and Indian signal fires were raised on Elliott's flanks and front. Despite Navajo warnings, the hard-riding riflemen succeeded in surprising a large flock which could not be driven to safety in time, and 6,000 sheep were captured at the lakes. The infantry arrived at noon after a hard and dusty march. Together the foot-soldiers and cavalry returned to camp near Chinle, after burning two fields in the vicinity of Cañon de Chelly's mouth.

On the morning of September 14, the line of march was taken up toward Fort Defiance with the rear guard constantly harassed by Indians. Slowed considerably by wounded and the captured stock, the column finally reached the valley of Pueblo Colorado (in the vicinity of present-day Ganado, Arizona) by three p.m. Here camp was pitched. Due to increased Navajo boldness, pickets were doubled, and cautioned not to strike matches or to smoke, instead "to lay close, and, if discovered, to change their location." The night passed uneasily, with the Indians occasionally firing into the camp. Next day the march was resumed, with the column heading in a northeast direction. This brought it back to Fort Defiance by four p.m., after a march of 28 miles that day. Results of the first scout of the war was meager. Only six Indians had been killed; one man and six women and children captured; four or five horses and the flock of

6,000 sheep taken. The troops lost two killed and several wounded. However, the expedition had not been in vain. From one of the captives, Miles learned of another Navajo deception. The corpse which had been brought to Fort Defiance as that of the slayer of Jim was in reality the body of a Mexican slave of a prominent Indian (either Vincente Vaca or Juan Lucero). Assistant Surgeon McKee had been right. The slave had been murdered the same morning he was brought in — for the express purpose of deceiving the white men.[23]

The day that Colonel Miles and his troops arrived at Fort Defiance General Garland relinquished command of the Department of New Mexico to Colonel Benjamin L. E. Bonneville and headed back to the states. Miles' actions in opening the war with the Navajos was immediately sustained by the new commander with these words:

> The murder of the Mexican captive, and the offering him as the murderer demanded, is an outrage of so heinous a character, that when the negotiations were closed, and the agent turned the matter into the hands of the military, you were right in pressing the demands by taking the field against them.[24]

To further support Miles, instructions were issued to the Assistant Adjutant General, to bring together all available forces for a final assault on Navajoland. By September 23 all earlier requisitions had been complied with: maps of the best quality had been forwarded to Fort Defiance along with the authority to hire thirty Zuñi or other puebloan guides. To assure the proper supervision of supplying the troops with essentials of war, Captain Van Bokkelen, Assistant Quartermaster of the Department, was sent to Fort Defiance. Additional troops were also on their way to strengthen the forces already in Navajo country. Major Electus Backus, with six companies of recruits and ordnance, were on the road from Fort Leavenworth and would arrive in the territory by October 1. Bonneville planned to commit these soldiers to the field as soon as possible.

The strategy of the forthcoming campaign was well laid. It was Bonneville's plan that the troops using Fort Defiance as a base of operations, would operate "among the Navajo planting grounds, on and about the river San Juan, and the mouth of Cañon de Chelly, with the view of forcing the Navajos further south, towards the Rio Chiquito Colorado."[25] Until such time as all the forces were concentrated, Colonel Miles was directed to undertake a second scout.

On September 29, the second expedition of the war marched from Cañon Bonito, this time bound for Chuska Valley. This force consisted of more than 300 men composed of three companies of Mounted Rifles, two of infantry, and Blas Lucero's New Mexican Spies.[26] Arriving at their destination, Captains Elliott and Averell were detached to raid the fields and flocks of Navajos residing in the area. That day more than a thousand sheep and nine horses were captured by the Mounted Rifles; and Elliott claimed to have killed two Navajos and wounded four more in a brief skirmish. On the morning of September 30, camp was moved to a lake one and half miles to the north, which Miles named for Captain Lucero. Here abundant wood and water was found and the horses given a well-earned rest after their long and fatiguing race the day before.

It was while the command recuperated at this point that Miles was informed by one of his guides of the existence of a "large lake," fifteen miles to the east beyond a high mountain, "where all the herds and Indians fleeing from the military would seek refuge." The commander immediately determined to organize a command and attack that night. Companies H, I, and F of the Mounted Rifles were selected, and a detachment of New Mexicans would go along as guides. All were placed under the leadership of Captain Lindsey. The detachment left camp at ten p.m., and reached the laguna five hours later. To the surprise of the troopers the lake was found to be dry and its shores abandoned. The trail that had been followed, however, showed signs of recent passage by large numbers of animals. Lindsey therefore pressed on in hopes of surprising the fleeing Navajos. About daybreak the pursuing Riflemen came to a deep cañon through which led a winding trail three-fourths of a mile in length — but so rocky and steep as to render its descent with horses very difficult. A smoke in the valley below convinced Lindsey to try; and men and horses made their way down as quickly and silently as possible. As the troopers approached the cañon, three mounted Indians — who were ascending the trail — immediately spread the alarm to other Navajos encamped below. Lindsey, realizing that the command had been discovered, ordered Lieutenant Lane forward with Company H. Word was then sent to the other units to follow as rapidly as possible.

Lane's command succeeded in overtaking the fleeing Indians. They dashed through the Navajos, cutting their stock off from escape. In so doing, the Riflemen penetrated deeper into the valley where the Indians were more numerous. As his command consisted of only thirty rank and file, Lane did not want to risk his men further in a needless pursuit. He took possession of a wooded knoll in the center of the cañon and awaited assistance. Captain McLane with Company I soon arrived after a full gallop in column of fours. Dismounting his men and forming a skirmish line, McLane cleared the cañon and collected the sheep and horses at its center. The Indians, beginning to appear in large numbers on the flanks, convinced the officers of the wisdom of not exposing their men further. Retreat was sounded. As the troopers made their way out of the gorge with the captured livestock, Lieutenant Averell arrived with the remaining

Company F.[27] The expedition once again reunited, proceeded out of the cañon, which was becoming increasingly dangerous.

Burdened with captured livestock as well as wounded men, Lindsey dispatched a message informing Colonel Miles of the command's inability to rejoin the main column. Receiving this note, Miles at once marched to the relief of his cavalry. Leaving Chuska Valley, he struck the Fort Defiance-Albuquerque road and there made a juncture with Lindsey on October 2. The latter was directed to encamp at "Twelve-Mile" Camp, south of Fort Defiance, while the remainder of the column proceeded to the post. Thus ended the second expedition against the Navajos. Results of this march were better than that of the first. More than 5,000 sheep and seventy-nine horses were taken from the Indians. Added to this score, a great quantity of corn had been destroyed; and Captain Lindsey during the attack had burned all the property found in the Indian camp, as well as the hogans reputed to have belonged to Chief Kayatano. The entire expedition succeeded in killing ten Indians, and probably wounded that many more.[28]

✕ ✕ ✕

By now Major Electus Backus had arrived in New Mexico; and Department Commander, Benjamin E. L. Bonneville, was ready to deliver the final blow against the Navajos. This time two powerful columns would strike the Indians simultaneously. By Special Order Number 91 (dated October 1, 1858), Backus was assigned command of the "Second Column," composed chiefly of his raw recruits. Dixon S. Miles would again lead his veterans from Fort Defiance.

The six companies of infantry and cavalry constituting Backus' command would rendezvous at Jemez on October 15.[29] The orders, which the newly-arrived commander carried, directed him to proceed from that pueblo and make a thorough examination of the country around Tunicha, from which it was believed hostile Navajos were making raids upon the Abiquiu-Jemez frontier. It was Bonneville's hope that by closely coordinating the efforts of Miles and Backus, such pressure could be brought to bear that it would be possible to "destroy and drive from that part of the country every vestige of this troublesome tribe."[30]

Marching from the Pueblo of Jemez, Backus and his column arrived at Tunicha on the morning of November 2, and united with the troops of Colonel Miles. A base of operations was to have been established at this point. However, suitable location for a depot could not be found, and that plan was abandoned. Accordingly, each soldier in the two columns received rations for fifteen days — sufficient enough to allow a passage through Navajo country. The two commands were then put in motion a few days later.[31] Backus marched through Cañon Blanco, about fifteen miles north of Tunicha; then through Washington Pass. Turning northward, the column skirted the eastern slopes of the Tunichas. In the meantime, Miles also moved through Washington Pass, and marched up the western side of the mountains. The commands again reunited at the northern extremities of the Tunichas and struck westward toward the cañon system of de Chelly. Passing along the northern rim of Cañon del Muerto, the troops reached its western mouth, near Chinle. Here word was received from Ute and New Mexican scouts that many Navajos had congregated to the west of the Hopi pueblos. From Chinle the march of the two columns was directed to Black Mesa, and thence toward the Hopi pueblos themselves. Movements of these troops through Navajoland was rapid and effective. Three hundred and fifty miles were covered during the scout. Four Indians were killed, and four more wounded; and nearly 350 head of Navajo livestock either captured or slaughtered by the soldiers.

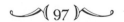

By early November several Navajo delegations had come into Fort Defiance seeking peace. This time both Miles and Indian Agent Yost were convinced the Indians truly desired peace. Both men realized that the imperative demands for the murderer of Jim had to be abandoned and they asked permission of their respective superiors to teminate the war. On November 6, the agent wrote to Superintendent Collins announcing his plans to confer with Colonel Miles "as to the propriety of calling in some of the chiefs of the tribe."[33] James L. Collins, however, believed that the Navajos had not been chastised enough; and he cautioned Yost not to be hasty in concluding the war:

> should you . . . ask a conference with the Navajo chiefs, let it be done with the concurrence of the military. If the war is prematurely closed, I do not wish it to be at the instance of our Department.
>
> ❊ ❊ ❊ ❊ ❊ ❊ ❊ ❊
>
> Confer with Colonel Miles . . ., and in all your communications with the Indians let them clearly and distinctly understand that they must give up their predatory habits, and that for the future, their conduct in this respect, will be strictly scrutinized, and the nation held responsible for all thefts committed by their people unless the guilty parties are given up for punishment.
>
> It should be the object of both departments [military and Indian] to close the war in such a way as will have a amicable effect upon the Indians, and this will be greatly promoted by letting them see that there is a harmonious action between us, and that the one stands ready to enforce the demands and requirements of the other.[34]

Shortly after this letter was written, Collins met with Colonel Bonneville. In the ensuing conference a complete reversal of stand occurred. Both men agreed that closing the war should be their sole responsibility, not that of the Navajo agent or the military commander at Fort Defiance. The superintendent therefore informed Yost not to do any more than "to agree to bring down to Albuquerque a deputation of fifteen or twenty of their chiefs . . . to meet Colonel Bonneville and myself."[35]

The letters transmitting these instructions, however, did not reach Fort Defiance in time, and Agent Yost and Colonel Miles took matters into their own hands. On November 20, a council was held with Zarcillas Largas, Armijo, Herrero, Barboncito, and other headmen, and an armistice of thirty days' duration was enacted. The chiefs agreed to deliver all stock taken from the military; a principal chief would be selected as spokesman for the entire tribe; the Navajos would deliver up the murderer if he should be caught; and a mutual restoration of captives would be made. At the end of thirty days the headmen would again meet with the military at Fort Defiance to form a new treaty of peace "on a sure basis; and which would be binding on the United States as well as the Navajos."[36]

Upon receipt of the armistice terms, Superintendent Collins and Colonel Bonneville were violent in their objections. Both men believed the Navajos had not been made to feel the full weight of United States power. The armistice, in its present form was totally unacceptable. The department commander and the superintendent felt that inhabitants of the territory should be insured maximum protection from the lightning-fast incursions of the Navajos. So too, the Indians should be forced to fully indemnify the citizens of New Mexico for all losses resulting from their raids.[37] Feeling that the security of the territory had been overlooked, Collins and Bonneville drastically revised the armistice terms by adding the following articles:

1. The establishment of another longitudinal line designating the eastern boundary of the Navajo domain.
2. Indemnification for depredations inflicted upon the citizens as well as Pueblo Indians since August 15, 1858.

3. The whole tribe would hereafter be held responsible for the actions of all its members.

4. Return of all captives held by the Navajos.

5. The murderer of the Negro boy would no longer be harbored or protected by any member of the Navajo tribe.

6. The United States government would retain the right to dispatch military expeditions and build posts in the Navajo country at any time and place.

7. The selection of a head chief to represent the entire tribe; and who would be empowered to act for it in all future negotiations.

8. Sandoval and his people would be permitted to reside east of the new boundary line.

On December 1, Collins mailed the armistice with its "amendments and additions" to Yost. Enclosed also was a letter severely reprimanding the agent for his actions:

> In your course as Navajo Agent . . . you have disregarded *both* my orders and suggestions. . . . You have allowed yourself to be put forward to close the war, and which you do without instructions or authority from me. . . . You knew that I do not intend that this responsibility should be thrown upon the Indian Department or that you should assume it yourself, which is the same thing.[38]

While Collins accused his agent of misconduct, the duration of the armistice was rapidly drawing to a close. The Navajos were naturally suspicious, and all endeavors to persuade the headmen to travel to Albuquerque to negotiate a final peace ended in failure. Forced to an alternative, a trip into Navajoland was scheduled by the commander of the department and the representative of the Indian Office.

Bonneville and Collins left Santa Fe on December 14. The journey to Fort Defiance was extremely hazardous and difficult. Winter, intensely cold, had set in, deep snow drifts obscured the road, and prolonged the travel. It took a week

for the party to reach their destination, and the headmen were summoned for a meeting four days later. On December 25, 1858, the final treaty was concluded. It was not the kind of peace treaty likely to restore mutual friendship, but rather one aimed at punishing the Indians for their wrong doings. The "amendments and additions" constituted the basis of the final agreement. This document specified that peace would be restored only if the tribe complied fully with its eight articles. An indemnity would be paid the citizens of New Mexico for all livestock losses sustained at the hands of the Diné — and this was calculated as amounting to over $14,000. The tribe as a whole would be held responsible for the actions of any of its members. All captives, "either Mexican or Pueblo" would be released from bondage. The murderer of Major Brooks' servant would not be harbored or protected by the tribe; and the United States would reserve the right to dispatch military expeditions into Navajo country at any time. A new chief, Herrero, was selected as headman, and hereafter would be regarded as central authority for the tribe. And Sandoval, who had always allied himself with the enemies of his people, was permitted to retain his residence near Cebolleta.

The most important and far-reaching article of the Bonneville Treaty — as it would be called — was the first of its clauses. This specified a radical change in the eastern boundary line of the tribal domain. The original line, established in 1855 by Governor Meriwether, was now moved still further to the west. It extended from Piscado Springs, near the headwaters of the Zuñi River, to Bear Springs, thence to Fort Defiance. From the post the boundary ran in a direct line to Chaco Cañon; and from there to the juncture of the Rio Tunicha and Rio San Juan. Hereafter, the Navajos would not be permitted to graze or plant — or even occupy — the land to the east of this new line. To prevent any infractions of the article, United States troops would have the

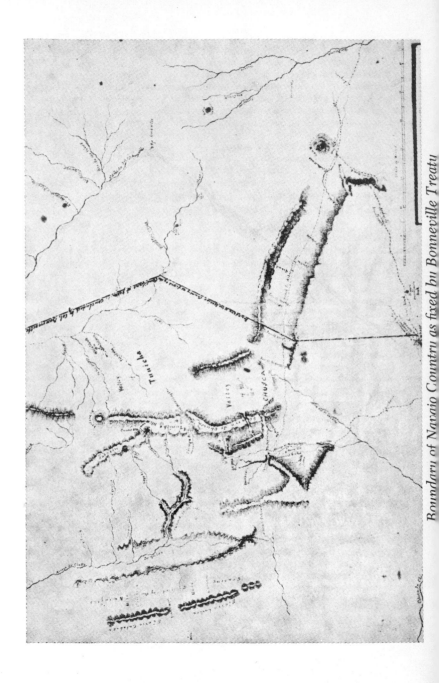

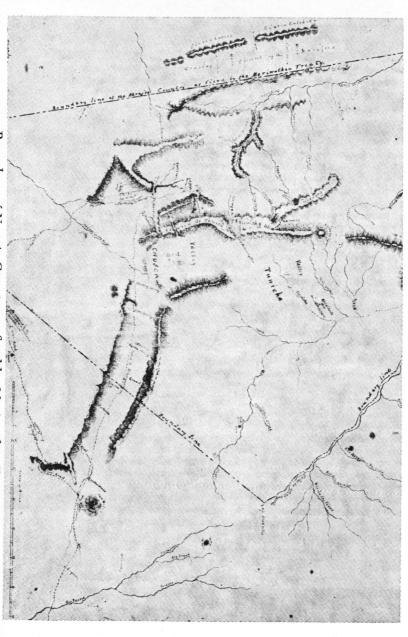

Boundary of Navajo Country as fixed by Meriwether Treaty

authority to destroy all livestock and crops found within the prohibited area.

It is obvious that the prime object of this stipulation was to punish the Indians to the fullest extent possible. In fact, Collins expressed the motivating idea behind formulation of the whole treaty with these words:

> They [the Navajos] must feel the effects of the war, and feel it deeply. They must feel that it is to their interests to remain at peace, and to give up their predatory habits, or they will continue to annoy us for the next twenty years.[39]

In theory, Collins' scheme of geographically restricting the Navajos sounded plausible. However, the superintendent failed to realize the limited grazing and agricultural land now available to the tribe — whose sheep holdings alone were estimated at as high as 250,000 animals. The principal grazing lands had always been east of the new line.[40] The plains of Tunicha and its adjoining mountains, as well as the Chuska Valley, furnished subsistence to thousands of sheep, goats and horses. The most fertile agricultural lands were also restricted. Collitas, Bear Springs, Chuska, Tunicha, Ojo Caliente, and Laguna Negra were no longer available for Navajo crops. Samuel Yost, perceptive to Indian wants, realized the consequences which might arise from prohibiting the use of land which was traditionally Diné. He spoke out against it — stating that the treaty stipulations were of —

> such a character that they cannot be endorsed by any enlightened mind, and if insisted upon will come in direct conflict with and defeat the whole policy of the government in its management of the Indians — will transpose the Navajos from the pursuits of industry and agriculture . . . to robbers and plunderers. . . . It will do this by depriving the best of the Indians of the grounds they cultivate and graze — whereon they raise corn and wheat enough to support the

whole nation — 12,000 souls, and sustain 250,000 sheep and 60,000 horses, thus forcing them either to violate the agreement forced upon them, or compel them to abandon cultivating the soil and stock raising or become pensioners on the government, or plunderers.[41]

Yost had good reason to make such predictions. Every foot of arable land possessed by the Navajos had been under cultivation, and areas which were not productive of crops served as grazing. Loss of their finest lands would be an insurmountable handicap to these Indians. It would now be only a matter of time before necessity compelled Navajos to violate the treaty and seek subsistence and plunder from ranchos and towns of New Mexico.

X   X   X

1. 35th Congress, 2nd Session, *House Executive Document,* Vol. II, Part II, pp. 283-284. Also John Ward to Samuel Yost, April 9, 1858; *Superintendency Records,* letters received from agencies, 1858.

2. This restlessness was partially induced by fear of Ute incursions. In January a party of forty Ute warriors crossed the Colorado below the mouth of the San Juan. They penetrated Navajo country as far as Cañon de Chelly, and there killed Pelon, a chief of considerable importance. In consequence of this, Major Brooks reported that many Navajos were living in such dread of the Utes, that they refused to farm north of Fort Defiance. Brooks to A.A.G., March 20, 1858; *Department of New Mexico,* LR.

3. 35th Congress, 2nd Session, *House Executive Document,* Vol. II, Part II, p. 288.

4. Brooks to A.A.G., April 4, 1858; *Department of New Mexico,* LR.

5. Lt. George McLane to Lt. William Dickinson, May 30, 1858, and Brooks to McLane, May 29, 1858; *ibid.* See also Joseph Fish, *History of Arizona* (unpublished mss., on file at the Arizona Pioneers' Historical Society, Tucson), p. 298.

6. According to the official report of Major Brooks, Jim upon being shot, attempted to extract the arrow himself. However, during his struggling, the Negro broke the shaft, leaving the point so deeply imbedded within his body that the post surgeon was unable to reach it with probes. Brooks to N. M. W. Craig, July 15, 1858; *Superintendency Papers,* LR.

7. *Ibid.*

8. Samuel M. Yost to James L. Collins, August 31, 1858; *ibid.*

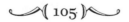

9. Brooks offered the name of an irregular company of New Mexicans from Albuquerque called "Lucero's Spies," as likely candidates for guides. The major stated that this group could be employed at a very low price, if a portion of the booty taken during the campaign was offered as payment for their services. Brooks to Col. L. Thomas, July 22, 1858; *Office of Adjutant General*, LR.

10. 35th Congress, 2nd Session, *House Executive Document*, Vol. II, Part II, p. 294.

11. *Ibid.*, p. 298.

12. Yost to Collins, September 9, 1858; *Superintendency Papers*, LR.

13. Report of Assistant Surgeon J. Cooper McKee, September 8, 1858; *ibid.*

14. Samuel M. Yost, ex-agent for the pueblo Indians and editor of the Santa Fe *Gazette*, was given the position of agent to the Navajos by Superintendent James L. Collins on August 10, 1858. He was instructed by Collins to Yost, August 10, 15, and September 9, 1858; all in *ibid.*

15. 35th Congress, 2nd Session, *op. cit.*, Vol. II, Part II, p. 308.

16. Departmental Order No. 4, September 8, 1858; *Department of New Mexico*, LR.

17. 35th Congress, 2nd Session, *op. cit.*, Vol. II, Part II, p. 309.

18. The appointment of Captain Kendrick to this position ended his life upon the frontier. He remained at the Military Academy until his retirement from the army in 1880. Samuel E. Tillman and Marvin R. Vincent, *Colonel Henry L. Kendrick, U.S.A.* (New York: 1892).

19. Miles to W. A. Nichols, September 8, 1858; *Department of New Mexico*, LR.

20. Lieutenant Walker of the Third Infantry was appointed adjutant to the command. Assistant Surgeon McKee acted as medical officer; and Captains Elliott, Hatch, and Lieutenants Lane and Averell commanded the Mounted Rifles, while Whipple and Hildt were in charge of the infantry. *Ibid.*

21. After passing partially through Cañon de Chelly, Colonel Miles noted that there was "little grass and no wood in the cañon, but good water." However, the colonel cautioned that "no command should ever again enter" the gorge. *Ibid.*

22. This location was probably Bekihatso Lake, and the series of small lakes and springs nearby.

23. Miles to Nichols, September 16, 1858; *Department of New Mexico*, LR. One of the captives, taken during this expedition, alleged that the body brought in as that of the murderer of the Negro boy, was actually a slave belonging to a prominent Navajo leader (either Vincente Vaca or Juan Lucero). The captive stated that the slave had been murdered the very morning he was carried into Fort Defiance, for the purpose of deceiving the Anglos. Yost to Collins, September 18, 1858; *Superintendency Papers*, LR.

24. 35th Congress, 2nd Session, *op. cit.*, Vol. II, Part II, p. 315.

25. *Ibid.*, p. 302

26. This expedition was organized under Order No. 12 (dated September 26, 1858). The contingent of Mounted Riflemen was composed of Company A (Captain Elliott), Company F (Second Lieutenant Averell), and Company I (Captain Lindsay). The infantry consisted of Lieutenant Whipple's Company B, Third Infantry; and Lieutenant Willard's Company K of the Eighth. *Ibid.*, p. 324-325. Also Miles to Wilkins, October 3, 1858; *Department of New Mexico*, LR.

27. Having heard the firing of Lindsay's troops, Averell with his forty-four men were endeavoring to reach the scene of combat. However, they too met with resistence, and were encumbered by 1,000 sheep which would have been lost, had not Lindsay sounded retreat and met F Company just at that time. Once back to safety a count was made of the troopers. Three men were missing — Sergeant John Thompson, and Privates Mauritz Paulman and William Nugent — all of Company H.

28. 35th Congress, 2nd Session, *op. cit.*, Vol. II, Part II, pp. 326-327.

29. The "Second Column," under leadership of Electus Backus, totaled 400 men. It was composed of Companies E and G, Mounted Rifles; D, Third Infantry; and B, I and E, of the Eighth Infantry. Acting as guides was a company of New Mexicans from Santa Fe, under command of José María Valdez, as well as a number of Utes from Abiquiu. It was October 18 before the troops finally reached their rendezvous at Jemez. *Ibid.*, pp. 319-320.

30. To protect those frontier towns which would be exposed to incursions of the Navajos by advance of the troops, Colonel Bonneville assembled companies E, F, I and K, Third Infantry; and stationed them at Los Lunas and Albuquerque. Bonneville to Backus, October 3, 1858; *Department of New Mexico*, LR.

31. Backus to W. B. Lang, November 19, 1858; *ibid.*

32. Backus to Wilkins, November 3, 1858, and Miles to Wilkins, November 3, 1858; *Superintendency Papers*, LR.

33. Yost to Collins, November 6, 1858; *Ibid.*

34. Collins to Yost, November 19, 1858; *Ibid.*

35. Collins to Yost, November 22, 1858; *Ibid.* Bonneville also sent similar instructions to Miles at Fort Defiance.

36. Copy of armistice inclosed with letter from Miles to Wilkins, November 20, 1858; *Department of New Mexico*, LR.

37. Collins to Mix, November 29, 1858; *Superintendency* Papers, LR.

38. Collins to Yost, December 1, 1858; *Ibid.*

39. Collins to Yost, December 1, 1858; *Ibid.*

40. In a letter to Agent Yost, Lieutenant Colonel Miles outlined the areas he considered as the finest grazing and agricultural lands of the Navajos: "I have the honor to state that the most favorable, extensive and with one exception only (the mouth of Cañon de Chelly) the best cultivable lands occupied

by the Navajos lies in Chuska Valley, Tunicha, Bear Springs, Ojo Caliente and Colitas, Laguna Negra, named in the order of the largest first.

"The principal grazing lands of the Indians seems to be the plains of Tunicha and the mesa of its mountains, Chuska Valley, and the Puerco of the West. There is extensive grazing on the mesas of Calabasas and Vica mountains, but water is very scarce, also fine grazing in Pueblo Colorado valley, from its head to where it ends in the valley of the Puerco.

"I will here mention that the largest and best lands under cultivation by the Navajos and also grazed on by them, *viz:* Colitas, Bear Springs, Chuska valley, Tunicha. Ojo Caliente, Laguna Negra, Cienega Negra, Cienega Juanico, lies east of a longitutional line passing through this Fort [Defiance]." Miles to Yost, December 20, 1858; *Ibid.*

41. Yost's letter (dated December 21, 1858) appeared in the Santa Fe *New Mexican.* The author found it as a clipping attached to a letter of J. L. Collins to J. W. Denver, January 13, 1859; *Ibid.*

VI

A TREATY IS BROKEN

FOR FOUR months following the conclusion of Bonneville's Treaty the Navajos attempted to satisfy its harsh demands. Beginning in January, tribal headmen sent into Fort Defiance small lots of livestock in an effort to repay the New Mexicans for losses which amounted to almost 6,000 animals valued at more than $14,000.[1] Several captives, who had been stolen at early ages from Rio Grande settlements, were also brought in. However, these individuals were now Indian in every sense of the word; and when given the choice of returning to their Mexican families or remaining with the Indians, they chose the latter. They had lived as Indians so long that they had lost the Spanish tongue and considered the vermilion mesas and cañons of Navajoland their true homes. When one captive was offered his freedom, he replied, "the Navajos were his brothers and his friends, and with them he desired to live."[2]

This evidence of good faith on the part of the headmen induced Superintendent James Collins to dispatch to Fort

Defiance the annuity goods which had been withheld from the tribe during the past conflict. He had intended to personally supervise the distribution. Business, however, had caught up with the superintendent; and his clerk, John Ward, was sent out in early April instead. Assisted by Major Oliver L. Shepherd, the new commanding officer of the post, Ward issued "a liberal allowance" of annuities to assembled tribesmen; and in return accepted a few more horses as further evidence that the headmen were at least attempting to comply with terms of the Bonneville Treaty.[3]

Complications, however, were looming large on the horizon of Navajo-Anglo relations. The December 25th treaty had never included the Diné's old enemies — the Utes. War parties still were being organized under the very eyes of the Ute Agent at Abiquiu throughout the early months of 1859. James Collins, fearing that this would lead to a renewal of warfare, requested in mid-March, a joint council of headmen from both tribes. To this meeting the Utes sent delegates from various tribal divisions. Kanyache, Sasaribo and Chichi-sobon represented the Mauhuache Utes. The Capotes sent their principal war chiefs, Tamuche, Pantalion, Tomasico and forty warriors. Representing the Navajos were Armijo, Manuelito, the aged Largas, as well as a number of lesser headmen. The council adjourned with both tribes promising to end their two-and-a-half year conflict and live once again in peace.[4]

No matter how well intending Navajo headmen were, they could never guarantee the conduct of the greater portion of their tribe. During spring months reports of raids and plunderings once again appeared. On May 13, Henry Connelly informed Collins that 2,000 sheep, belonging to Felipe Chavez, had been driven off; and that two herders employed by the Padillas lay dead. The slaying of the two *pastores* threatened to lead to open reprisals by the New Mexicans. There were bitter complaints voiced against the military and civil administrators when demands for the murderers of these men were not pressed — as had been done in the case of Major Brooks' Negro servant.

Ute-Navajo relations once again were strained. From Abiquiu, Agent Albert W. Pheiffer reported that raids had been perpetrated by the Navajos within three miles of his agency. Incensed at this infraction of the recent agreement between the two tribes, the Utes were now preparing for war.[5]

James Collins was now convinced that Navajo leaders had little or no influence; and on May 29 he informed Commissioner Greenwood that "the influential men seem entirely unable to control the dishonest portion of the tribe, and in many cases it is believed . . . they connive at the robberies committed by their people."[6] The raids against New Mexican flocks substantiated the superintendent's belief that the armistice and treaty had been too hasty; and he suggested more stringent measures be taken against the tribe:

> It is true that since the conclusion of peace the conduct of the chiefs had led me to hope that the tribe would profit by the lesson they had received. But their chastisement must be more severe, they must be well punished and thoroughly humbled before we can expect better conduct from them.[7]

Although Collins acknowledged that reports of recent Navajo depredations might have been exaggerated by New Mexicans, who hoped for greater indemnity and a justifiable cause for launching reprisals; still he believed that a show of force was necessary to force tribal compliance with treaty terms.

✗   ✗   ✗

By mid-May Colonel Bonneville had taken steps to force the Indians into line. An expedition was planned and organized, under the command of Major John S. Simonson[8] of the Mounted Rifles. His orders were to execute a movement

through Navajoland as a demonstration of the might of the United States Army, without actually bringing on a full-scale war. On June 12, Simonson proceeded to Abiquiu and assumed command of troops assembling at that frontier town. The expedition, numbering 700 men, would march in two columns for Fort Defiance. The portion of the command assembling at Las Lunas would march by way of Laguna and Cubero on June 17. The other column, commanded personally by the major, would take the road from Abiquiu to Cañon Bonito, via Ojo Caliente, crossing the Tunicha Mountains twenty-five miles northwest of Washington Pass.[9]

Once in Navajoland, it was the intention of Major Simonson to remain there until fall, visiting the various localities inhabited by the more troublesome bands. James Collins was desirous that the Indian Department be represented on the expedition — to prove to the Indians that both branches of the government were working harmoniously together. He therefore instructed Agent Alexander Baker (who already was at Fort Defiance) to accompany the military on their tour of Indian country.[10] The orders which Collins issued to the agent were straight to the point, for he did not want a renewal of the conflict which had arisen between himself and Yost:

> You will ... cooperate with Major Simonson and his command in demanding a fulfillment of the stipulations referred to. No deviation from a strict compliance will meet the approval of the Indian Department. Should the Indians refuse or hesitate it is expected that the troops will take the alternative of making reprisals from the flocks of the tribe to the full extent of the property lost.[11]

Major Simonson reached Fort Defiance about the first of July, and a meeting was immediately held with the headmen. The Indians were instructed to carry word to other chiefs, requesting them to assemble for a series of "talks" before scouting parties were dispatched.

Between July 5-14, Simonson and Baker held three councils with the Navajos. The first two meetings effected little, owing to poor attendance of the headmen, who were afraid to approach too near the post. To dispel any suspicions that Navajos might still harbor, the last meeting (July 14), was held in a wooded area, about a mile from Fort Defiance; and was attended by Herrero, Zarcillas Largas, and a number of other prominent chiefs.[12] At this council "an article of agreement" was put forward for the signature of the headmen. This document was intended — if signed by the Navajos — to bind them to the restoration of all the property stolen (or its equivalent) since the conclusion of peace, as well as that stolen by them since August 15, 1858. However, Herrero and Zarcillas Largas had seen enough of these pieces of paper and knew how much reliance the Anglos put upon them; and they persuaded the other headmen not to sign the "agreement." But the chiefs did pledge verbally to repay all they had stolen.[13]

Agent Baker and Major Simonson, however, had little confidence in this pledge. Both men believed the Navajos had no intentions of returning the stolen stock until they were forced to do so. It was, therefore, definitely decided to make a demonstration against the Indians to prove to them that the army was sufficiently strong to force a compliance of any terms. On July 18, two detachments left Fort Defiance to reconnoiter the Navajo country. The first column, commanded by Brevet Major Oliver Lathrop Shepherd, consisted of companies B, K, and a portion of G, Third Infantry; and companies H and part of G of the Mounted Rifles. This column marched westward toward the Hopi villages and the mountains beyond. The second command was placed in charge of Captain John G. Walker; and consisted of companies C, G, Third Infantry; and company K and a detachment from E, Mounted Rifles. Since this column would pass through what was believed to be the more densely populated

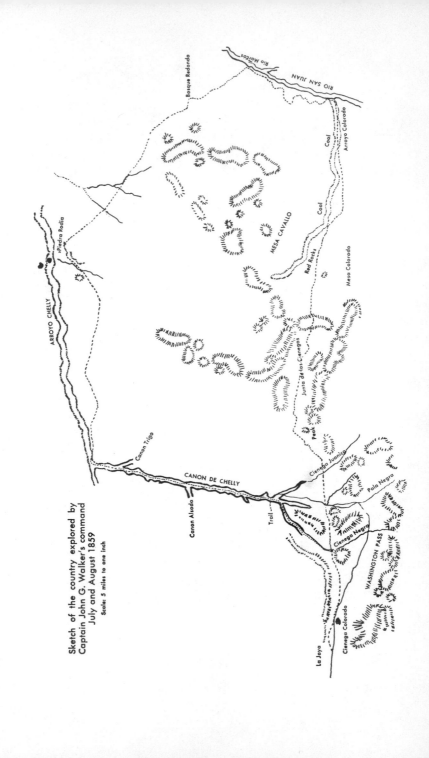

Sketch of the country explored by
Captain John G. Walker's command
July and August 1859

Scale: 5 miles to one inch

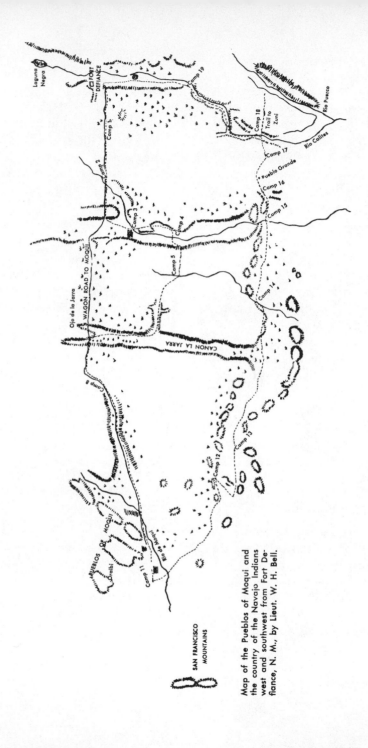

Map of the Pueblos of Moqui and the country of the Navajo Indians west and southwest from Fort Defiance, N. M., by Lieut. W. H. Bell.

portion of the Navajo country, Agent Baker would accompany it in hopes of conferring with the Indians. Walker's column marched toward Cañon de Chelly, passed through that chasm without molesting the planted fields there, and struck northward toward the Rio San Juan. This stream was followed for some ten or fifteen miles before the command again turned southward — crossing the Tunicha Mountains, which impressed Agent Baker as "the most beautiful country I have ever seen in this territory."

The great numbers of Indians encountered during the seventeen day trip convinced Baker beyond a doubt that the tribe was more populous than the previous estimates of 12,000-15,000. Immense herds of horses, sheep and goats proved to the agent that here lived a people actually more prosperous than heretofore believed; and they were capable of immediate repayment of any debt. However, the majority of Navajos with whom the agent conferred with during his excursion had no conception of the military strength of the United States government; and in fact, had held tenaciously to the idea that the Diné were as numerous as the newcomers. For these reasons the agent's report fully concurred with the views of Superintendent Collins:

> It is perfectly useless to postpone a settlement of the present difficulties with them [the Navajos]; the longer it is put off the more trouble you will have in the end. Now is the time to take a decided stand with them, while the army is in their country.[14]

Despite the large concentration of troops in Navajoland there was a hesitancy on the part of military leaders to renew hostilities. The majority of lesser officers at Fort Defiance felt that the demands being pressed against the tribe were unjust; and that many reports of New Mexican losses attributed to Navajos had been falsified or padded. Regardless of these beliefs, James L. Collins still clung to his stand that the Indians must be punished for their failure to comply exactly with the terms of the Bonneville Treaty. Additional robberies attributed to the treacherous Diné, as well as the murder of two Mexicans near Albuquerque during the first week of September, further enraged the superintendent. On September 17, Collins wrote to Commissioner Greenwood that in his opinion —

> the only policy . . . that can be adopted for the successful management of the Navajos, should be based upon a rigid enforcement of all their treaty obligations. We should never allow a murder or robbery to go unpunished; each violation of law or treaty stipulation should be followed by prompt and immediate chastisement. They deserve no mercy at our hands, and should be taught to expect none.

In the meantime temporary Agent Alexander Baker had been replaced by the permanent appointee, Silas F. Kendrick, who had arrived at Fort Defiance in early September. The new agent was carefully instructed by Collins not to waver in carrying out the demands. Kendrick set to work diligently to extract retribution from the Navajos, and thus avoid war. Shortly after his arrival at Fort Defiance, the agent held a series of councils in rapid succession. Because of the reluctance of tribesmen to come into the post, a meeting was held at Laguna Negra on September 15, at which Herrero, Ganado Mucho, Zarcillas Largas and between 400 to 500 others attended. Through an interpreter, the new agent emphasized the importance of Navajos paying the claims against the tribe. Because the headmen assembled during this parley constituted but a small segment of the influential leaders of the tribe, Kendrick proceeded to Cañon de Chelly on September 18. There, he remained for four days, visiting with the Indians and examining their planting grounds. In councils, he again emphasized the fact that unless the treaty was complied with, their crops and flocks would be destroyed.

It was during his talks at Cañon de Chelly that Kendrick learned of outside influences at work attempting to turn the tribesmen against the United States Government. Headmen had informed the agent that Mormons from Utah had been at work among them. This religious sect, which had fled persecution in Illinois and Missouri, and founded their Zion in the desert of the Great Basin, was now under attack by the United States Army. Consequently, missionaries who in the past had preached salvation, were now acting as spies attempting to stir western tribes against the "Gentiles." Kendrick was informed that Mormons had advised Navajos not to give up any more sheep or horses — "as the Americans were cheating them out of their land, timber, grass and livestock."[16] The agent, however, assured Superintendent Collins that he would do his best "to induce this unfortunate race, not to follow these deluded people."[17]

Before concluding his visit to Cañon de Chelly, Silas Kendrick appointed September 25 as time for still another meeting at Laguna Negra; and the Navajos promised to send runners to inform all the scattered portions of the tribe of the council, so that as many headmen as possible would be there. Unlike his other "talks," during which he faced the Indians alone, Kendrick now invited Major Simonson and Captain Walker.

Early on the morning of the day set for the parley, the agent, together with the two officers and an escort of fifty mounted troops, proceeded to the council site, where they found about 150 Indians assembled. The headmen were addressed by both Simonson and Walker, who urged upon them the wisdom of meeting their obligations. Agent Kendrick concluded by informing the Navajos they had thirty days longer in which to send in their indemnities.

During the next month a small quantity of livestock was delivered to Kendrick but not without complaint. The Navajos bitterly protested that their people had been killed, their property stolen, and they had not been offered compensation for any part of their losses. Regardless of what they had sustained, they were required to pay for claims — the half of which, they alleged, were fictitious. By the expiration of the period allowed, the Navajos had delivered only 19 horses and 130 head of sheep. According to the agent's calculations, the value of these animals did not amount to more than one-tenth of the amount of outstanding claims — which exceeded $14,000.

Thus disappointed in his hopes that the Navajos would still comply with treaty stipulations, Kendrick, on October 25, officially laid his charges in the hands of the new military commander of Fort Defiance, Major O. L. Shepherd (who had replaced Major Simonson):

> Having used every means within my power as agent for the Navajo Indians to obtain from them a compliance with the stipulations . . ., and these means having entirely failed to induce such compliance. It now becomes my duty under my instructions from the Superintendent of Indian Affairs . . . to bring officially to your knowledge the delinquency of the tribe, and to apply to you as the commanding officer . . . at this post to enforce the provisions of that engagement or treaty.[19]

✂   ✂   ✂

In early November an escort was furnished Agent Kendrick so that he could conduct livestock, which the Indians had relinquished, safely to Albuquerque, to be either sold or delivered to persons having suffered losses.[20] During this trip an incident occurred which, together with others, greatly precipitated matters with the Indians. The first night after leaving Fort Defiance the Navajos stampeded all but eighteen horses which the agent had charge of. The following morning an Indian on horseback, carrying two rifles, was discovered lurking about the camp. With promises of protection, Kendrick lured the buck into camp. When questioned about the guns, the Navajo stated that he had found the weapons, but would cheerfully give them up for "some trivial reward." The officer in charge of the escort induced the Indian to take a letter to Fort Defiance informing Major Shepherd of the loss of the horses. The Indian faithfully performed the mission — though somewhat tardily. In recompense for his trouble, Major Shepherd ordered a severe flogging administered to the Indian's bare back. As this Navajo belonged to the band of Ganada Mucho — one of the most faithful friends of the Anglos — this wanton beating greatly shook the confidence which this band harbored for United States authority.[21]

Agent Kendrick returned to Cañon Bonito on December 18. Shortly thereafter several leading Navajos came to him begging that the tribe be permitted until January 1 to satisfy the indemnification demands. But Kendrick replied that he no longer had control in the matter, and that they would have to apply directly to the post commander. From that time until mid-January few Indians ventured into the post; and the atmosphere of Anglo-Navajo relations carried the current of impending storm.

At sundown on January 15 Juanico, a Navajo headman, appeared on the hill overlooking the fort, desiring to confer with the agent. Kendrick, suspecting treachery, requested the Indian to come into the fort. When the latter refused, an interpreter was sent to inquire the object of his visit. The Indian revealed that parties of Navajos had been passing his ranchería all day, going in the direction of the grazing camp, seven miles from the post — as if intending to attack the military herd. This information was immediately communicated to Major Shepherd, who dispatched a detachment of thirty men to strengthen the guard at that point. Next morning another chief, Agua Chiquito, came into Fort Defiance, and informed Kendrick that Herrero, "Head Chief" of the tribe, was instigator of the impending attack.

The information which the two Indians relayed was correct. Just after sunrise on the morning of January 17, the cattle herd was attacked by 200 Navajos. The raid would have succeeded had it not been for the reinforcement of the guard. The warriors were beaten off by the vigilant soldiers — with only a few oxen lost. However, on their retreat, the Indians attacked a wood detail of four soldiers, and killed three. At noon the same day still another detachment from Fort Defiance, which was sawing lumber three miles distant, was also surprised. Again Anglo soldiers paid with the blood of another man killed and one wounded. The Navajos tried desperately to cut off the much-needed supplies now en route to the virtually beseiged troops at Cañon Bonito. The quartermaster train, sent out from Albuquerque, was constantly harassed by Indians as it snaked its way deeper into Navajoland; and would probably have been lost altogether had it not been for the presence of an escort of forty-two men under the command of Lieutenant William Dickinson.[22]

With eruption of war with the Navajos came a widening of the breach between the Indian Department and the Military. The incident which severed all connections between the two, occurred on January 20. Early that morning the friendly chief, Agua Chiquito, again made his appearance on the brow of the hill overlooking the fort and was invited into the post by Major Shepherd on assurance that he would not be hurt. This headman, however, appeared anxious to talk only with Kendrick; and when the latter proceeded to confer with the Indian, through an interpreter, the officer abruptly interrupted the conference and informed the agent that he was in command, and that the representative of the Indian Department was hereafter not allowed to hold conversation with any Navajo without his permission. Shepherd then endeavored to "talk" with Chiquito. When the Indian did not show an interest in what the commander was saying, Shepherd became enraged and ordered him to leave the post. As the Indian turned to go, the major instructed the sentries to fire on him. Agua Chiquito, however, quickly darted from the post and made his way to safety.

These actions of the military commander at Fort Defiance had alienated the last vestige of Navajo goodwill; and in his final report, Agent Kendrick bitterly complained:

"Up to this occurrence Agua Chiquito, Ganado Mucho, Juanico and several other influential members of the tribe, had given every evidence of their sincere desire to bring their people to an amicable adjustment of the difficulties and had rendered many valuable services to me and also to the military . . . There was every reason to believe in and rely upon their good faith, and they were extremely anxious to second and advance the views and purposes of the Government to best of their ability. But since this treatment of Agua Chiquito, not one of these Indians has returned to . . . the fort or to seek any communication with me or any other white man. Evidently their good confidence in the good faith of the Americans is entirely destroyed, and if they have not become active combatants themselves, they cannot be expected again to cooperate with us."[23]

Following the alienation of Agua Chiquito, Major Shepherd wrote to the agent, again warning him not to confer with the Indians; and that if the instructions were violated he would be ordered from the post. Kendrick, since his arrival in Navajoland had not attempted to tread upon military toes. When councils were held, he journeyed to them without escort; he accepted whatever quarters were provided for his agency; and had always informed the post commander of any actions taken by the Indian Department. Silas Kendrick felt that Shepherd's actions and subsequent letter was a direct affront to himself and a hindrance to the endeavors of the Office of Indian Affairs — as well as a treacherous act which put the army little above the savages they were now fighting. Agent Kendrick could not leave the major's note unanswered; and he accordingly responded in writing:

SIR: I have just received your note of today informing me that war now exists with the Navajo Indians, and that I am prohibited from holding within this garrison, any intercourse with this tribe, and that the first violation of this order, I must be prepared to leave the post.

It seems that a change has taken place in your mind since this morning. I asked you to let me talk to the Indians [in] your presence and you refused. I give you notice now, as I told you today, that I will talk to them when I please outside of the post.

If your note is intended as a threat I pass it by unnoticed as one would the passing fly that should perchance light upon his head. I will discharge my duty as agent regardless of consequence.

I will now notify you that your conduct in reference to the Indians — the Navajos that you invited into the post this morning and other circumstances shall bring you officially before the proper tribunal for adjustment.[24]

As war now existed with the Navajos, Agent Kendrick saw little use in remaining at Fort Defiance. On January 23, he requested permission of Superintendent Collins to return to Santa Fe, which was accordingly granted on February 5.[25]

X X X

New Mexico was now in the grip of another full-scale Indian war. News of Navajo depredations poured in daily. The commander of the military department, Colonel Thomas T. Fauntleroy, however, remained inactive. The forces stationed throughout the territory had never been so strong. Twenty-two companies of infantry and mounted troops were at the immediate disposal of the commander — if and when he chose to move. Despite the availability of 1800 fully equipped soldiers, Fauntleroy hesitated, and requested authority to call upon the governor for an additional 1,000 volunteers, as well as recruitment of 400 Utes.[26] In the meantime, Fauntleroy informed the commandant of Fort Defiance that no expedition would be launched at that time against the Navajos. However, the troops at that post must keep communications open to Albuquerque.[27]

Such hesitancy on the part of the army, together with increasing livestock losses, created considerable agitation from the general population of the territory. Public opinion was vociferous in protesting the inadequate protection along the frontier. By spring this feeling was becoming so intense it was venting itself in the organization of irregular companies to invade the Navajo country. The Territorial Assembly, influenced by popular demand, authorized the organization and conduct of an independent campaign. Governor Abraham Rencher signed a bill raising two companies of militia, each 100 men strong, and armed them. The Utes, who had always sided with the New Mexicans against the Navajos, were also advised to raid their southern neighbors. At Abiquiu, Agent Albert W. Pheiffer openly encouraged his charges to conduct attacks; and his agency was used as a rendezvous for combined expeditions of New Mexicans, Utes, and even Apaches.[28]

In the meantime, Navajo raids in the vicinity of Fort Defiance became better organized and more frequent. On February 8, the cattle guard, consisting of three commissioned officers and forty-one privates, were attacked at Ewell's Camp by an estimated 500 Navajos, who were finally repulsed after a two-hour battle. The lines of communication with Albuquerque — the supply depot for the garrison — were constantly cut by the marauders. It was with great difficulty the four companies comprising the garrison were able to keep their livestock intact, or to provide adequate escort for the quartermaster trains which supplied the fort.[29]

Regardless of increased pressure upon the already over-burdened troops at Fort Defiance, orders were dispatched from department headquarters directing Company G of the Third Infantry to proceed on April 21 to Ojo del Oso, where a new post was being constructed as another barrier to Navajo incursions.[30] The Indians witnessed the weakened state of the post, and launched an attack directly at the fort nine days later.

About four o'clock on the morning of April 30, an estimated 1,000 Indians closed in upon Fort Defiance. Because of the terrain surrounding this fort, Navajos were able to approach from three sides undetected. With war-whoops and yells, the warriors attacked. Through the corrals they poured — driving in the sentries. The three companies comprising the garrison were instantly turned out, and took their positions of defense. A part of Company C, Third Infantry, attempted to get into the kitchen gardens on the west side of the post, but were driven back to the sheltering walls of the bake-house and laundress' quarters by the heavy fire of Navajos screened behind fences and wood piles.

For a while it looked as if the Navajos would take Fort Defiance. Warriors seemed to be everywhere. Indians had penetrated the sutler's store and were rifling the goods stored in the back rooms. They were behind and in the post's out-houses. Frantically the troops endeavored to stem the tide which threatened to engulf them. Lieutenant Whipple, with E Company, was detailed to clear and secure the magazine, corrals, and stables containing the officers' mounts and work teams. On the east side of the post, Company B, under Lieutenant Dickinson, took up a position between the fort and the abrupt hill rising behind.

By dawn the Navajo attack was spent, and the Indians were withdrawing up the hillsides, leaving their dead behind. Lieutenant Hildt was ordered to take Company C and pursue the retreating savages. This order, however, was countermanded when the advancing troops were mistaken for Indians and fired upon by soldiers in the post below. When light enough for the troops to distinguish one another, Company C was again deployed along with B Company to clear the mesa tops to the east and north. The Navajos as usual, faded away before the advancing soldiers, and the latter returned to the post with nothing to show for their labors.[31]

This brazen attack upon Fort Defiance acted as a stimulus for army operations. On May 4, the Adjutant General of the Army ordered that the post be not abandoned "for the time being;"[32] and Secretary of War J. B. Floyd issued the following declaration:

> Active operations will be instituted against the Navajos as soon as the necessary preparations can be made. A winter campaign *with infantry*, if inaugurated with secrecy and prosecuted with vigor, will prove the shortest and most effectual plan of operations.[33]

For the next two months the United States Army in New Mexico geared itself for a full-scale campaign, the likes of which the territory had never before witnessed.

X X X

1. S. L. Kendrick to O. L. Shepherd, October 25, 1859; *Superintendency Papers,* LR.

2. S. M. Yost to J. L. Collins, January 14 and 18, 1859; *Superintendency Records,* Letters received from agencies.

3. Collins to C. E. Mix, May 22, 1859; *Superintendency Papers,* LR.

4. On March 20 Collins informed the Commissioner of Indian Affairs that he had been anxious to close the war between the two tribes ever since he came into office. However, the attempts which he had made ended in failure, "owing to the evil influence of bad disposed Mexicans." While the war continued, the New Mexicans exercised an unhealthy influence over both tribes by offering an outlet for stolen property and captives. Collins to J. W. Denver, March 20, 1859; *ibid.*

5. One Ute chief informed Pheiffer that he considered the peace with the Navajos broken, and by "the beginning of the other moon he would have his people ready to invade Navajo country, together with the soldiers and

New Mexicans." Pheiffer to Collins, May 6, 1859; *Superintendency Records,* Letters received from agencies. Also Pheiffer to Collins, May 15, 1859, Henry Connelly to Collins, May 13, 1859; *Superintendency Papers,* LR.

6. Collins to Greenwood, May 29, 1859; *Superintendency Papers,* LR.

7. Collins to Mix, May 15, 1859; *ibid.*

8. A distinguished officer of the Mounted Rifles, Major John S. Simonson received his captaincy of that regiment in May 1846. He was breveted major on September 13, 1847, for gallant and meritorious service at the Battle of Chapultepec. On September 16, 1853, he received a regular commission as major.

9. Simonson to Wilkins, July 5, 1859; *Department of New Mexico,* LR.

10. Alexander Baker was appointed temporary Indian Agent to the Navajos on April 22, 1859. He filled the vacancy left by the resignation of Agent Cowert, who had replaced Samuel Yost during the winter of 1859. Collins to Baker, April 22, 1859; *Superintendency Papers,* LR.

11. Collins to Baker, June 12, 1859; *ibid.*

12. Simonson to Wilkins, July 17, 1859; *Department of New Mexico,* LR.

13. See report of Alexander Baker, September 1, 1859, in *Annual Report of the Commissioner of Indian Affairs* (Washington: 1859), p. 716. Also Baker to Collins, July 17, 1859; *Superintendency Records,* Letters received from agencies, 1859.

14. Baker's report, *ibid.,* pp. 717-719; also *Fort Defiance Post Returns,* July 1859; Baker to Collins, *ibid.* For details see: Walker to Edson, August 3, 1859 and Shepherd to Edson, August 7, 1859; *Office of Adjutant General,* LR.

15. Collins to Greenwood, September 17, 1859, in *Annual Report of the Commissioner of Indian Affairs, ibid.,* pp. 706-707.

16. Reports of Mormon activity among the Navajos was nothing new. As early as March 1856, Henry L. Dodge had claimed to have talked with Indians attending Mormon councils. These Navajos stated that missionaries had been very interested about "the Americans that had a fort in Navajo country." The Mormons also asked why the Navajos did not drive the American soldiers out of their country, "for if they were permitted to stay they would take the entire land."

During 1856 both Dodge and Major Kendrick reported seeing "a few fine rifles silver mounted, tobacco, blankets, among the Navajos near Moqui," allegedly traded from Mormons. In January of 1858, General John Garland informed the Adjutant General of the Army, that there was every reason to believe that much of the difficulties with the Navajos were instigated by Brigham Young and his missionaries. Garland believed the Latter Day Saints were trying to bring about a peaceful settlement between the Utes and Navajos in an attempt to turn the two tribes against the United States government. See Report of Secretary of War in 35th Congress, 2nd Session, *House Executive Document,* Vol. II, Part II, p. 282.

17. Kendrick to Collins, September 24, 1859; *Superintendency Records,* Letters received from agencies, 1859.

18. Kendrick to Collins, *ibid.* Kendrick to Greenwood, October 4, 1859; *Superintendency Papers,* LR. See also Report of Silas F. Kendrick of Navajo Affairs, 1859-1860 (dated February 25, 1860) in *ibid.*

19. Kendrick to Shepherd, October 25, 1859; *ibid.*

20. The animals which Kendrick was to deliver consisted of nineteen horses and 130 sheep which had been turned over by Navajos before the October 25 deadline, as well as sixty-four horses and 130 goats subsequently returned. See Report of S. F. Kendrick on Navajo Affairs, *op. cit.*

21. Kendrick, Report on Navajo Affairs, *ibid;* also Kendrick to Collins, January 6, 1860; *Superintendency Records,* Letters received from agencies.

22. *Fort Defiance Post Returns,* January 1860; also Kendrick, Report on Navajo Affairs, *ibid.*

21. Kendrick, Report on Navajo Affairs, *ibid;* also Kendrick to Collins, January 6, 1860; *Superintendency Records,* Letters received from agencies.

22. *Fort Defiance Post Returns,* January 1860; also Kendrick, Report on Navajo Affairs, *ibid.*

23. Kendrick, *ibid.*

24. Kendrick to Shepherd, January 20, 1860; *Superintendency Papers,* LR.

25. Silas Kendrick arrived in Santa Fe in early March, and assumed the duties of Pueblo agent. On May 3, 1860, he requested a leave of absence due to poor health. He had contracted an "ulcerating affection of the thoat" from the constant exposure endured during his last winter in Navajoland.

26. James Collins was suspicious of Fauntleroy's motives for recruiting volunteers and in delaying the campaign — a delay which if persisted in might prove disastrous to frontier settlements. On February 10 the superintendent wrote to Commissioner Greenwood: "I fear Fauntleroy is influenced in making this call for volunteers by a party of men, some of whom as well known to you, who have been engaged in speculating in land warrants. These men have been constantly courting his favor. . . ." Collins to Greenwood, February 10, 1860; *Superintendency Papers,* LR.

27. Fauntleroy to Shepherd, January 27, 1860; *Department of New Mexico,* LR.

28. Collins opposed employment of Utes as guides and trackers against the Navajos. This practice, as in the past, invariably resulted in the bartering of Navajo captives. A. W. Phieffer to Collins, December 18 and 29, 1859; also Collins to Greenwood, January 8, 1860; *Superintendency Records.*

29. *Fort Defiance Post Returns,* February 1860.

30. The detaching of Company G left only B, C, and E, of the Third Infantry at Fort Defiance. *Ibid.,* April 1860.

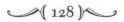

31. The account of the attack upon Fort Defiance can be found in the report of O. L. Shepherd (dated May 7, 1860) in Annual Report of Secretary of War, 36th Congress, 2nd Session, *Senate Executive Document,* Vol. I, pp. 52-56.

32. *Fort Defiance Post Returns,* June 1860.

33. J. B. Floyd to Fauntleroy, July 9, 1860; Annual Report of Secretary of War; 36th Congress, 2nd Session, *Senate Executive Document,* Vol. I, pp. 59-60.

Cañon de Chelly

VII

GATHERING OF A STORM

FOLLOWING the instructions of Secretary of War J. B.
Floyd, reshuffling of military units in the southwest was
rapid and efficient. The Fifth and Seventh Infantry regiments, three companies of the Tenth Infantry, and two companies of the Second Dragoons were transferred from Camp
Floyd, Utah, to duty in New Mexico. By end of August, six
companies of cavalry and nine of infantry were awaiting
orders and a commander to lead them into Navajoland.

As the attention of the "reluctant" department commander, Colonel Thomas Fauntleroy, could not be turned
from the many details attending the reorganization of military personal under his jurisdiction, the impending Navajo
campaign was entrusted to another field officer. On August
21, 1860, orders were dispatched from army headquarters
at Santa Fe, selecting the commander of the Navajo Expedition — and an excellent choice it was. Colonel Edward
Sprigg Canby — then stationed at Fort Garland — had
many years of military experience behind him. Upon gradua-
tion from West Point in 1839, he had served in Florida

against the Seminoles; had been with General Scott in Mexico; and knew what southwestern frontier duty was. Canby's instructions from Fauntleroy were direct to the point, yet flexible enough to give the colonel full control over the troops now placed under his command:

> The Department Commander directs me to say that he has decided to commence active operations against the Navajos at once, and he wishes you to conduct them.
> Therefore you will move from Fort Garland as soon as possible to Fort Defiance via Abiquiu taking with you G company, Second Dragoons, one of the companies of the Tenth Infantry now at Fort Garland and as many spies and guides as you think necessary.[1]

On September 9, Colonel Canby left Fort Garland with a column of 138 men. Eight days later he reached the town of Abiquiu.

Two other columns were also converging on Navajoland, and would meet at Fort Defiance. Major Henry Hopkins Sibley of the Second Dragoons, and brother-in-law of Canby, had left Albuquerque on September 12, with four companies of cavalry and one of infantry, as well as twenty guides under Blas Lucero. This column's route lay through the fertile Tunicha Valley, and over the old military road through Washington Pass to Fort Defiance. At the same time that Canby left Fort Garland, Captain Lafayette McLaws had marched from Fort Craig, with one company of cavalry and two of infantry; and had taken up the route to Navajoland by way of the Zuñi Pueblos.[2]

Before Colonel Canby could resume his march to Fort Defiance, where he would take command of all the columns then converging on Navajo country, he would first have to secure the "eyes and ears" for his troops. Department commander, T. T. Fauntleroy, had already made the initial arrangements for obtaining the services of Ute guides and New Mexican auxiliaries. On September 4, a letter had been dispatched to Superintendent of Indian Affairs, James L. Collins, requesting the aid of Ute agents, Christoper Carson and A. W. Pheiffer. A day later Fauntleroy had Collins' answer:

> ... The Navajcs have reached a point that makes them the common enemy of both Indians and white men and it seems proper that they should make common cause against them.
> ... I have reason to believe that both the agents in charge of the Utahs will be willing to accompany the Expedition, but of that will be matters for their own choice ...[3]

In addition to the Utes and regular troops, 500 Pueblo Indians were organizing to war against the Navajos. Still another force of 800 New Mexicans were being readied by Governor Abraham Rencher — and much against the wishes of many military officers, who feared that volunteers would only complicate matters with the Navajos.[4]

By September 18 Canby had secured from Agent Pheiffer enough Ute guides; and on the following morning the column left its encampment upon the Rio Chama, and took up the march to Navajoland by way of Cañon Largo. Two weeks later Canby and his troops arrived at Cañon Bonito — after a march that was anything but uneventful.

In his first report· of this Navajo campaign, the colonel wrote that his initial "operations have resulted in trifling success — one Navajo warrior was killed by the spies ... one the 1st inst.; six [squaws] in the meleé could not be distinquished from the warriors were killed by the troops and spies in a conflict with a superior force of Navajos on the 2nd inst., and about 60 or 70 horses ... captured." Most important of all, however, was the information that Canby derived from Ute guides and captured Navajos. The march of Major Sibley through the Tunicha Valley, a few days previous, had, according to informants, forced the Indians in that area to flee westward toward the region of Black Mesa and the inaccessible areas around Navajo Mountain. It would be toward these points that Canby would direct his operations, in hopes of inflicting a decisive blow against the Diné.[5]

By October 12 two powerful columns, each numbering 270 men, had been equipped for the difficult campaign ahead. Major Sibley took one command (the Second Column), and on October 10 marched to the mouth of Cañon de Chelly at Chinle, by way of Pueblo Colorado. The First Column, commanded personally by Colonel Canby, would move a day later toward the northern rim of that great cañon; and thence to a point of juncture with Sibley near Chinle. From the west entrance of the cañon, the two commands would operate in concert, moving in the direction of the northern reaches of Black Mesa, which Canby called Sierra Limitar. A third and somewhat smaller column, under the command of Captain Lafayette McLaws, would march from Fort Defiance on October 13. Its operations would be along the western base of the Chuska-Tunicha Mountains and in the neighborhood of the head of Cañon de Chelly, to prevent the return of Navajos fleeing from their haunts due to operations of the two other commands.[6]

✄   ✄   ✄

Major Sibley's command was well supplied and equipped to open any campaign — provided it was against a foe that could be seen, and in a country where cavalry mounts could be sustained. Early on the morning of October 10, this hard-fighting and still harder-drinking southern officer filed out of his camp near Fort Defiance with two companies of cavalry (I, Second Dragoons; and B, Regiment Mounted Rifles), and three of infantry (B, G, Fifth Infantry; and K, of the Seventh). The long column moved toward the country lying south of Cañon de Chelly; and by nightfall of the first day had reached Pueblo Colorado — the mid-point between

Fort Defiance and the cañon system of de Chelly. It was there the command rested.

Only one day had passed and the troops were already exhausted. Not a drop of water had been found along the march, and the fine, red sand of the Navajo country caked in the nostrils of both men and horses. But what was most odd was that about Pueblo Colorado — an area which had always supported a large Indian population — not a Navajo was seen. In fact, Sibley wrote in his official report, that "no evidence of recent occupation by Indians were found."[7] This absence of Navajos, and still greater lack of water, would repeat itself regularly day after day, destroying the morale of troops and sapping the strength of horses.

For four days Major Sibley and his column pushed onward to effect juncture with Canby's forces near Chinle. On October 15 Sibley arrived at the mouth of Cañon de Chelly, and made camp in some "old fields." There his exhausted command rested for three days awaiting Canby. With the uniting of the First and Second Columns on the 18th, operations were commenced on a much wider scale. Early next day the column turned northward, following the Arroyo Chelly over a trail that Sibley described, as being "very heavy and distressing to the animals." Two more days were spent plodding along the Arroyo Chelly through "a most picturesque region of red sandstone formations."

On October 22 the entire column left the Rio Chelly and ascended, by a difficult trail, the mesa lying to the west. Over irregular sandstone outcroppings, the command picked its way for about six miles to the "Cienega Bonito." At this point the entire cavalry force (I, G, Second Dragoons and B, I, Mounted Rifles) was placed under the command of Henry Sibley, with orders to make a night march southward to the mid-point of Black Mesa, thirty-five miles distant — and "there ascend the mesa and move westward to Cañon Limitar [now known as Klethlana Valley], destroying or driving before him any Navajos that might be found on the route." The infantry in the meantime, would move directly to the cañon's mouth, near present-day Marsh Pass, and intercept any Indians fleeing toward the Rio San Juan.

Sibley set out at dusk and rode until 3:30 a.m., at which time he halted and rested his men briefly. At dawn the march was resumed. Only one mile was covered, however, before a large herd of horses and several flocks of sheep were discovered; and the hard-riding troopers rounded up 200 horses 2,000 sheep, besides killing five Navajos who opposed their charge. Three squaws and two children were also captured — and they revealed that this band was Delgadito's, one of the wealthiest leaders of the Navajo tribe.

Following this engagement, Sibley and his men moved up Klethlana Valley; and on October 26 met Canby and the infantry somewhere near Marsh Pass. The next four days were spent examining the cañons and red sandstone mesas of the Segi country, as well as the gray northern rim of Black Mesa. On November 2 the march was resumed toward Fort Defiance; and four days later the command was back at that post. Thus far the campaign had done little to humble the Navajos. In fact, it had been disastrous to the army. When Major Henry Sibley penned his official report of operations, he revealed the full impact which this fatiguing campaign had upon troops under his leadership:

> I deeply regret to report the complete exhaustion of the cavalry horses, and the entire inefficiency of the four companies which have been actively employed in this campaign since the 12th of September for any further active service.[8]

✂   ✂   ✂

Meanwhile, to the east of Canby and Sibley, the Third Column had been carrying out its assigned duties. Companies E, Mounted Rifles, and A and I, Seventh Infantry, with a detachment of New Mexican guides, had left Fort Defiance on October 13, under command of First Lieutenant Tilford.[9] From Cañon Bonito this column proceeded to La Joya, near Laguna Negra, thence to Whisky Creek, a tributary of the Rio Chelly. There the command remained until October 17 in hopes of apprehending Navajos fleeing from Canby's operations along the north rim of Cañon de Chelly. However, not an Indian or fresh trail of Indians, were discovered.

On the morning of October 17, Tilford broke camp upon Whiskey Creek and marched toward the confluence of Wheatfield Creek and the Rio Chelly — at the eastern end of Cañon de Chelly. There Tilford's New Mexican guides discovered what appeared to be a large trail of Indians, not more than a few hours old, leading into the great gorge. The mounted troops were rapidly deployed, and for four or five hours the trail was followed. The Indians were finally caught up with and surprised. They turned out to be, however, no more than two men (who escaped), and one squaw, who was captured along with their livestock — thirty horses and forty sheep.

However, the race after these Navajos was not as futile as it might seem. The squaw revealed what appeared to be vital information. She substantiated Canby's earlier assumption that the main part of the tribe had fled westward beyond Cañon de Chelly, where she said, "all of the wealthiest and most important men of the tribe with their flocks and herds were." Why these Indians would abandon their prime grazing grounds in the higher elevations of the Chuska-Tunicha Mountains was now clearly apparent.

New Mexican irregulars were combing the mountains along the eastern border of Navajoland. A few days previous Chief Mariano Martinez had been killed in the Chuskas; and the great orator and tribal leader, Zarcillas Largas, had been slain near the mouth of Cañon de Chelly. The

Navajo's dreaded enemies, the Utes, led personally by Agent Pheiffer, had harassed Navajos living between the Rio San Juan and the Carrizo Mountains; and had captured large numbers of horses and sheep.[10] With this information, Tilford decided not to risk his command in the upper reaches of Cañon de Chelly, but instead convey the news to his superiors at Fort Defiance.

✄ ✄ ✄

Results of operations during September and early October did not measure up to Canby's expectations. In fact, the Navajos' innate ability to evade the troops greatly exasperated the colonel. He had never before seen Indians such as these. For as Canby complained to the Assistant Adjutant General:

> I entered upon this campaign with the belief that as it was not the policy of the Navajos to fight, they would not fight unless driven to points from which they could not escape or pressed to do so in defense of their families and flocks. Our recent operations have shown that even when pressed to the extreme limits of their country, they still have the means of escape, and that they will abandon their families and their flocks, rather than fight even with inferior numbers.[11]

The Navajos' amazing ability to vanish before pursuing columns of soldiers; the extreme ruggedness of their redrock homeland; and almost total lack of forage and water, which wasted the grain-fed and coddled cavalry mounts, convinced Canby that this tribe could not be subjugated by just one, two, or even three campaigns. Instead, the army would have a task which must be pressed home with vigor during all seasons. No periods of rest must be allowed these Indians. They would have to be hounded and hunted from their places of concealment. Their herds and flocks slaughtered or driven away. Only then would the Navajos submit.

But how was Canby to accomplish this? His companies of cavalry were now afoot, or nearly so. Thus far, his operations had succeeded in killing only thirty-four Indians, and capturing about 8,000 head of livestock (the greater portion of which had been taken by Utes) — a mere fraction of total Navajo wealth. And soon Navajoland would be blanketed with a thick mantle of snow, greatly curtailing army operations.

Canby proposed to hurdle these obstacles by garrisoning strategic points with strong infantry contingents. The Chuska and Tunicha Valleys were suggested as points from whence troops could easily strike the eastern Navajos. As both Forts Defiance and Fauntleroy would be snow-bound, Canby wanted to establish "a depot to the west of Zuñi," within reach of Navajo winter grazing grounds; and from which operations could be extended down the Little Colorado River.[12]

By December 1, department commander Fauntleroy had sustained Canby's decision to use infantry exclusively against the Navajos.[13] Therefore, two companies each, of the Second Dragoons and Mounted Rifles were relieved and ordered to Albuquerque. A depot to the west of Zuñi, however, would pose too difficult a logistic problem; and the newly established Fort Fauntleroy would thereafter be headquarters for all future movements against the Diné.[14] In mid-November six companies of the Navajo Expedition were rapidly transferred from Fort Defiance to the new post at Bear Springs. The forces remaining at Defiance would, in the meantime, do no more than harass the Navajos in the vicinity of that post, and attempt to drive them and their flocks into the mountains, where inclement weather would do the rest.[15]

Throughout December Canby confined his movements to the immediate neighborhoods of Forts Defiance and Fauntleroy. Scouting parties, led by Ute and New Mexican trackers, were kept constantly afield, searching the country for hiding places of the Navajos. The Zuñi Mountains and the mesas bordering the Rio Puerco and Chuska Valley were scoured. From Fort Defiance columns searched the country adjacent to the Little Colorado and in the vicinity of the Hopi villages. Although these scouts were not attended by any striking results,[16] the Navajos were kept perplexed and their activities greatly hampered. They now lived in constant dread of surprise and attack; and thus were always on the move, rarely spending more than one or two nights in the same place.

By end of December Canby believed the majority of Navajos desired peace; and that the tribe had been broken up by military operations into small groups, "destitute of stock and resources of any kind." Already Navajo delegations, making overtures for peace, had come into Fort Fauntleroy; and the colonel cautiously appointed January 12 as time for a general council to discuss armistice terms.[17]

As the council date drew near, many prominent Navajos arrived at Fort Fauntleroy. The rising war chief, Manuelito, conservative Armijo, and Ganado Mucho, always the friend of the Anglos were there, as well as Herrero, Barboncito, Delgadito, and the son of the late Zarcillas Largas. Throughout the council the military commander was emphatic and unrelenting in his terms — the armistice would be only a partial one. Peace would be granted to Navajos living west of Fort Fauntleroy. Operations would still be conducted to the east, where Canby believed most of the hostiles resided. The Indian delegation was warned: "that if they permitted any *ladrones* [thieves] to take refuge in the country exempted from operations, their conduct would be regarded as a breach of faith."[18] The Navajos consented to all that Colonel Canby dictated, and even pledged help in driving the *"ladrones"* from the tribe. This cooperation convinced Canby that peace could once again be restored; and he appointed February 5 as date for still another council to consider terms of a final treaty.

✗   ✗   ✗

For a week prior to the council Navajos began to assemble in great numbers near Fort Fauntleroy. By the first week of February, 2,000 Indians were encamped about Ojo del Oso, and many more were on their way in. When the treaty council opened on February 5, Canby was disappointed, however, to see only a small minority of the tribe's headmen present. Herrero Grande, Herrero Chiquito, Ganado Mucho, El Barbon, Barboncito and Vincente were the principal headmen present — far less than half the chiefs desired by Canby. For the benefit of those absent chiefs, many of whom were reported detained by deep snows now blanketing Navajoland, as well as Canby's own desire to have as many Navajo leaders represented as possible, the council was postponed for ten days.

By February 15, twenty-four chiefs had assembled — to Colonel Canby's satisfaction. The treaty that was put forward was far different from all previous agreements with this tribe. Canby did not press the Indians for immediate approval and signature. Instead, he only explained the document, and then gave the headmen sufficient time to show their good faith, and secure signatures of the majority of tribal leaders. Because Canby believed the Diné to be impoverished by the recent military campaign, as well as past ones, he did not attempt to exact conditions which would be impossible for the tribe to meet, and the subsequent enforcement of which would inevitably lead to renewed hostilities. Only six conditions — and liberal ones at that — did he present to the Navajos:

> 1. Any aggressions by the Navajos against the peoples of Zuñi, Moqui, the New Mexicans or other Indian pueblos and tribes would be considered as a breach of peace.

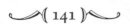

2. All chiefs signing the treaty would agree to submit unconditionally to United States authority, and would be held responsible for the acts of all their people.

3. The chiefs agree to make war upon the "ladrones," and carry that war on until all are suppressed.

4. The chiefs shall not let any of the ladrones reside in their country, nor shall they let their people steal. They furthermore promise to indemnify all losses occasioned by Navajo theft.

5. The chiefs shall immediately collect their people and establish them in the country west of Fort Fauntleroy, and until otherwise stipulated none will be allowed to live or graze in the country east of that post.

6. Whenever the government of the United States is satisfied that the Navajo people will conform in good faith to the conditions of the treaty; put an end to their depredations and live in peace . . ., measures will be taken to render them any assistance that may be necessary to place them in the same condition with other nations under the protection of the government.

Within two weeks of initial presentation, this treaty had been signed by thirty-two headmen, and Colonel Canby was confident that a lasting peace could be secured. In fact, both he and Fauntleroy had deemed the peace lasting enough to order the final abandonment of Fort Defiance. Throughout late March and early April, material and supplies were transferred from Defiance to Fauntleroy. Finally, on April 25, 1861, the last troops were withdrawn from Cañon Bonito, and the old army quarters turned over to the Navajos.[20] The regular garrison at the new post near Bear Springs, and for that matter the whole Navajo Expedition, was considerably reduced when Canby transferred his operations southward to Apache country. The campaign in Navajoland had come to an abrupt end with the movement of the entire Seventh Infantry regiment to the Tularosa.

The abandonment of Fort Defiance and transfer of troops elsewhere was perhaps too hasty, for there were influences at work — many traditional — which would never allow peace. As always there was that element among the New Mexican population that overlooked any treaty or agreement of peace between the United States Government and the Indians. The slaveraiders and horse thieves were still very much at work. In late February a party of thirty-one New Mexicans from Taos were apprehended by military patrols, with six Navajo squaws in their possession. They also admitted killing one man and six women and children before obtaining their captives. This party of slave-raiders brutally demonstrated the general feeling prevalent among frontier settlements, when they "openly avowed their intentions to disregard the treaty made with the Navajos, and on their return home, to organize a new expedition to capture Navajos and sell them."

Throughout March other large scale inroads were made by New Mexicans. The band of Ganado Mucho was attacked and fifty of its horses stolen. Fifteen Navajo rancherías near the northern extremities of the Tunichas were also attacked by New Mexicans, probably from Cubero.[21] If these disruptive incidents had been the work of a few lawless individuals, who were always to be found where quick profits could be made, they might have been overlooked by the army. However, the magnitude and organization of these raids upon the Navajos reflected the fact that public sentiment — at least in frontier towns — was not at all behind Canby's treaty.

Colonel Canby was fast realizing how devastating these wanton acts were to the peace, for on February 27 he wrote to Fauntleroy:

Those and other occurrences of minor importance indicate, I think, a settled disposition on the part of some of these people to protract the Navajo troubles indefinitely.

For myself I shall have no hesitation in treating as enemies of the United States any parties of Mexicans or Pueblo Indians who may be found in the country assigned to
the Navajos.[22]

✗ ✗ ✗

Colonel Canby, however, was destined never to have the
opportunity to take measures he deemed necessary for
securement of a permanent peace with the Navajos. Far to
the east and south of New Mexico another conflict of far
greater scope was gathering. With the election of Abraham
Lincoln to the presidency, the question of Negro slavery and
state's rights was brought once and for all to a head.
Throughout January one southern state after another declared its independence — South Carolina, Mississippi, Florida, Alabama, Louisiana, Georgia — and on February 1,
Texas.

In New Mexico as elsewhere, the effects of succession
were immediately apparent and hard felt. Army officers by
scores resigned their commissions to take up the cause of
their native states and beloved South. Colonel Thomas
Fauntleroy resigned as department commander on March
25; his successor, Colonel Loring, followed suit sixty days
later. And Major Henry H. Sibley also departed from the
territory after leaving these remarks with soldiers at Fort
Fillmore: "Boys, if you only knew it, I am the worst enemy
you have!"

Command of the United States Army in New Mexico fell
to the next senior officer — the mild mannered, plain appearing and "prudent," Edward R. S. Canby. His task of
reorganizing the scattered troops would not be an easy one.
The Army in New Mexico was struck by one of the worst
epidemics of demoralization in its history. By summer of
1861 the weak and scattered companies throughout the territory found themselves with pay half a year in arrears. The

sustained droughts which had struck New Mexico for the past eighteen months had left the cavalry with few serviceable mounts.

At the very moment that Canby was attempting to mold his troops into some semblance of an army, Henry H. Sibley, now a brigadier general, was before Confederate President, Jefferson Davis, outlining a grandiose scheme. Sibley viewed the southwest as a gigantic recruiting ground. The 86,000 population of New Mexico; the Mormons of Utah, still smarting from their persecutions by gentiles; and the thousands of miners of California and Nevada, would surely swell Southern ranks. The fertile soil of California would be ideal for extension of the plantation system, and the abundance of mineral wealth of that vast area would fill the Southern treasury. Sibley visualized Arizona and New Mexico as a spring-board for military expansion into Mexico; and the 1200 mile long California coastline (including Baja California) would forever break the Union blockade and bring European recognition of the Southern cause. This scheme, as visionary and farfetched as it might seem, could very well be the most important single move the South ever made.

By June 1861 Sibley was on his way back to Texas with Jefferson Davis' authorization to undertake the conquest of the "Desert Southwest;" and by the close of that year, 3500 Texans of "the best that ever threw a leg over a horse or that had ever sworn allegiance to any cause," were on their way northward, up the Rio Grande Valley. Sibley's words uttered that day at Fort Fillmore had indeed come true.

News of the impending Texas invasion set Canby feverishly to work. From the War Department he secured authority to raise four regiments of New Mexican volunteers; and by end of September, Canby had fourteen ill-equipped companies, on enlistments as short as six months. Not able to muster a full four regiments, the department commander organized these volunteers into two units — the First and Second New Mexico Volunteers.

To lead these regiments, Canby picked men whom he knew commanded respect and loyalty. Christopher "Kit" Carson, veteran of Rocky Mountain fur trade, explorer and Indian fighter, and more recently Indian Agent for the Utes, was chosen to head the First Regiment. The command of the Second went to an almost equally illustrious New Mexican. As a man of unquestioned Union loyalities, an able administrator, publisher and politician from Santa Fe, Miguel Piño would also prove an excellent field officer.

Canby, however, knew that he would require additional aid to hold New Mexico against the rising Confederate tide. In desperation he enlisted the aid of volunteer forces being mustered in Colorado. It was also essential, not only to the Army in New Mexico but to the preservation of the Union, that the overland route to California be kept open and protected. But to accomplish this Canby would need still more troops. A brigade of California volunteers was mustered for this expressed purpose and placed under the command of a man who was no stranger to the southwest. Colonel James H. Carleton, veteran of Plains service, had come to New Mexico in the spring of 1852. For five years he served against the Navajos and Apaches. In 1858 Carleton was transferred to California, but was now to return to New Mexico — there to shape the territory's destiny in years to come.

While awaiting reinforcements, Canby shifted his troops, withdrawing units from isolated posts such as Fort Fauntleroy (now renamed Fort Lyon for obvious reasons) and concentrated them at more strategic points. Forts Fillmore, Stanton and Craig — posts that would feel the brunt of Texas invasion — were strengthened. The Confederate tide, however, was strong and rapid. It swept up the Rio Grande during summer and fall of 1861, engulfing Fort Fillmore, causing Fort Stanton to be abandoned; and claiming the territory's nerve centers of Albuquerque and Santa Fe. However, Brigadier General Henry Hopkins Sibley was never to realize his dream of conquest. From out of the west marched the "California Column" under command of Colonel James H. Carleton; and from the north came the Colorado Volunteers led by Colonel John B. Slough, to crush the Texans at Glorieta Pass in February 1862.[23]

✂ ✂ ✂

1. Orders No. 187, August 21, 1860; *Department of New Mexico*, LR. Also Report of Secretary of War, 36th Congress, 2nd Session, *Senate Executive Document*, Vol. I, pp. 62-63. For a very excellent biography of Canby consult Max L. Heyman, *Prudent Soldier: A Biography of Edward R. S. Canby* (Glendale: 1959).

2. Col. T. T. Fauntleroy to Lt. Col. S. Thomas, September 9, 1860; *Department of New Mexico*, LR.

3. D. H. Maury (A.A.G.) to J. L. Collins, September 4, 1860; Collins to A.A.G., September 5, 1860; *ibid.*

4. Collins to Greenwood, September 8, 1860; *New Mexico Superintendency Papers*, LR.

5. Canby to A.A.G., October 4, 1860; *Department of New Mexico*, LR.

6. Canby to A.A.G., October 5, 1860; *ibid.*

7. Sibley to A.A.G., November 12, 1860; *ibid.*

8. The account of this portion of Canby's campaign has been taken from the report of H. H. Sibley to Lt. L. Rich, November 12, 1860; Canby to A.A.G., November 8, 1860; *ibid.*

9. In the absence of Colonel Canby, Captain L. McLaws assumed command of Fort Defiance. McLaws subsequently delegated the command of the "Third Column" to Lt. Tilford.

10. Tilford to E. J. Cresey, October 20, 1860; *ibid.*

11. Canby to A.A.G., November 21, 1860; *ibid.*

12. *Ibid.*

13. On December 1, Fauntleroy informed Adjutant General of the Army, Col. L. Thomas, that "future operations of this campaign against the Navajos will be carried on by infantry entirely." Fauntleroy to Thomas, December 1, 1860; *Records of the Office of Adjutant General*, LR.

14. Canby to Capt. J. C. McFerran, November 22, 1860; *Department of New Mexico*, LR.

15. Canby to Capt. H. R. Selden, November 24, 1860; *ibid.*

16. An idea of the results of December operations against Navajos is given by Colonel Canby, when he wrote: "On December 14, Lt. Stith, 5th

Inf., surprised a camp of Navajos on the Puerco, 30 miles S.W. of Fauntleroy, capturing several women. On December 24, a party of Indians surprised 16 miles northeast of Fauntleroy, one women, wounded and 1 horse killed. On 29th, 30th, 31st of December, 1 warrior killed, 3 women, 9 horses and 120 sheep and goats captured in Chuska valley." Canby to A.A.G., January 6, 1861; *ibid.*

17. Canby to A.A.G., December 23, 1860; *ibid.*

18. Canby to A.A.G., January 14, 1861; *ibid.*

19. Canby to A.A.G., February 6, 1861; *ibid.*

20. Canby to A.A.G., March 11, 1861; *ibid.* Also *Fort Defiance Post Returns,* April 1861.

21. Canby to A.A.G., February 27, March 11 and 18, 1861; *ibid.*

22. Canby to Fauntleroy, February 27, 1861; *ibid.*

23. This summary of the Confederate invasion of New Mexico has been taken, for the most part, from two very excellent studies: Robert L. Kerby, *The Confederate Invasion of New Mexico and Arizona, 1861-62* (Los Angeles: 1958); and William A. Keleher, *Turmoil in New Mexico, 1846-68* (Santa Fe: 1952). The latter work, besides giving a very clear picture of events during the Civil War, delves into the problems presented by the Navajos during this twenty year period. It is a work that no serious student of southwestern history can do without.

VIII

THE LONG WALK INTO CAPTIVITY

INDIAN depredations greatly increased during the time New Mexico was being torn asunder by civil and military strife occasioned by the Texas invasion. Navajos on the west, Mescalero Apaches to the east, and Comanches and Kiowas ran riot in the south. Raids became so frequent and intense that a great many people were impoverished by livestock losses, and many farms and settlements were abandoned.[1] As never before the people of New Mexico looked to the United States Army for deliverance.

By fall 1862 the new military commander of the territory, James H. Carleton — now promoted to rank of Brigadier General — had formulated plans for reduction of the Indian menace. To punish and control the Mescaleros, he ordered Colonel Christopher Carson, with five companies of the First New Mexico Volunteers, to reoccupy Fort Stanton in the heart of Apache country. To support Carson's movements, other troops were detailed to cooperate — "yet to be independent . . ."

It was General Carleton's plan to trap the Apaches within a pincer movement. On October 11 Carleton requested Colonel Joseph R. West, commander of the newly established District of Arizona, to issue orders for two companies of First Cavalry California Volunteers and twenty Mexican guides, to move by way of Dog Cañon and operate to the east and southeast of Mescalero haunts. At the same time, Captains Roberts and Pishon's companies of the same regiment, together with twenty "firstrate" Pueblo Indians and Mexicans from Isleta, Socorro and San Elizario, would proceed to the north of the Apaches. Both commands were given strict instructions not to hold any talks with the Indians — as this would be a war of extermination. Carleton was emphatic when he ordered: "The men are to be slain whenever and wherever they can be found. The women and children may be taken prisoners . . ., they are not to be killed."[2]

Five months later the Mescaleros had been humbled. On February 1, 1863, General Carleton reported to the Adjutant General of the Army, Brigadier General Lorenzo Thomas, that "the Mescalero Apaches have been completely subdued."[3] Already 350 of the tribe had surrendered, and the remainder had fled across the border into Mexico, or joined Gila Apaches in the White Mountains.

Carleton had foreseen the results of his campaign and carefully began planning for establishment of a post to receive and watch over Apache prisoners; and on November 4, 1862, he directed the issuance of Special Orders Number 193:

A board of officers, to consist of Lieutenant Colonel Dodd, 2d Colorado volunteers, Surgeon James M. McNulty, 1st Infantry California Volunteers, and First Lieutenant Cyrus H. De Forrest, 2d Colorado Volunteers, will convene at Bosque Redondo, on the Pecos River, New Mexico, on the 15th of November, 1862, or as soon thereafter as practicable, and proceed to select the exact site of Fort Sumner, the new post recently ordered to be established.[4]

One month later the board of officers had accomplished their task. They had carefully and dispassionately inspected that portion of the Pecos River Valley known as Bosque Redondo. For fourteen miles, above and below that clump of cottonwoods from whence the location derived its name, the terrain was scanned and measured. When the board submitted its report to Carleton, however, there was little in it to please the general:

> The advantages of the site and its immediate vicinity are that the ground is above the land of the highest floods; it commands a view of the plain for two or three miles in every direction; it is convenient to the water and cottonwood, and the grazing in the vicinity is good.
>
> It has the following disadvantages: it is remote from the depot of supplies [Fort Union], and from the neighborhoods that supply forage. Building material will have to be brought from a great distance. The water of the Pecos contains much unhealthy mineral matter. A large part of the surrounding valley is subject to inundation by the spring floods.
>
> In view of the disadvantages of the location, the majority of the board respectfully recommend that the junction of the Agua Negra and Pecos Rivers, be selected as the site of Fort Sumner, for the following reasons: the supply of good timber for building and firewood is convenient to the site. The water is pure and abundant. The grazing is very fine. None of the neighboring country is subject to overflow....[5]

Regardless of what the board advised, Carleton had made up his mind. Fort Sumner would be situated at Bosque Redondo in east-central New Mexico, 165 miles from Santa Fe. He had been over the ground in 1852, and again in 1854 — and both times had considered the area of strategic importance. The Pecos rising in the mountains near Santa Fe,

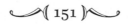

was deemed by Carleton, to be of sufficient volume to supply the needs of both military garrison and the contemplated Indian reservation. Located in a large oblong valley, having the river as its western boundary, Fort Sumner was perfectly situated geographically for settlement of one of the most troublesome of tribes. To the east and south rose a low mesa which extended and blended into the Staked Plain. The country to the north and west was open for many miles, and the nearest settlement was fifty miles away. So too would Fort Sumner stand as a barrier to the marauding Comanches and Kiowas, who had long used the area as a rendezvous for organization of raids into New Mexico. Furthermore, Bosque Redondo lay in the path of a great plunder trail which swept from the northern end of the territory far into Mexico. Establish Fort Sumner at Bosque Redondo, and the Mescaleros, Comanches, Kiowas, and other Plains and mountain tribes would forever be blocked in their devastating raids south of the border. Based upon these facts, Carleton's decision was well taken. Only future events would demonstrate the wisdom inherent in it.[6]

X X X

While Mescalero Apaches were being driven to their "brutal senses," Carleton was carefully working out his policy relative to the management of the Navajos. By application of force-of-arms, Carleton and his troops would gather this tribe together "little by little, on a reservation, away from their haunts, and hills, and hiding-places of their country, and then . . . to be kind to them; there teach their children how to read and write; teach them the arts of peace . . .; the truths of Christianity. Soon they would acquire new habits, new ideas, new modes of life; the old Indians [would] . . . die off, and carry with them all the latent longings for murdering and robbing; the young ones [would] . . . take their places without these longings; and thus, little by little, they [would] . . . become a happy and contented people, and Navajo wars [would] . . . be remembered only as something that belongs entirely to the past."[7] To all outward appearances the beautiful prose of Carleton was enough to convince even the most skeptical of his "humanitarian intentions."

The commandant of the Department of New Mexico, however, may very well have had other reasons for commencing a campaign against the Navajos. Like many other officers of that day, James H. Carleton was bitten by the mineral bug. His letters to the adjutant general of the army, the commander-in-chief, and the secretary of war, outlined grandiose schemes for advancement of mining and commercial endeavors in New Mexico. To Carleton, as well as to the newly appointed Governor, Henry Connelly, the Navajos and Apaches occupied one of the richest mineral and grazing regions on the continent — and their removal was imperative for advancement of New Mexico. Carleton, in his visionary manner, believed these human obstacles could in time be overcome, and the wealth tapped would "bring the great railroad over the 35th parallel, and thus unite the two extremes of the country by bars of steel, until, from the Atlantic to the Pacific, we become homogeneous in interests as in blood." To Carleton, Governor Connelly, and practically every member of the Territorial Assembly, the price of removing both the Apaches and Navajos was not too high.[8]

By September 30, 1862, Carleton had informed the Adjutant General of the Army of the preliminary steps he intended to take toward bringing these Indians to their knees. Lieutenant Colonel José Francisco Chavez, Governor Connelly's step-son and second in command to Kit Carson, would soon move into Navajo country with four companies of the newly raised Fourth New Mexico Mounted Rifles; there to establish and garrison a post on the eastern slopes of the Zuñi Mountains, somewhere in the vicinity of Ojo del Gallo. The general location for this proposed fort — which would be christened Fort Wingate — had been selected by General Canby a year previous, and upheld by Carleton as an ideal location from whence troops could "perform such services among the Navajos as will bring them to feel that they have been doing wrong."[10]

After informing the Adjutant General of his intentions, Carleton acted fast. Seven days later Special Order Number 180 was issued, authorizing selection of the exact site of Fort Wingate:

A board of officers, to consist of Captain Henry R. Seldon, United States Fifth Infantry, Assistant Surgeon Joseph C. Bailey, medical department, United States Army, and First Lieutenant Allen L. Anderson, Fifth United States Infantry, acting as lieutenant of engineers will proceed to the Navajo country, and near the headwaters of the Gallo, select the exact site on which Fort Wingate should be established.[11]

The site chosen was ideal. The locality was a broad valley at the headwaters of the Ojo del Gallo, about 85 miles west of the Rio Grande, and four miles south of present-day Grants, New Mexico. The valley spreading out in two directions below the post (one branch leading toward Zuñi, the other to Acoma and Laguna) afforded fine pasturage. The plans of the post were designed so that it would cut the cardinal points at right angles. A large parade ground would separate officers' quarters from company barracks. A row of sycamore trees was projected, and once planted around the borders of the post, would assure "a cooling shade of a hot summer's day."[12]

Although construction of Fort Wingate was begun immediately, erection of actual living quarters was a slow process. A letter by Captain J. C. Shaw, commander of Company A, published in the *Alta California*, revealed actual conditions under which troops lived while the post was being built:

> The fort looks vastly fine on paper, but as yet it has no other existence. The garrison consists of four companies of my regiment — the Fourth New Mexico Mounted Rifles — and we live on, or rather exist, in holes or excavations, made in the earth, over which our cloth tents are pitched. We are supplied also with fire places, chimneys, etc., and on the whole, during the beautiful pleasant weather of the past few weeks, have enjoyed ourselves quite well. Our camp presents more appearance of a gipsy encampment than anything else I can compare it to.[13]

Under the able direction of Chavez and regimental quartermaster, First Lieutenant Benjamin Stevens, Fort Wingate began to take shape by spring of 1863. More than 250,000 feet of lumber was salvaged from the abandoned Fort Lyon (Fort Fauntleroy);[14] and 25 citizens and 75 soldiers were kept constantly on extra-duty as carpenters, millwrights, masons and timber cutters. A contract was awarded to Messrs. Pool & McBride for the manufacture of 380,000 adobe bricks for erection of officers' quarters, quartermaster's storerooms, hospital, and other buildings.[15]

✂   ✂   ✂

The Navajos, observing the activity at Wingate and hearing reports of what was happening to their cousins, the Mescaleros, began to wonder if the same fate was about to befall them. A delegation of eighteen headmen, led by Delgadito and Barboncito journeyed to Santa Fe during December to plead with Carleton for peace. The general, however, sternly told the headmen, "that they could have no peace until they would give other guarantees than their word, that peace should be kept; to go home and tell their people so; that we [the Army] have no faith in their promises. . . ."[16]

Hearing this, the chiefs sullenly returned to their tribesmen, to await their fate.

By mid-March 1863, Carleton had 400 Apaches interned at Bosque Redondo, where it was hoped they would be gradually civilized to a point where they could plant crops and "become like the Pueblo Indians."[17] Now that the Mescaleros were pacified, troops would be available to campaign against the Navajos. The strategy to be used against these Indians was simple and basic. First destroy their means of subsistence; hound and harass them during fall; and then deliver a hard, masterly stroke against the tribe when they would feel it the hardest — during dead of winter.   .

Throughout spring, troops were withdrawn from Apache country, preparatory to a move on Navajoland. On April 11, Carleton instructed Carson to begin assembling his guides and trailers; and authority was granted to employ "ten of the *best* Ute warriors . . . and four of the *best* Mexican guides from the Abiquiu area."[18]

Three days later, Carleton left Santa Fe for Fort Wingate to personally inspect the new post and gather additional information for the campaign, which would commence as soon as grass was sufficient to support cavalry mounts. Returning from his tour, the general knew that still another post must be established deep in the heart of Navajoland, if his scheme was to be successful. On June 15 he directed issuance of General Order Number 15, which specified creation of another board of officers to select the site of a second post. Major Henry D. Wallen, Surgeon James B. McNulty, Acting Engineer, Brevet Captain Allen L. Anderson and Assistant Adjutant General Benjamin C. Cutler would proceed with Kit Carson and his regiment to Pueblo Colorado, near present-day Ken-lee-chi, Arizona. There, the terrain would be mapped and marked for a new post, named in honor of Carleton's predecessor — R. E. S. Canby. The same orders which authorized this board of officers and selection of a site for Fort Canby, also formally marshaled military forces against the Navajos:

It is therefore ordered, that Colonel Christopher Carson, with proper military force proceed without delay to a point in the Navajo country known as Pueblo Colorado, and there establish a defensible depot for his supplies and hospital; and thence to prosecute a vigorous war upon the men of this tribe until it is considered at these headquarters that they have been effectually punished for their long continued atrocities.[19]

At the same time, the garrison at Fort Wingate was strengthened by addition of companies F, E, and H, First New Mexico Volunteers — a total of 315 men. These troops would support and cooperate with Carson's troops; alternating their scouts so that at least two companies would be in the field at all times.[20]

However, careful inspection of the area around Pueblo Colorado revealed total lack of those essentials necessary for maintenance of a post in that isolated part of the country. Water and grass were insufficient for support of troops and their animals; and the rough terrain rendered approach to the proposed fort exceedingly difficult for wagons. Therefore, Cañon Bonito, the site of old Fort Defiance, was decided upon as depot and operational headquarters for Carson's troops.[21]

Carson knew that the Navajo campaign would fail unless experienced guides and trackers, who knew the ways and haunts of the Diné, were available. Having been Ute agent for a number of years, Kit was already aware of the great animosity which these mountain Indians harbored for the people across the Rio San Juan. He further knew of the intermittent wars which the Utes had carried on with their pastoral foes, and had even aided in their cause. The Utes were therefore Carson's first choice; and on June 17 he requested Carleton's permission to employ 100 auxiliaries from that tribe. The request was immediately forwarded to the Adjutant General of the Army with Carleton's endorsement: "The Utes are very brave, and fine shots, fine trailers, and uncommonly energetic in the field. The Navajos have entertained a very great dread of them for many years. . . . One hundred Ute Indians would render more service in this war than double their number of troops."[22]

Even before this request reached Washington, the Diné's old enemies from across the Rio San Juan had struck. At the very time that Carson penned his letter, large concentrations of Utes were ranging Navajoland in search of captives and livestock.[23] Indeed, the coming Navajo campaign left an open season for that most vile of merchants — the slave procurer. Navajo country was now alive with not only Indians bent on rapine and pillage but with New Mexicans seeking women and children. Companies of irregulars were being organized and equipped with the blessings of General Carleton. Again, those frontier towns of Cubero, Cebolleta and Abiquiu were serving as jumping-off points for these slave-raiders disguised as "volunteer troops." One such company in particular would be highly successful in the months to come. The unit recruited by Ramón A. Baca, of Cebolleta, would stand out above all others because, as Indian trader Nathan Bibo wrote: "they became familiar with the country and the Indian hiding places. . . . They took hundreds of prisoners, who, as was the custom . . ., were sold as domestics all over the territory, sometimes at very high prices."[24]

As an upstanding citizen of the Territory of New Mexico, Christopher Carson sanctioned the conduct of these volunteer companies as they bartered away the lives and freedom of hundreds of Navajo children. In true mountain man fashion, Carson wanted to reward his Utes for "their continued zeal and activity" by permitting them to retain women and children. The "Rope Thrower" — as Carson was called by the Navajos — was convinced that captives disposed of in this manner would be better off than at Bosque Redondo — as the Utes would sell them to Mexican families who would care for them. Thus they would, in his words, "cease to require any further attention on the part of the Government." Carson also advocated distributing captive Navajos as servants in order to break up "that collectiveness of interest as a tribe which they will retain if kept together" at Bosque Redondo.[25] These ideas, however, were promptly altered when Carleton informed his subordinate that —

> all prisoners which are captured by the troops or employes of your command will be sent to Santa Fe, by the first practicable opportunity after they are, from time to time, brought in as prisoners. *There must be no exception to this rule.*[26]

X   X   X

By mid-summer all preparation for the Navajo roundup had been completed and the troops were ready to take the field. The burned and ruined buildings of old Fort Defiance had been rejuvenated, and christened Fort Canby.[27] On June 23, Carleton instructed Colonel J. Francisco Chavez, the commander of Fort Wingate, to send word to Delgadito and Barboncito — the two headmen who had begged peace for their people — that the war was about to commence. All Navajos not wishing to engage in hostilities would be given until July 20 to come into either Forts Canby or Wingate with their families; and there await transferral to a new reservation being set aside for them along the Pecos River. After that day, wrote Carleton, *"every Navajo that is seen will be considered as hostile and treated accordingly;* that after that day the door now open will be closed."[28]

In accordance with these orders, the "door" was slammed shut on the date specified. Colonel Carson struck the first blow by ordering out small detachments from Fort Canby to harass the Navajos. Throughout the closing days of July, the First New Mexico Volunteers and their Ute auxiliaries did a thorough job. Thirteen Indians were reported killed in these initial operations of the war, and more than twenty women and children captured. But perhaps the most important accomplishment was the destruction of virtually all Indian fields and planting grounds within a forty mile radius of Cañon Bonito. Carson personally reported that about 2,000,-000 pounds of Navajo grain were destroyed by his troops.[29]

This war, however, would not be conducted in the hit-and-miss pattern of previous campaigns. Carleton knew that large movements of troops were ineffectual against a people who would appear one moment and than vanish into inaccessible country. This time the war would be carried to the Navajos in Indian fashion; and in well written prose Carleton outlined his strategy:

> The troops must be kept after the Indians, not in big bodies, with military noises and smokes, and the gleam of arms by day, and fires, and talk, and comfortable sleep by night; but in small parties moving stealthily to their haunts and lying patiently in wait for them; or by following their tracks day after day with a fixedness of purpose that never gives up. . . .
>
> An Indian is a more watchful and a more wary animal than a deer. He must be hunted with skill; he cannot be blundered upon; nor will he allow his pursuers to come upon him when he knows it, unless he is the stranger.[30]

Post commandants were instructed to send out small units, carrying their rations in haversacks and upon mule back. These units would vigilantly watch all springs and water holes known to be frequented by Indians. Throughout August troops from Canby and Wingate scouted the interior of Navajoland, while companies from Forts Bascom, Stanton, Sumner, and from Albuquerque and Los Pinos, were stationed in passes of the mountains forming the Navajo-New

Mexico frontier to intercept Indian raiding parties returning from the Rio Grande Valley. To stimulate the soldiers of Carson's command to greater activity, Carleton authorized establishment of a bounty for each horse, mule and sheep captured from the Navajos. A bonus of twenty dollars would be paid to any and all soldiers delivering to the chief quartermaster, sound and serviceable horses and mules. For all sheep turned over to the chief commissary officer, a dollar a head would be paid.[31]

Despite this preparation and stimulus to army zeal, small parties of Navajos and Apaches still committed depredations. In fact, more than 10,000 animals were driven away from Rio Grande settlements in August alone. Harassed by incessant pursuit, most Navajos had little time to engage in pilfering livestock. They thought only of escape from a relentless foe. Some joined with the few remaining hostile Mescaleros. Others moved with their families and flocks to the west of Hopi; still others crossed the San Juan. But the majority of Navajos remained in the redrock country so long familiar to them. Carleton, fearful that small parties of Navajos might travel southward to the Gila Apaches, cautioned Brigadier General Joseph R. West to be on the lookout for Navajos. West was also advised to take steps to meet the increased depredations which were expected as coming snows forced Indians out of the mountains in search of subsistence.[32]

By mid-October the Carleton policy had taken its toll upon the Navajos. With their fields ruthlessly burned and their herds driven away or slaughtered — the Diné now faced starvation as sure as the snows would come. On October 21 a Navajo delegation arrived at Fort Wingate, desiring peace. Unlike other wars with the tribe, this time there would be no cessation of hostilities with appearance of the first Indian delegation. They were informed that there was no choice in the matter: "All must come in and go to the Bosque Redondo, or remain in their own country at war." The delegation, however, was informed that those Navajos who voluntarily surrendered would be sent to a new reservation — and there fed and clothed. They would furthermore, be permitted to retain all stock (except those animals belonging to the government). But the more recalcitrant members of the tribe, who refused to obey the "new policy," would feel the arm of the American military as never before.[33]

So far, results of the campaign had not measured up to Carleton's expectations. Only 180 tribesmen had surrendered — indeed a poor showing for a "policy" upon which rested the future economy of New Mexico, if not the very military reputation of its instigator. Instead of giving themselves up, Navajos merely disappeared like magic before the troops; or taunted and jeered the soldiers out of rifle shot. Discouraged at the poor results, Carleton attempted to appeal to Navajo reason. On November 22 he dispatched a party of four Indians from Fort Sumner to carry word to their people of the comforts awaiting them at Bosque Redondo.[34] The *jornada* of this delegation, headed by Delgadito, effected little. Depredations were still increasing as the coming winter forced Navajos to look elsewhere for food to sustain their starving families. In late December, Navajos attacked the herds belonging to the Mescaleros interned at Fort Sumner.[35] On January 3, a quartermaster train bound for Fort Canby was waylaid by an estimated 150 Indians, who killed the wagon master, Powell Russell, wounded two others, and drove off three lead wagons and twenty mules.[36]

Navajos now had another enemy to contend with. Their land was now in the grip of winter. Crops and herds had been drastically reduced by Carson and his troops; and the Diné had no chance to store away food enough to sustain them through the ensuing cold months. Now was the time for Carleton and Carson to strike — while snow fall deeply obliterated forage for the remnants of Navajo stock. On January 6, two commands left Fort Canby to deliver a blow at that traditional target of Navajoland — Cañon de Chelly. Ex-Ute agent and now Captain, A. W. Pheiffer, with Company H, and thirty-three men of Company E, First Cavalry, New Mexico Volunteers, rode for the east entrance of Cañon de Chelly — today known as Cañon del Muerto. The other command — and by far the largest, totaling nearly 400 men — was personally led by Kit Carson. This column would strike at the west entrance of Cañon de Chelly, near Chinle; and between the two units, the Navajos within their "natural fortress" would be bottled-up.

Spirits of the volunteers were high that crisp, cold morning as they filed out of Canby. No doubt many hoped this would be their last Indian scout; and they perhaps expressed their sentiments with a song especially composed for the occasion:

> Come dress your ranks, my gallant souls, a standing in
>   a row,
> Kit Carson he is waiting to march against the foe;
> At night we march to Moqui, o'er lofty hills of snow,
> To meet and crush the savage foe, bold Johnny Navajo,
>   Johnny Navajo! O Johnny Navajo![37]

The snow lay six inches deep, causing Pheiffer's troops to cover only nine miles the first day, and seven the next. By January 8 his weary volunteers were approaching the Chuska Mountains. The snow deepened, and the march became increasingly difficult. For the next two days Captain Pheiffer was compelled to divide his command into three parties. An advance guard of fifteen men, equipped with picks and shovels, broke trail for the main command, and the rear guard followed with the supply mules.

Finally, on January 11 the east entrance was reached. Pheiffer knew from long experience the hazards lying within this Navajo sanctuary, and instructed his men carefully before commencing the passage next day. The command would be kept as close together as possible, moving as one body through the cañon. The advance guard would be entrused to the leadership of Lieutenant Laughlin; the rear of the column, with its precious supply animals, would be commanded by Lieutenant C. M. Hubbell. The march through the cañon to the west entrance, where a juncture with Carson was planned, was not to be an easy task. Roads in that gorge were non-existent. Horses and mules floundered under their heavy loads, and broke through the ice covering of the creek, causing many a painful fall.

Pheiffer had penetrated Cañon del Muerto but a short distance before encountering Navajos. Like mountain cats, the Indians began appearing on rocky ledges high above the volunteers. They threw rocks, cursed the New Mexicans, and threatened vengeance in every variety of Spanish they could master. The troopers, however, were unable to reach the illusive and troublesome Indians; and only two bucks and one squaw, who "obstinately persisted in hurling rocks and pieces of wood," were killed, and six others captured. As night came on, Pheiffer encamped in a secure spot on the cañon floor, "where plenty of wood was to be obtained — the remains of old Indian lodges."

Meanwhile, volunteers under the command of Kit Carson, had arrived at the west entrance of Cañon de Chelly, after an equally difficult trip through deep snow. On the same day (January 12) that Pheiffer began his passage of Cañon del Muerto, Kit reconnoitered the cañon's southern rim before commencing full scale operations the next day. The near perpendicular walls, falling for a thousand feet or more, convinced Carson of the futility of locating a trail to the bottom of the gorge, whereby he could flank and surprise the Indians.

On the morning of January 13 Carson divided his force. Companies B and G, under leadership of Captain Asa B.

Carey, would proceed along the south rim of Cañon de Chelly, while companies C and D, commanded by Captain Joseph Barney, would attempt to march along the northern rim. Carson, growing anxious for word from Pheiffer's troops, decided to accompany Carey in hopes of meeting the lost unit. For nearly two days they moved cautiously along the south edge of the great chasm, approaching nearly to its eastern entrance. Carson found not a trace of Pheiffer. He did learn, however, that this reputed Navajo citadel could be flanked without much trouble — at least along its southern rim.

On their return to the main camp at Chinle, Carson and Carey were greatly relieved to find Captain Pheiffer and his lost command resting easily. Reasons for the two units not meeting now was very apparent. The Cañon de Chelly system consisted of two huge gorges — Cañons de Chelly and del Muerto. Pheiffer had marched down the latter, thus eliminating all possibility of meeting Carson, who was making his way along the southern rim of Cañon de Chelly.[38]

While the troops rested that night, three Navajos came into camp under flag of truce. They requested permission to surrender with their families. Through an interpreter, Carson told them that they had until ten a.m. the next morning — ". . . after that time, if they did not come," he informed them, "his soldiers would hunt them down." Next morning — before the designated time — sixty ragged and starving Indians arrived; who in Carson's words, "expressed their willingness to emigrate to the Bosque."

These Navajos stated that they would have gladly surrendered earlier had they not thought that this war was one of extermination. Owing to Carson's scorched-earth policy, many of their women and children had already died of exposure and starvation. As this party of Navajos desired to return for the rest of their band, Carson granted them freedom to do so, and directed them to assemble at Fort Canby in ten days.

Having accomplished all he could at Cañon de Chelly, Kit wanted to be present when the Navajos began to arrive at Canby. On January 15 he set out on the return journey to the post, taking with him the majority of his command. He left, however, a unit of seventy-five men under Captains Carey and Pheiffer, to march through the cañon, destroying as many hogans and peach orchards as they could find. After consultation with Pheiffer, Carey decided to travel the south branch of the gorge (the northern, today known as Cañon del Muerto had been Pheiffer's route). On January 16 the command moved out. Throughout that day, Indians were seen in the rocks overhead and hovering about the rear of the column as it performed its work of destruction. Late that afternoon, Navajos began to come into camp in such large numbers, that by nightfall Carey counted 150 adults as well as many children. This pitiful group of hungry, cold natives were informed that unless they tendered their "full and complete submission," all would be treated as enemies, hunted down and destroyed like predatory animals. Permission, however, was granted many Navajos to return for their families — provided, as Carson stipulated — they would come into Fort Canby in ten days.

With the command's arrival at the east entrance of Cañon de Chelly on January 17, its task of laying waste to the orchards — the pride of Navajoland — had been completed. Carey and Pheiffer then struck a direct line of march for Cañon Bonito, and reached Fort Canby the following day.[89]

✗   ✗   ✗

The Diné had been hit, and hit hard, by Carson and his troopers. Hogans, orchards, and fields had been laid waste, and flocks too large to drive in had been ruthlessly slaughtered by the army. Inclement weather had added to the

Indians' miseries. The Navajos were now left but two choices — surrender and be fed by the army, or retreat deeper into the recesses of their land, there to grub out a subsistence on piñon nuts and wild potatoes. Many chose the latter and migrated, with what flocks they could preserve, deeper into the maze of cañons which characterized their homeland. Some pushed northward into the extremely broken country around Navajo Mountain. Others forded the Rio San Juan and sought sanctuary to the north of that river. Still others made their way to the west, beyond the Hopi villages, or to the south, where they joined their cousins, the Apaches. But the majority of those who did not surrender did what all peoples do when faced with a disaster of this kind. Instead of fleeing into unknown country, they remained close to the redrock land they knew best, ever vigilant against surprise and lurking death which existed in the form of Utes, Puebloans, and the blue-clad New Mexicans.

By February 1, the more destitute Navajos began to arrive at Canby and Wingate. During the first week of that month almost 800 Indians were awaiting transfer to Fort Sumner.[40] Thirty days later this number had swelled to 2,500, and still Navajos arrived. A letter to the editor of the Santa Fe *Gazette* illustrates the rapidity with which the number of Indians increased:

> There are at this moment a hundred campfires sparkling amongst the hills of Cañon Bonito and within five hundred yards of this post. These fires are built by peaceful Navajos who have been arriving daily in large numbers.... It is a happy omen.... There are now about 1600 Indians here, and perhaps an equal number on their way to Fort Wingate so that at the rate they arrive daily we will in less than three weeks have about five thousand on the reservation.[41]

On March 4 more than two thousand Indians began their "Long Walk" from Canby to Fort Sumner, taking with them

473 horses and 3,000 sheep. Perhaps this group was lucky, for subsistence was dwindling at the posts in Navajoland; blankets were practically non-existent — and the results were inevitable. In little over a week's time 126 Navajos died of dysentery and exposure at Fort Canby. Flour had been furnished to those Indians leaving for Bosque Redondo without a word as how to prepare it for consumption. They ate it raw or mixed with water as a gruel. Unaccustomed to this type of fare, many doubled up with the cramps of dysentery and crawled to the side of the road to perish. Those Navajos unable to resume their march were shot, perhaps mercifully, by their blue clad escorts. Of a party of a thousand Indians sent to Fort Sumner, its officer in charge reported ten individuals dying on the road between Los Pinos and Fort Canby — there was no mention of the number which must have perished during the remainder of the journey.[42] Still the Navajos continued to surrender, for they had no other choice — surrender or die a lingering death by exposure and hunger.[43]

The continual stream of Indians now traveling the 400 miles which separated their homeland and the Bosque Redondo impressed Carleton. His "policy" was at last paying dividends; and on February 7, he reported to the Adjutant General the favorable prospects ahead: "I believe this will be the last Navajo War. The persistent efforts which have been and will continue to be made can hardly fail to bring in the whole tribe before the year's end."[44]

However, the large numbers of Navajos now at Fort Sumner or on the way greatly perplexed General Carleton. The ever-increasing number of hungry, ragged Indians were beginning to tax the quartermaster department to the utmost. Dilemma of feeding the thousands of mouths was now upon the shoulders of the department commander. He sought relief from the situation by directing the commanding officer of Fort Wingate not to keep excessive numbers of Indians at that post, but to move them at once to the Rio Grande, where supplies could be more easily procured.[45]

The number of Navajos at Fort Sumner were threatening to grow beyond Carleton's earlier estimates of 5,000 for the entire tribe. As February drew to a close, he began worrying as to how the army was going to feed them all. On February 25 he directed Major Henry Wallen, commander of Fort Sumner, to "make timely estimates for the bread and meat and salt required for all these Indians, and have a margin of food on hand for at least fifty days. There must be no mistake about having enough for them to eat, if we have to kill horses and mules for them."[46] Three days later Carleton again wrote to Wallen instructing him to purchase all stock from the Navajos that were not for breeding.[47]

Throughout the territory, newspapers heralded Carleton's Indian policy; and urged farmers to increase their agricultural output to meet the crisis. Even the Santa Fe *New Mexican*, who in a few months would be the "policy's" bitterest opponent, called upon the people to raise all they could:

> Carleton now has at Fort Sumner, and under his control destined to that place, about 3,500. Provisions such as corn, meal, flour, etc., they must have from the government for a time. This will increase greatly, the demand for these articles. Prices will necessarily be very favorable to the producer. We advise our friends, and the farmers everywhere . . . to sow all the wheat, and plant all the corn they practicably can. A ready market and paying prices will surely be at hand.[48]

X   X   X

Meanwhile, Navajos continued to come in, spurred on by the constant raids of Utes and Pueblo Indians, who prowled the Navajo country in search of booty and slaves. In mid-April, 2,400 men, women and children commenced their "Long Walk" of more than 400 miles to the flat, wind-swept reservation situated on the open plains east of the Rio Grande. It was this trip which would forever be remembered in sadness by the Diné. The traumatic experience of being uprooted and transported from a country that was their sacred home to a land alien to them, would forever be indelibly stamped upon their minds. The hardships endured, along with suffering and death which many a Navajo met, would be remembered painfully as — THE LONG WALK.

That April the weather was very inclement. Heavy snow fell, and ensuing gales piled drifts over roads which the Navajos must take. The Indians, many nearly naked, packed into quartermaster wagons, or forced to walk behind the lumbering vehicles, suffered the agonies of frost bite. Dysentery occasioned by eating army fare, or contracted at the unsanitary assembling point of Los Pinos, took its toll. The route of the Long Walk was marked by the frozen corpses of Indians, who, too fatigued to go on, had crawled to the wayside to die.

Carleton was by now so worried, that he sent James L. Collins as a special messenger to Washington D.C., to seek an interview with the Adjutant General of the Army, Lorenzo Thomas. The message which the ex-superintendent of Indian Affairs presented was brief, but to the point: "Now, when they [the Navajos] have surrendered and at our mercy, they must be taken care of — must be fed, clothed, and instructed. . . . These six thousand mouths must eat, and these six thousand bodies must be clothed."[49] Through Collins, Carleton pleaded for two million pounds of breadstuffs to subsist the Navajos now in the hands of the army. According to Carleton, this amount of food need not be sent at once — but in installments of 500,000 pounds — the first to start at once; the next to reach New Mexico in August; and the rest to follow by November. This amount, Carleton hoped, would sustain the Indians until their crop "comes off" in 1865.

In the short span of two weeks the Indians at Fort Sumner doubled in number. Six thousand Navajos, not to mention the 400 Apaches, were now concentrated on the banks of the Pecos. The situation had become desperate. Endeavoring to overcome the serious food shortage, Carleton directed, on March 25, that troops throughout the department be put on half rations. To keep track of existing supplies he ordered that "on the last day of each month, the commander of every military post and camp within the department will send direct to department headquarters an exact account of all subsistence stores on hand, and a list of all troops, employes, laundresses, and servants who receive rations by issue, purchase, or otherwise. . . ." Carleton further advised post commanders to carefully "husband their provisions" to prevent serious privation and want.[50]

At the same time that troops were receiving half-rations, the Indians at Bosque Redondo were receiving smaller allotments of food. Major Henry Wallen received emphatic instructions as to the amount of subsistence to allot his charges:

> The Indians are to be fed at the rate of *one* pound for each man, woman and child per day, of fresh meat, or of corn, or of wheat, or of wheat meal, or of corn meal, or of flour, or of kraut, or of pickles. . . . Or in lieu of any one of these articles, half a pound of beans or of rice, or of peas, or of dried fruit.[51]

In this hour of despair, when it appeared that his dreams of civilizing the Indians of New Mexico would crumble for lack of food, Carleton was saved. His constant pleadings, and his personal "bearer of dispatches," James L. Collins, had succeeded. Although not able to obtain as much as he originally requested, Carleton did secure 500,000 pounds of flour from commissary stores in the District of Colorado. Two thousand head of cattle would also be forwarded to

New Mexico by October; and additional supplies were expected momentarily at the Colorado River port of Fort Yuma.[52] With these stores, Carleton would be able to feed both his troops and Indians, and at the same time save his "Indian policy."

✄ ✄ ✄

1. Carleton to L. Thomas, September 30, 1862; *Office of Adjutant General, LR*. Also *Report on the Condition of the Tribes, 1867* (Washington: 1867), p. 98. Hereafter cited as *Condition of Tribes.*

2. Carleton to West, October 11, 1862; *Condition of Tribes,* p. 99.

3. Carleton to Thomas, February 1, 1863; *Office of Adjutant General, LR.*

4. *Condition of Tribes,* p. 238.

5. Report of Board of Officers convened to select site of Fort Sumner (dated December 4, 1862); *Department of New Mexico, LR.*

6. Carleton to L. Thomas, November 9, 1862; *Condition of Tribes,* p. 101. For further description of Bosque Redondo see: George Gwyther, "An Indian Reservation," *Overland Monthly* (Vol. X, January 1873), p. 127; also Report of Captain F. McCabe in *War of the Rebellion: Official Records of the Union and Confederate Armies* (Series I, Vol. XLVIII, Part I), pp. 524-525. Latter work hereafter cited as *Official Records.*

7. Carleton to L. Thomas, September 6, 1863; *Office of Adjutant General, LR.*

8. Although Navajo country possessed little actual mineral wealth, still it had not been explored sufficiently at that time, to ascertain the fact. Carleton had every reason to hope for active mining operations, once the Navajos had been removed. Many of his letters resounded with plans to meet this end. On May 10, 1863, Carleton wrote Major General Henry W. Halleck, General-in-Chief of the Army, that "among all my endeavors since my arrival here . . . has been an effort to brush back the Indians . . . so that the people could get out of the valley of the Rio Grande, and not only possess themselves of the arable lands in other parts of the territory, but, if the country contained veins and deposits of precious metals, that they might be found." *Condition of Tribes,* p. 110.

One month later, Carleton again wrote Halleck, reiterating his belief that great mineral wealth existed in Navajo country. "There is every evidence that a country as rich if not richer in mineral wealth than California, extends from the Rio Grande, northwestwardly, all the way across to Washoe." *Ibid.,* p. 114.

The fact that Governor Henry Connelly also sustained Carleton's plans for tapping the mineral wealth thought hidden in Navajoland, is exemplified in his speech before the Legislative Assembly in December 1863, in which the governor stated, that the "Navajos occupy the finest grazing districts within our limits, and . . . infest a mining region extending two hundred miles north by . . . the same extent east and west . . . [thus] an immense pastoral and mining population is excluded from its occupations and the treasures of mineral wealth that are known to exist . . . have remained untouched. The public interest demands that this condition of things should cease to exist.

"The policy of locating the Indians [at Bosque Redondo] should not stop with the Navajos and Mescalero Apaches. It should be applied to all the tribes of New Mexico and Arizona. Peaceful if possible, forcibly if necessary. Too long have they roamed lords of the soil over this extensive and valuable tract of country. They are entitled to a portion of it for their maintenance, but to no more. . . ." For full text of Connelly's speech see: Santa Fe *New Mexican,* December 12, 1863.

9. José Francisco Chavez was born at Los Padillas, Bernalillo County, New Mexico, on June 27, 1833; and was the son of Mariano and Dolores Perea de Chavez. His grandfather, Don Francisco Xavier Chavez was the first governor of New Mexico under the Mexican Republic in 1822.

Oddly enough, J. Francisco Chavez was educated in Anglo-American schools. He attended preparatory schools in St. Louis, Missouri, and then took a course at the College of Physicians and Surgeons in New York City. For additional details see: J. Francisco Chavez folder, Carl Hayden Biographical Collection; Arizona Pioneers' Historical Society, Tucson.

10. Fort Wingate was named in honor of Captain Benjamin Wingate, Fifth U.S. Infantry, who died of wounds sustained during the Battle of Valverde. *Condition of Tribes,* p. 99; also Albuquerque *Rio Abajo,* June 23, 1863.

11. *Condition of Tribes,* pp. 237-38.

12. *Rio Abajo,* June 23, 1863.

13. Shaw's letter (dated December 21, 1862) appeared in the San Francisco *Alta California,* March 13, 1863.

14. Lt. Col. J. F. Chavez to Capt. B. C. Cutler, November 7, 1862; *Department of New Mexico,* LR.

15. *Rio Abajo,* June 23, 1863.

16. Carleton to Thomas, December 20, 1862; *Office of Adjutant General,* LR.

17. Carleton to Thomas, March 19, 1863; *ibid.*

18. *Condition of Tribes,* p. 108.

19. General Orders No. 15, Headquarters, Department of New Mexico (dated June 15, 1863); published in *Rio Abajo,* June 30, 1863, p. 4.

20. *Ibid.*

21. *Rio Abajo,* August 11, 1863. Also Capt. A. B. Carey to Capt. J. C. McFerran, July 23, 1863; *Department of New Mexico,* LR.

22. Carleton to Thomas, June 17, 1863; *Office of Adjutant General,* LR. See also: *Condition of Tribes,* p. 114.

23. Throughout summer of 1863 small parties of Moache and Tabe-quache Utes daily returned to their agency at Abiquiu from forays into Navajoland. They proudly exhibited numerous scalps and scores of prisoners, as well as thousands of sheep and horses taken from Navajos. Steck to Carleton, August 6 and 12, September 3, 1863; *Department of New Mexico*, LR.

24. Nathan Bibo, "Reminiscences of Early Days in New Mexico," Albuquerque *Evening Herald*, June 11, 1922.

25. Carson to Carleton, July 20, 1863; *Official Records*, (Series I, Vol. XXVI), pp. 233-234.

26. *Condition of Tribes*, p. 128.

27. Carey to McFerran, July 29, 1863; *Department of New Mexico, LR.*

28. *Condition of Tribes*, p. 116.

29. Carson to Cutler, January 3, 1864; *Department of New Mexico, LR.*; also *Rio Abajo*, August 11, 1863.

30. Carleton to Col. Edwin A. Riggs (commanding Fort Craig), August 6, 1863; *Condition of Tribes*, p. 124.

31. *Ibid.*, pp. 128-29.

32. *Ibid.*, p. 132.

33. *Ibid.*

34. *Ibid.*, pp. 144-45.

35. *Ibid.*, p. 151.

36. General Orders No. 4 (dated February 18, 1865); *Official Records* (Series I, Vol. XLVIII, Part I), p. 899.

37. This poem, "Johnny Navajo," appeared in the *Rio Abajo*, December 8, 1863. From its rhythm, it very likely was written to fit one of the Irish *"Come-All-Ye"* ballads, so popular during that day.

38. At the time of Carson's campaign, the name Cañon de Chelly usually embraced both gorges, although the northern or left hand branch, was referred to as Cañon del Trigo. It was not until 1886 that del Muerto was applied to the cañon by archaeologist James Stevenson, who found many remains of the prehistoric Anasazi in the caves and rock shelters lining its walls.

39. This account of Carson's operations in Cañon de Chelly has been taken from: Report of Captain A. W. Pheiffer, January 20, 1864; Carson's Report, January 23; and the Report of Capt. A. B. Carey, January 21, 1864; all in *Official Records* (Series I, Vol. XXXIV, Part I), pp. 71-79.

40. On February 2, 200 Navajos were forwarded to Los Pinos, the receiving center on the Rio Grande, where they could be fed cheaply. On that same day, Chief Delgadito arrived at Fort Wingate with 680 tribesmen. See General Orders, No. 4 (dated January 8, 1864); in *ibid,* (Series I, Vol. XLVIII, Part I), p. 901.

41. *Weekly Gazette,* March 5, 1864.

42. General Orders No. 4 (February 18, 1865); *op. cit.*

43. Following Carson's roundup, Navajos poured into Fort Canby in such numbers that the colonel deemed it expedient not to send out scouting parties, for fear of hostile encounters with incoming Navajos.

44. *Condition of Tribes,* p. 157.

45. *Ibid.,* p. 159.

46. *Ibid.,* pp. 158-59.

47. *Ibid.,* p. 161.

48. *New Mexican,* March 5, 1864.

49. *Condition of Tribes,* p. 167.

50. General Orders No. 8 (dated March 25, 1864); *Official Records* (Series I, Vol. XXXIV, Part II), pp. 733-34.

51. *Condition of Tribes,* p. 170.

52. *Ibid.,* p. 173.

Sketch of Fort Sumner, 1864

James H. Carleton

Indian awaiting rations at Issue House. On horse in center is Major McCleave, post commander of Fort Sumner.

The large building in background, with open gates, is the Indian Commissary at Fort Sumner.

Artist concept of Fort Canby at the site of old Fort Defiance

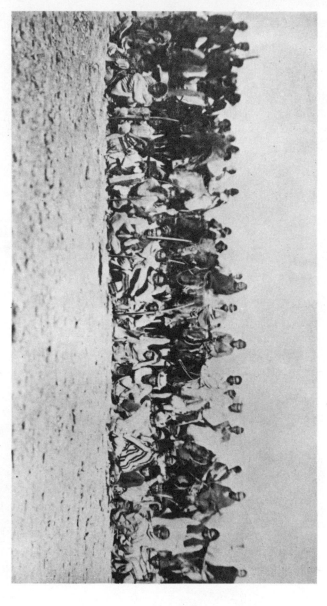

Navajos gathered for counting at Fort Sumner

Courtesy National Archives

Seated Navajos allegedly accused of counterfeiting ration tickets

Navajos gathered at Indian Agency, a few miles from Fort Sumner

Navajo Camp Scene at Bosque Redondo

Building company quarters at Fort Sumner

The Indian Commissary at Fort Sumner

An Indian work detail assembled at the farms, Fort Sumner

Courtesy National Archives

Soldiers of Company B, First New Mexico Volunteers at Fort Sumner.

Counting Indians at Bosque Redondo

Courtesy National Archives

Indians receiving ration tickets at Office of Provost Marshal, Fort Sumner.

Inside courtyard of Indian Commissary and Quartermaster storehouse.

Company quarters, Fort Sumner

IX

"FAIR CARLETONIA"

G ENERAL CARLETON was firmly convinced that Bosque Redondo, situated as it was on the edge of a vast expanse of uninhabited land — the Llano Estacado — was the only location for internment of New Mexico's most troublesome residents. He had early recognized the close affinity in language between the Navajos and Apaches, and was led to believe that both tribes could be settled harmoniously together.

By fall of 1863 the Mescalero campaign was at an end, and 425 members of that tribe were residing at Fort Sumner. These Indians, under direction of their agent, Lorenzo Labadie, showed considerable promise as agriculturalists. They had already dug an irrigation ditch (called an *acequia*) which diverted much of the Pecos River onto several corn fields. In early September the first Navajo contingents were forwarded to Fort Sumner. Ironically, they were the same band which resided near Cebolleta, and who, under the leadership of Sandoval, had been so helpful to Mexican and Anglo-American authorities.

With removal of the *Cebolleteros* to Fort Sumner, the Bosque Redondo period began in the lives of the Navajos. This first group, numbering only fifty-one individuals, were treated kindly. Carleton instructed the post commander to assign these Indians land, where they would be by themselves and would not come into conflict with the Mescaleros, who far out-numbered them.[1]

By end of the year Fort Sumner was nearly completed and ready to meet Carleton's needs. Seven spacious adobe buildings, of five rooms each, had been constructed and set aside as officers' quarters. Six more buildings, each housing 100 enlisted men, were also standing. There was a hospital of twenty-four beds; a large adobe bake house, as well as a three-room guard house. Four storehouses, 175 by 36 feet, were sheltering quartermaster and commissary supplies; and three stables, of 100 horses each, afforded protection from the winds which blew off the Staked Plain.[2] Now, the army in New Mexico was ready to do its part in helping settle the Apaches and Navajos on this reservation.

✂   ✂   ✂

On January 15, 1864, Secretary of the Interior, J. P. Usher, laid before President Lincoln the recommendation for establishment of a forty-square-mile reservation with Fort Sumner as its center. By the following day the Chief Executive had approved the document, and Bosque Redondo was recognized as the official reservation for the Apaches of New Mexico — without any mention of the tribe which soon would displace the Mescaleros.[3]

Although Lincoln had given his blessing to the scheme, General Carleton had undertaken his "Navajo policy" without having necessary funds and sustenance on hand to support those Indians when once confined at Bosque Redondo. Nor had he the wholehearted support and approval of all civil branches of government. The commander hoped that the Office of Indian Affairs would assume the duty of caring for the Navajos, as they were doing with other New Mexican tribes. The Indian Office, however was in dire financial straits. The New Mexico Superintendency, was at that time, unable to carry on its administration duties relative to lesser tribes, let alone more than 8,000 Navajos.

By January 1864 the Navajo campaign was at its height and arrangements had to be made for feeding of tribesmen as they came in. Crops must be planted soon, for the growing season was already well advanced. Vital agricultural implements, however, were lacking. Not even plows, shovels and hoes were procurable in adequate quantities. Time was precious and crops had to be sown immediately. Carleton feverishly dispatched letters and orders requesting seeds, tools; and directed the enlargement of the farms commenced by Apaches the year before. By late February two large "breaking-up" plows had been procured from Colorado and rushed to Fort Sumner, and two more were being constructed at Fort Union. It was hoped that soon eight plows would be kept constantly at work preparing the land for corn.

To furnish necessary water to the parched earth, an irrigation system of immense size and capacity was projected. On February 25· Carleton instructed the post commander, Major Henry Wallen, to construct "an *acequia-madre* of great capacity and length, so there will be no doubt of the supply of water being adequate to your needs."[4] To supervise the tremendous task of digging new irrigation ditches, laying out fields, as well as final planting operations, Carleton selected a person of considerable agricultural experience and skill — Captain William Calloway.

Under Captain Calloway's direction the *acequia*, dug by Apaches the year previous, was enlarged and lengthened to water an additional 1,500 acres lying between the Apache farm and the post; and by February this tract of land was deemed sufficient for the Navajos. The arrival, one month later, of 3,000 tribesmen quickly changed the situation. More land would have to be set aside for the increasing number of Indians. Carleton pleaded with the post commander to do his utmost in meeting this crisis:

> It will require the greatest effort and most careful husbandry to keep the Indians alive until the new crop matures. Every Indian — man, woman, or child — able to dig up the ground for planting, should be kept at work every moment of the day preparing a patch, however small. What with ploughing, spading and hoeing up ground, with the labor of the troops and the Indians, you must endeavor to get in at least three thousand acres. It will surprise you to see how much can be done if the bands are properly organized, and all the officers go out and set the example of industry. The very existence of the Indians will depend upon it, and they should understand that now.[5]

Implicitly following Carleton's orders, Calloway commenced a new irrigation system five miles above the post. In less than a month an *acequia* twelve feet wide and over six miles long had been completed — and this with only fifty spades to work with. Fifteen miles more of secondary ditches radiating from the *madre* canal were also dug by Calloway's Navajo laborers.

Once the precious flow of the Pecos had been diverted onto the parched lands, small tracts of ten to twenty-five acres were allotted the Indians for cultivation. A great portion of this land, however, was covered by tangled growths of mesquite that "had to be grubbed out" before the earth could be turned with a plow. Calloway set his Navajos to this task with neither axes nor picks. With their bare hands the Indians scratched the dirt from the roots, and with stones and pieces of wood they beat down and broke the tough roots.

This process often compelled an Indian to work all day on the roots of a single mesquite plant. However, by Navajo perseverence and industry, Calloway succeeded in clearing and planting 3,000 acres to corn, beans, melons and pumpkins.[6]

Despite the strenuous labor which the newly arrived Navajos were subjected to, it would be months before crops matured. Something had to be done now to feed these people, or Carleton would have thousands of dead Indians upon his hands. Subsistence was scarce even for his troops, and much of the food issued was contaminated with ground plaster, dried bread and rat droppings, and caused dysentery among the Indians. Many Navajos, who had never seen or tasted white men's food, knew nothing about preparing it. They ate their meager rations uncooked. When Carleton was informed of this, he quickly directed Wallen to instruct the Indians how to prepare their food; and in an effort to cut costs, the department commander suggested that Navajos be shown how to brew *atole* or porridge and soup.[7]

Not only were Navajos close to starvation but many were "quite naked." The Superintendent of Indian Affairs, Doctor Michael Steck, could do nothing to meet Carleton's frantic requests for blankets. For that matter, Steck had left his superintendency to seek council in Washington D.C. as to what his duties were, now that the army had assumed control of Indian Affairs in New Mexico. The departure of the superintendent greatly perturbed Carleton, who felt that the Indian Department should at least pull their weight in the "policy" which he was so desperately trying to put into effect. On February 7 Carleton wrote the Adjutant General of the destitute condition of his charges, and complained of the apparent lack of interest demonstrated by the Indian Office:

I beg respectfully to call the serious attention of the government to the destitute condition of the captives, and beg for authority to provide clothing for the women and children. . . . Whether the Indian Department will do anything for these Indians or not you will know. But whatever is to be done should be done at once. At all events . . . *we can feed them cheaper than we can fight them.*[8]

If the Superintendent of Indians could not or would not do anything, then Carleton would try his best to alleviate the sufferings of his Indian captives. He instructed Wallen to issue Navajos "all the hides and pelts of the cattle and sheep which are killed . . . for the manufacture of parflesh to make soles for moccasins." If enough leather could not be obtained, Wallen was given permission to purchase what he could from army contractors.[9]

By mid-March more than 5,000 Indians were encamped for twenty-five miles above and below Fort Sumner. Never in the history of New Mexico had so many Indians been assembled in one area — and never before had the essentials for sustaining so many been so lacking. The appeals for food, clothing and Indian goods which constantly went out are indicative of the desperate situation then at hand:

> There are now at and en route to Fort Sumner . . . about 5,000 Navajo Indians who are entirely destitute of everything and it is of *vital importance* that all articles which you have in store such as spades, hoes, wool cards, shears, ploughs, leather, tin cups and pans, brass kettles, butcher knives, awls and awl handles, axes, hatchets, and indigo; also such articles for clothing that is absolutely necessary for their comfort be sent to them at the earliest practicable day. The farming implements cannot be purchased in this country and therefore I respectfully request that all articles above mentioned may be sent immediately to the Bosque Redondo that the Indians may commence to plant.[10]

To shelter Navajos from the bitter cold winds blowing off the Staked Plain, Carleton authorized distribution of condemned army tents. However, the majority of these had been cut up and converted into sacks to transport and store grain. Carleton quickly seized upon an alternative — and to his way of thinking — a much more adequate solution to the settlement of these Indians. On February 28 he informed Wallen that the Navajos "must be settled in a pueblo town." Already layout of this "Navajo pueblo" had taken shape in the fertile mind of Carleton, and he wrote:

> The buildings should be but one story high, and face to the *placitas*. By a proper arrangement — dead-wall on the outside, and the buildings arranged so as to mutually defend each other in fighting on the parapets — a very handsome and strong place could be made by the Indians themselves. . . . By having a judicious site selected, and the spare time of the families spent in putting up their houses, by next winter they can all be comfortably sheltered. Then to have trees planted to make shade, and I fancy there would be no Indian village in the world to compare with it in point of beauty.[11]

Carleton wished that this proposed "Navajo pueblo" be placed close to the *acequia madre;* and that each family be given separate plots to farm close by.[12]

The Navajos, however, balked at prospects of living in the closed atmosphere of a village community. Accustomed to living in small bands, composed of related members, they instead wished for something more reminiscent of what they once had. When questioned as to their wants, most tribesmen expressed desire to have a series of small villages, each under control of their most powerful and influential leaders, *viz.:* Herrero Grande, Delgadito Grande, Ganado Blanco, Delgadito Chiquito, El Barboncito, El Barbon, Narbona, Juhadore and Largo.

Carleton was perfectly willing to let the Indians have what they desired; and that summer Colonel Christopher Carson was recalled from duty at Fort Canby and entrusted with the task of supervising construction of ten villages.

These settlements were no sooner commenced than serious difficulties arose. Navajos, imbued with deep-seated fears of the dead, refused to occupy quarters where death had occurred. In their own country, when a member of the family died, the dwelling was immediately abandoned and destroyed. Now the fear of *Chindi* was threatening to destroy the very organization of the tribe at Bosque Redondo.

Carson had never before come to grips with the formidable enemies of tradition and superstition. He tried repeatedly to reason with the Navajos, and convince them they had nothing to fear in a house where death had stalked. To the Diné, death and departed spirits were a very real thing, and as expressed by Ganado Blanco, this fear had "grown with their growth and strengthened with their strength." But the army was just as stubborn in their beliefs that the Indians should be settled in villages, and a solution was at last arrived at. Adobe dwelling for the Indians would be abandoned, and Navajos would be permitted to retain their traditional "huts." Their hogans, however, would be placed in uniform rows with good intervals and wide streets. One end of each row would be left open for those Indians desiring to move. Then when death struck, a family could immediately destroy their home and move to the end of their row, where a new dwelling would be erected.[13]

✗   ✗   ✗

While Carleton was endeavoring to settle the Navajos upon the Rio Pecos, and instill in them concepts of "peaceful pursuits," other hazards were arising which threatened his policy. Ever since the first Navajo contingents arrived at Fort Sumner, Superintendent Michael Steck had refused to assume responsibility for their care. Although he concurred with Carleton on the wisdom of confining the Indians of New Mexico to reservations as the only means of securing a permanent peace, the superintendent could not accept administration of the territory's largest tribe. His superintendency had little funds with which to feed and clothe a tribe as large as the Navajos. Steck had, therefore, informed the Apache agent at Fort Sumner, Lorenzo Labadie, not to take charge of the Navajos unless a "positive arrangement" was made with the military department, whereby provisions would be furnished in large enough quantities to sustain the tribe.[14]

In October 1863 Michael Steck made his first visit to Bosque Redondo. After observing condition of the post and speaking with both Apache and Navajo leaders, he confessed to Carleton that he approved "most cordially" of the policy being pursued. Furthermore, Steck expressed opinion that the Bosque was the "only suitable place in New Mexico for a large Indian reservation."[15] The superintendent, however, must have inwardly doubted the reservation's ability to maintain large numbers of Indians, for on his return to Santa Fe, he requested the opinion of John A. Clark, Surveyor General of New Mexico, as to the amount of arable land at the forty-square mile reserve. Surveyor General Clark's letter of reply substantiated Steck's fears:

> I reply to your enquiry, as to how much *arable* land would be included in a limit forty miles square — Fort Sumner . . . being the center. I have to state that the public surveys in this district have [not] been extended over the country described, and the only positive information I have, in relation to the character of the land in question, I derived from personal observation during a visit to Fort Sumner in the month of March last. I was on and along the Pecos River for a distance of seven or eight miles above and below the Fort, and estimated the arable land within that distance at 4,000 acres. . . .[16]

Surveyor General Clark's letter did much to shape the future attitude and actions of Michael Steck. In November the su-

perintendent journeyed to Washington, where he conferred with Bureau of Interior officials. During his visit to the capital, Steck changed his tune regarding the Indian policy being pursued by the army in New Mexico. He now made a rapid about-face, and openly criticized the actions of General Carleton. On December 10 he wrote to Commissioner William P. Dole, expressing his true feelings about settling a large number of Indians upon the Pecos:

> ... I regard the location of [Bosque Redondo] as one of the best that could be made in New Mexico for a limited number of Indians. In the language of General Carleton, "the Bosque Redondo is far down the Pecos on the open plain where these Indians can have no lateral contact with settlers." This the Hon. Commissioner is aware would be an important consideration in the selection of a permanent home for the Indians. East and west of the Bosque, no settlement can be made for the distance of seventy-five miles, being arid plains, north the nearest settlement is 45 miles, and south it is not probable permanent settlement will ever be made as the salt plains in that direction render the water of the Pecos unfit for use.

While Steck concurred with the selection of Bosque Redondo for a reservation for a "limited number" of Indians, he found serious objections, which he felt would ultimately defeat the whole program of internment of a large Indian population in that area.

> ... I beg leave to differ with him [Carleton] as to the practicability of removing and settling the Navajos upon it, for the following reasons. First, the arable land in the valley is not sufficient for both tribes; and secondary, it would be difficult to manage two powerful tribes upon the same reservation. This reserve as proposed is within the country claimed by the Apaches, and to remove the bands, viz.: Jicarilla, Mescalero and Mimbres upon it, and divide the bands so as to give each family a farm large enough to eventually enable them to maintain themselves, will occupy

the whole valley. From my own observation upon a recent visit I am of opinion that 6,000 acres is a fair estimate of the amount of land susceptible of cultivation. This is also the opinion of John A. Clark, Surveyor General of New Mexico ... The three bands of Apaches will number at least 2,500 souls, and allowing five to a family and dividing the arable land equally would give each family ... about twelve acres—an amount quite small enough to maintain them.

The Navajos it is well known number about 10,000 . . . If you take into account further that they own thousands of horses, and not less than 500,000 sheep, the impracticability of locating them upon a reservation of forty miles square, with 6,000 acres of arable land or even double that amount is so apparent that I need offer no arguments to prove it.[17]

Thus Superintendent Steck endeavored to point out to the Commissioner the physical impossibility of locating all of New Mexico's Athapascan-speaking peoples upon the Bosque Redondo. He forsaw conflicts which would inevitably result, when the Mescaleros, a plains oriented tribe, was confined to the same reservation with the Navajos, a semi-sedentary and far more numerous people. Steck diligently urged the Office of Indian Affairs to consider the adoption of two separate reservations: one for the Apaches at Bosque Redondo, and the selection of an adequate reserve for the Navajos in their own country.

When news of Steck's sudden opposition to Bosque Redondo reached Carleton, the general was aghast. A few months previous both men had met at Fort Union and had, to all outward appearance, departed in total agreement with the policy being pursued. In an attempt to protect his moves and justify his actions, Carleton wrote to Adjutant General Lorenzo Thomas on January 12, 1864, stating that his plan for establishment of the reservation was unanimously endorsed by the legislature, late Superintendent of

Indian Affairs James Collins, Kit Carson and Doctor Michael Steck — in short, "every intelligent man in the country approves it."

As far as the quantity of arable land at the reservation, Thomas was informed that there was more than enough in the immediate area. Even if there wasn't, added Carleton, land at Bosque Grande, twenty-five miles further down the river, could be used.[18] Carleton believed that if Steck successfully thwarted his plans, it would be most unfortunate for New Mexico. The great thoroughfare over the 35th Parallel would be interrupted. Those imaginary gold fields which Carleton constantly harped about, could not be worked; and the Navajo wars would continue for the next twenty years.

Evidence presented by Michael Steck, however, shattered Carleton's plans for immediate support of Navajos by the Indian Department. On March 4 Commissioner William P. Dole informed Secretary of the Interior, J. P. Usher, of the points against settling Apaches and Navajos together on the same reservation; and advised the Department of the Interior not to assume responsibility for Navajos at that time.[19] The army would therefore, continue to administer affairs of those Indians settled upon the Pecos River; and the gulf would continue to widen between Carleton and representatives of the Office of Indian Affairs in New Mexico — as the latter opposed the general's every move to force the Navajos onto the forty-square mile preserve originally alloted to the Apaches.

By mid-May Carleton and Governor Henry Connelly were convinced that the major portion of the Navajos had surrendered, and those remaining in their old country were too few to cause any trouble. Accordingly, a proclamation was issued announcing "a suspension of arms in the prosecution of the war against the Navajo tribe." Thereafter all forays by citizens against tribesmen remaining in Navajoland would be prohibited.[20]

Although the war had officially closed, Indian depredations continued at an alarming rate. Needless to say, they were always laid to the machinations of Navajo marauders, whom it was claimed, still remained in large numbers in their redrock sanctuaries. The same week that Connelly's proclamation was issued, Ute Agent, José Mansanarez informed Michael Steck of alleged Navajo depredations against citizens of Tierra Amarilla. The agent also related that a party of New Mexicans had, a few weeks previous, conducted a reprisal expedition against the Indians. This party, according to Mansanarez, penetrated beyond the Hopi villages in their search for captives and booty. However, they soon regretted having done so, for they found themselves surrounded by over 200 mounted Navajos. The expedition finally fought their way out of the trap after killing eighteen Indians. This account and the postscript which Mansanarez added, gave every indication that Navajoland was still very much alive with hostiles:

> I have been informed by various members of one of the expeditions against the Navajos which were out during the months of February, March and April, that they believe that a majority of the hostile Navajo warriors are still in their country.[21]

This letter added fuel to Steck's opposition to "Fair Carletonia" — as Bosque Redondo was beginning to be contemptuously called. In another letter to Commissioner Dole, the superintendent took the liberty to attack assertions of Carleton supporters, who claimed that few Navajos remained in their old country. He explained that facts of the case pointed to a completely different viewpoint. The tribe, contended the superintendent, was not anywhere near subdued; and the vast majority of its warriors were still in their own country. Those already at Bosque Redondo were of the poorer class who had willingly surrendered upon promise of food. The rich and by far the most powerful portion of the tribe remained where they always had been. As proof of this, Steck enclosed Mansanarez's letter and informed the commissioner of what he had been told by a delegation of Hopis now at the superintendency. This group of puebloans, according to Steck, has reported "that the wealth and power of the Navajos had scarcely been touched."

To Michael Steck this was proof enough. It would be impossible to remove so large a tribe as the Navajos — and to attempt it would only result in immense costs to the government. Those Navajos already at Bosque Redondo, insisted Steck, were being fed at a rate of at least $50,000 monthly, and if the number of Indians were doubled — as surely they would be if the whole tribe were rounded up — supplies could not be furnished by a territory that was already being drained dry by military needs.[22]

The picture painted by Superintendent Steck was gloomy but true. Carleton believed that the Navajos numbered no more than 8,000 — which the army could easily maintain at Bosque Redondo on short rations until crops matured. Major Henry Wallen, however, had found through experience that feeding even 6,000 was extremely difficult. Since inception of the roundup, Indian rations had been but a pound of breadstuffs per day for every man, woman and child — an amount that Carleton deemed sufficient. Yet many Navajos appeared undernourished and deaths from malnutrition among infants and children were not uncommon. These Indians had to have meat if they were to live, work, and quell their emotions and restless murmurings to return to their beloved redrock country. On April 1, 1864, Major Wallen requested Carleton's permission to issue more provisions. Nine days later came the good news: "it is possible that we may be able to get meat so as to give them a pound apiece per day, if the whole animal . . . be issued." In the meantime, Wallen would issue beans once a week; and the Indians would be taught by military overseers to prepare their food according to white man's formulas, so that the most nutriment could be extracted. To relieve anxieties among the headmen, many of whom were voicing desires to return with their people to Navajoland, Carleton instructed they be given coffee and sugar — "in all not to exceed eighty rations per day."[23]

Shortly thereafter, leaders of both Apaches and Navajos were summoned by Wallen to a general council. There, the welcomed news of increased rations was announced; and the post commander requested the Indians to wait patiently for arrival of adequate quantities of foodstuffs. In the meantime, they and their families must be prudent and see that not an ounce of subsistence was wasted. They all must believe that the government would eventually make them comfortable on their reservation, which according to Wallen, "was situated on the best lands in New Mexico." When the council adjourned the headmen must have departed with the feeling — however temporary — that their people would soon have enough to eat. They would be patient and work stoically to increase the yield of their farms in this new and foreboding land.

By mid-summer the quota of 3,000 cultivated acres had been reached. Crops were coming in splendidly and a bountiful harvest was everywhere in prospect. The corn alone was expected to yield twenty-five to thirty bushels per acre — a total of 84,000 bushels. Considering the extraordinary handicaps under which the Indians worked to reach this goal — scarcity of tools, lateness of season, militant drivings of army officers — this was an astonishing accomplishment.[24]

Headway was at last being made in obtaining those vital goods without which any Indian policy would collapse. In Washington, Carleton's personal emissary, James Collins, had done his job well in convincing government legislators and officials of the War Department that Bosque Redondo must have their support. On April 5 Secretary of Interior

Usher submitted to Congress a recommendation for a $1,000,-000 appropriation.[25] By late July New Mexico had received news of passage of a bill "to aid in the settlement, subsistence and support of the Navajo Indian . . ." Two capable men were appointed by the Secretary of the Interior as special commissioners to purchase Indian goods with the appropriated funds. William B. Baker and Colonel J. H. Leavenworth, both men of high business capabilities and possessing considerable experience in the administration of Indian affairs, would select goods and provisions from mid-west and eastern markets and ship them overland as soon as humanly possible.[26]

✗ ✗ ✗

When it seemed that the dreams of James Carleton were at last reaching fruition, fate stepped in and dealt a lethal blow. The reservation's three thousand acres of prime agricultural land held every promise of a fine yield. Shortly after the corn had tasselled the crop was struck by a cut worm, or "army worm" as it was called, that ate the ears away, unmercifully destroying months of superhuman effort, and threatening ruin once again to Carleton's policy and starvation to the Indians. As though this were not enough, in late October the nearly-matured wheat was drenched and beaten down by an unprecedented series of severe storms which destroyed over half of that crop. The counties of Taos, Mora, Rio Arriba and San Miguel — counties where Carleton hoped to purchase grain to replace that destroyed during the summer, had also been hit by hailstorms and harsh early frosts which destroyed nearly all of their corn and bean crops.

"Fair Carletonia" was nearing the brink of ruin. The reservation was virtually without subsistence, and the number of Navajos there were fast approaching the 8,000 mark. The interruption of government trains bringing much needed supplies, by Kiowa and Comanche war parties heightened the desperate situation. This was indeed the time that would test Carleton's genius for logistics. On October 22 the new commander of Fort Sumner, Brigadier General Marcellus M. Crocker,[28] received a letter from Carleton which put into effect the first in a series of moves to overcome the plight:

> I find that in my judgment it is all-important to reduce the ration of breadstuffs to twelve ounces per day, and to have issued eight ounces of meat per day — twenty ounces of solid food in all — until we can hear from the proposals for furnishing wheat, etc. . . . We shall strain every nerve to get a plenty but as we may encounter delays which would perhaps be fatal to the Indians, unless this precaution were taken.

Carleton then instructed Crocker to assemble headmen of both tribes and inform them of reasons for ration reductions.[29]

By now the Indian population of Bosque Redondo was over 8,000 — a number which taxed Carleton and the army in their quest for food. No more Indians must be sent in. The commanders of Fort Wingate and the forwarding post of Los Pinos,[30] were sent explicit orders to hold all Navajo prisoners where they were until further orders; and allow them the same rations as their brethren at Fort Sumner.

At Bosque Redondo Navajo murmurings and complaints grew louder, and parties of Indians began to slip off the reservation, either in quest of food or endeavoring to make their way back to their traditional homeland. Believing the only answer to restlessness was more work, Carleton ordered *acequias* enlarged, new fields cleared and plowed preparatory to early planting.[31] At least 9,000 acres — triple the acreage which had previously been planted — would go under the plow in hopes of furnishing all Indian wants, as well as that of the garrison at Fort Sumner. Blight of the "army worm" and consumption of much of the surviving corn by hungry Indians, who ravished the fields before the ears filled, convinced Carleton never again to trust in one crop alone. This time at least 3,000 acres would be reserved for wheat which matured early. The land could then be sown to beans during the summer months.

Not only was Carleton making frantic plans for cultivation of foodstuffs but he was also endeavoring to have enough fuel on hand to meet wants of both troops and Indians. Brigadier General Crocker was instructed to give his personal attention to the planting of at least 5,000 trees which someday would replace the dwindling supply of mesquite and cottonwood.[32]

The dire straits which "Fair Carletonia" was now in gave its opponents ammunition in their battle against military authorities of New Mexico. During summer of 1864 the Santa Fe *New Mexican* began to change its tune. This newspaper's praise for Carleton and his Indian policy diminished. Instead, accounts of alleged Navajo outrages filled its pages. In all likelihood, Navajo depredations were continuing and were probably at an all time high. Carleton was charged repeatedly with being "too lenient" in his policy.[33] Parroting Superintendent Michael Steck, the *New Mexican* contended that interests of the territory demanded Navajos be located west of the continental divide, upon the Little Colorado or Rio San Juan in their own country — instead of upon the Pecos. On October 28 the paper stated: "The white man should not be overlooked or his rights ignored, nor should every interest of the territory be permitted to suffer because one man has in opposition to the almost unanimous will of the people, conceived the idea of bringing the curse to their prosperity into our midst; making one of our most fertile valleys an asylum for the Indians of another territory; removing them from 300 to 400 miles east against the current of emigration and improvement. . . ."

The fact that Navajos were not yet self-sufficient at Bosque Redondo was a vulnerable point of attack for the *New Mex-*

can: "They cannot be subsisted on less than one pound of beef and one pound of flour per day each. The cost of these two articles alone, delivered at the reservation, will be about forty cents. This sum multiplied by 8,000, and the product by 365, gives the nice little sum of $1,168,000. The Navajos themselves say that about one-half the tribe is at the Bosque . . .; remove the whole tribe, and the cost of feeding them will be . . . $2,336,000. . . ."

When the pro-Carleton *Gazette,* edited by ex-Superintendent James Collins, came to the general's defense with the illogical excuse: that the "army worm blight" had been produced by recent rains, its opponent published a well-written attack — which made both Carleton and Collins look ridiculous.

> The name of the eminent naturalist who discovered that the "wet engendered a worm that destroyed the Indian crops at the Bosque," should be enrolled with that of Baird, Henry, and Audubon; won't the *Gazette* do him justice, it is due to science; let the world know we have men of research in New Mexico, as for ourselves we make no pretensions to a profound knowledge of natural history. We shall not, therefore, attempt a learned disquisition upon that terrible scourge, the corn worm. But having what we consider reliable information, as to the cause of the present high prices of provisions; and the threatened starvation and distress among the people. . . .

The "reliable information" which the *New Mexican* wrote of pointed to the Navajo, or *vermix carletonianus,* as the Indians were labeled. Continuing the attack, the article pointed out the unusual habits of this animal:

> One of his peculiar characteristics is his fondness for [sheep]. Heretofore he has been considered a wanderer; but recently under the auspices of General Carleton, U.S. Volunteers, his ravages have been confined to the Bosque Redondo where it is well known his destruction upon commissary stores alone have cost Uncle Sam over $2,000,000.

He is not only a carnivorous animal destroying millions of sheep, and thousands of horses, mules, and cattle, as the destruction of hundreds of the fortunes of our people in the history of the past will prove, but at this time his graniverous qualities are being exhibited to such an extent as to threaten a total destruction of the corn, wheat and beans of the country. Look to your stores of provisions People of New Mexico. The *vermi carletoniani* are multiplying upon your border to an alarming extent, and God only knows how soon your scanty stores will be attacked by this terrible enemy; already the prices are beyond your reach and are becoming higher and General Carleton's policy says this destroying worm must *live* if you should starve.

By late October 1864 Carleton was truely hard pressed. Crops had failed, civil authorities were pointing up his mistakes and appropriated Indian supplies had not reached New Mexico. It seemed as though every obstacle had been thrown in the path leading toward settlement of the Navajos. The Congressional bill appropriating $100,000 for clothing and maintenance of these people had passed on July 1. As yet not a yard of cloth, blankets or spades had reached the territory. Carleton had received word that goods bought by these appropriations had left Fort Leavenworth on the first of October. With good luck they would be in New Mexico by December — just when the Navajos would need them most. In the meantime, 4,000 sheep purchased by the quartermaster department would have to furnish wool and meat for the cold and hungry Indians.[34]

In accordance with instructions received in August, Michael Steck would proceed to Fort Union to meet the train of Indian goods. The superintendent would then personally accompany it to Fort Sumner, and there supervise its distribution to the Indians. By late November the goods had arrived in New Mexico. To forestall possibility of future disagreement, Brigadier General Crocker was cautioned by his superior to afford Dr. Steck every assistance in your power to enable him to carry out the wishes of the Commissioner of Indian Affairs in the distribution of these goods. . . . If the superintendent wishes to examine into the condition of the Indians under your charge and to go among and talk with them, you will permit him to do so. . . .[35]

These orders, however, were somewhat altered on December 9 when Assistant Adjutant General Benjamin C. Cutler informed the post commander that

about one year since, [when] Dr. Steck . . . went to the Bosque Redondo, he caused the Apaches to become discontented, by telling them that they could go to their own country to make mescal. If the doctor pursues any such course during his present visit, or talks with the Navajos in any manner to make them unhappy or discontented, he will be required at once to leave the reservation.[36]

Following instructions, Steck proceeded to Fort Union; and on December 11, William Baker turned the Navajo train over to his custody.[37] By January 1 the wagons had arrived at Bosque Redondo, and their loads of blankets, shoes, tools and beads had been distributed to the Indians. The accompanying cattle, which were scheduled to be slaughtered as food for Navajos and Apaches, were turned out to graze and fatten first. In all, Steck spent four days quietly examining the reservation. He prudently reserved comment until he returned to Santa Fe. Once back in the capital, however, the superintendent took the liberty of reporting to the Commissioner of Indian Affairs, that he was "more than ever satisfied that the reservation at Fort Sumner will be a failure for so large a number of Indians. The Navajos are now leaving in small parties. They are all dissatisfied and can only be kept upon the Pecos by force. . . ."[38]

✗   ✗   ✗

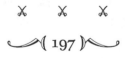

1. *Condition of Tribes,* p. 133.

2. National Archives, Records of the War Department, *Office of Quartermaster General,* Record Group 92; Consolidated Correspondence File Relating to Fort Sumner, New Mexico.

3. J. P. Usher to William P. Dole, January 16, 1863; *Superintendency Records,* LR; also *Annual Report of Commissioners of Indian Affairs 1865,* p. 20.

4. *Condition of Tribes,* p. 159.

5. *Ibid.,* p. 164.

6. Santa Fe *Weekly Gazette,* September 21, 1864.

7. *Condition of Tribes,* p. 165.

8. *Ibid.,* p. 157.

9. *Ibid.,* p. 161.

10. H. B. Bristol to Acting Superintendent Baker, March 17, 1864; *Superintendency Papers,* LR.

11. *Condition of Tribes,* p. 161.

12. *Ibid.,* p. 165.

13. Carson to Carleton, July 14, 1864; *Official Records* (Series I, Vol. XLI, Part II), p. 192. See also Santa Fe *Gazette,* October 8, 1864.

14. Steck to Carleton, September 6, 1863; *Superintendency Papers,* LR.

15. *Condition of Tribes,* pp. 155-156.

16. J. A. Clark to Steck, October 21, 1863; *Superintendency Papers,* LR.

17. Steck to Dole, December 10, 1863; *Ibid.*

18. *Condition of Tribes,* p. 155.

19. Dole to Usher, March 4, 1864; *Superintendency Records,* LR.

20. Santa Fe *New Mexican,* May 14, 1864.

21. Mansanarez to Steck, May 19, 1864; *Official Records* (Series I, Vol. XLI, Part II), pp. 900-901.

22. Steck to Dole, May 28, 1864; *ibid.,* pp. 899-900.

23. *Condition of Tribes,* p. 175.

24. Carson to Carleton, July 14, 1864; *Official Records* (Series I, Vol. XLI, Part II), p. 192.

25. It was hoped by Carleton and others favoring Bosque Redondo, that $100,000 would provide the Indians with essential items of clothing and hard goods. Colonel Carson had previously submitted a list of items which he felt must be obtained. This list was carried to Washington by James L. Collins, and submitted to officials of the Department of the Interior. Many of the items listed and their quantity present an idea of the destitute condition of the Navajo captives: 100 pieces of red standing; 15,000 yards unbleached domestic (wide and heavy); 5,000 yards blue denim; 5,000 pairs Mackinaw blankets; 2,000 Mexican blankets; pick-axes; at least 300 stout hoes, spades and long-handled shovels; 12 breaking-up ploughs, and 12

smaller ploughs; axes, hatchets, scissors, butcher-knives, beads, looking-glasses and paint. 38th Congress, 1st Session, *House Executive Documents, No. 70,* pp. 1-4.

26. Dole to Steck, August 28, 1864; *Superintendency Records,* Letters received by Commissioners. See also Santa Fe *New Mexican,* September 2, 1864.

27. *Condition of Tribes,* p. 207. Also Santa Fe *Gazette,* October 8, 1864.

28. Marcellus M. Crocker assumed command of Fort Sumner in early fall of 1864. Less than a year later Crocker was relieved of command, and reassigned to duty with the Army of the Cumberland.

29. *Condition of Tribes,* pp. 200-201.

30. Fort Wingate was now the only post in Navajoland. Fort Canby was evacuated on October 8, 1864; and its garrison transferred to Fort Union and its materiel to Wingate. See Special Orders No. 38 (dated October 8, 1864); and Carleton to Eaton, September 7, 1864; *Official Records* (Series I, Vol. XLI, Part III), pp. 719-720, 98.

31. Special Orders No. 37 (dated September 19, 1864); *Ibid.,* p. 261.

32. Crocker to Cutler, September 28, 1864; *ibid.,* pp. 463-64; *Condition of Tribes,* p. 210.

33. Santa Fe *New Mexican,* August 19, 1864.

34. *Condition of Tribes,* pp. 207-9.

35. *Ibid.,* p. 121.

36. *Ibid.,* p. 212.

37. While on its last leg of the journey, this train was in charge of Agent John Ward. Steck, in hopes of receiving further instructions by mail from the Commissioner of Indian Affairs, had journeyed to Santa Fe. Finding no letters from Washington, he immediately left for Fort Union, where he again took charge of the train. Steck to Dole, December 11, 1864; *Superintendency Records,* LR.

38. Steck to Dole, January 1, 1865; *ibid.*

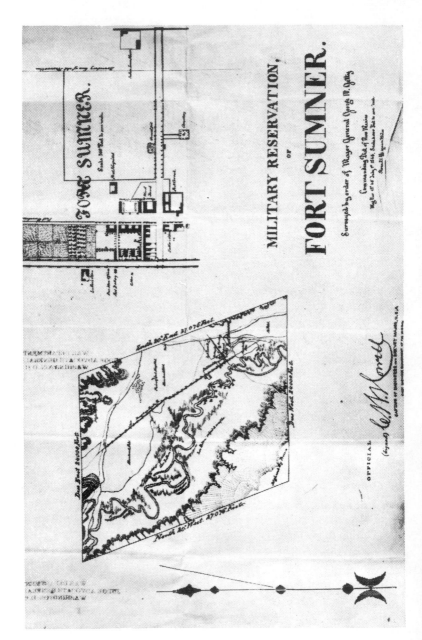

MILITARY RESERVATION,
OF
FORT SUMNER.

X

CONFLICTS ALONG THE PECOS

THE INDIAN GOODS purchased from the $100,000 congressional appropriation, and delivered to Fort Sumner by Doctor Steck, were carefully inspected by army personnel. By Special Order Number 133 (dated December 20, 1864), a board of officers consisting of Captains Henry B. Bristol, Lawrence G. Murphy and the post sutler, was authorized to be present at the distribution; and to witness the manner in which the annuities were passed out. On December 23 the board examined and counted the agricultural implements, blacksmith tools, as well as other items.

The board of inquiry found that many articles purchased from the appropriation were, in the opinion, of no use to the Indians. Such things as nails, iron, blacksmith tools and leather, they asserted, could have been dispensed with altogether — thus saving a considerable sum. The board also found that many articles were purchased at prices which hinted — "that the purchasers were either culpably negligent, or entirely regardless of the interests of the Government and of the Indians." Blankets, for example, were bought at an average price of $18.50 per pair by the Office of Indian Affairs, while those purchased by ordnance and quartermaster departments were furnished at $5.85 per pair — and the latter were as good, if not superior to blankets purchased for the Indians. The officers believed that equally extravagant prices were paid for other items, but this could not be positively determined at the time.

From data collected, both Murphy and Bristol concluded that $30,000 would have covered the cost of all Indian goods distributed by Superintendent Steck. Post sutler J. L. LaRue also inspected the wagon loads, and furnished a still higher estimate of $40,000.[1] Concluding the inspection, the officers submitted their reports to General Carleton. By mid-January the department commander had read the papers; and they were again forwarded — this time to his superior in Washington with the following notation:

> If, general this is to be considered as a specimen of the manner in which the intentions of Congress in making appropriations are to be carried into practical effect, it would be well for that honorable body, when considering the matter with reference to how much of that appropriation would reach that point aimed at by them, to leave a wide margin for what in target practice is technically called 'the drift.'[2]

As these reports would inevitably cast unfavorable light upon the Office of Indian Affairs, Doctor Steck attempted to counter the charges. On February 15, 1865, he sent his copies of the board's report — *with comments* — to Commissioner Dole, so that the latter could "draw his own conclusions." Steck insisted the reports were "full of errors calculated to deceive, and no doubt intended to reflect upon the Indian Department." The superintendent maintained that the estimates were carelessly made — without the data necessary to assemble an impartial report. The blankets, Steck defended, were purchased in the east where prices were considerably higher; and the estimates of Mr. LaRue were based upon inspection of little more than half the articles actually bought. In other instances, insisted Steck, the army had given the Indian Department credit with issuing more annuities than were purchased, as well as listing items not belonging to the appropriations.[3]

The dispute over the December deliverance of Indian goods resulted in final severance of cooperation — whatever little existed — between the Office of Indian Affairs and the military in New Mexico. The gradual buildup of mutual grievances which had existed for more than a year, finally came to a head with expulsion of Mescalero Agent, Lorenzo Labadie, from the Fort Sumner reservation, a month after the board's report was forwarded to Washington.

Since Bosque Redondo had always been under strict control of the military, the wishes and feeble power of the Indian Office and its New Mexican representatives could be superseded at any time by the commanding officer. With arrival of the first Navajos at Fort Sumner, land which had been cleared by Mescalero Apaches was turned over to the intruders — much to the dismay and alarm of Agent Labadie. The Apache agent endeavored to induce Navajos to move off the ground that he felt properly belonged to his charges. In March 1864 Major Henry Wallen informed Carleton that the agent was "making the Navajos unhappy" by attempting to persuade them to move. The department commander issued immediate instructions to watch Labadie's actions closely. Should the Mescalero agent continue to spread discontent among the Navajos, he would be ordered off the reservation.[4]

From the first instance of conflict between Labadie and the army, matters grew continually worse. In months to come correspondence between Carleton and the post commander hinted of a definite plot afoot to oust the agent from the reservation. The agent's large flock of sheep grazing within

reservation limits, to which he occasionally added to by purchasing animals from the Indians, was first to fall under the prying eyes of the military. On September 12 General Carleton directed Captain H. B. Bristol to investigate the matter; and to notify the agent that he could no longer graze within the area controlled by the army. Furthermore, the agent would not be permitted to purchase "an ounce of food from the Indians, nor under circumstances a single sheep."[5]

While the Apache agent's grazing rights were being restricted, his duties as administrator of 400 Indians was being closely scrutinized. More than six months previous, Kit Carson, while supervising Navajo labor, remarked about the apparent lack of progress which Apaches were making agriculturally. Kit quickly detected the Mescalero's aversion to labor; and he claimed that only 160 acres had been planted by them — most of which had been accomplished by Mexican labor hired by Labadie. Very critical of the agent for not making a better showing, Carson wrote Carleton that with the "facilities which have been afforded this gentleman, and the number of farm hands employed by him . . . a far greater amount of labor [should have been] performed, even without any assistance from the Indians."[6]

The fact that Labadie naturally sided with Superintendent Steck in the fight against Carleton only made his position at Fort Sumner all the more precarious. Every instance of army mismanagement, trouble with the Indians or infringement upon Office of Indian Affairs rights, were promptly reported by Labadie to Santa Fe. Indeed, it was little wonder that Carleton wanted to remove this virtual thorn in his side.

The department commander, however, would soon have his hour of reckoning with the agent. In mid-March 1865, Second Lieutenant Edwin J. Edgar, who commanded the picket guard at the post, inspected several wagons belonging to the Apache agent. The lieutenant's report at last furnished an air-tight case against Labadie:

I today, made an examination of certain wagons in possession of Lorenzo Labadie, Indian agent, coming from Fort Sumner and discovered the following articles being conveyed in them — *viz.*: two sacks of corn, and a number of agricultural implements consisting of plows, shovels, pickaxes and hoes, all of which I believed to be the property of the United States.

When questioned about his cargo, Labadie frankly admitted that these articles were not his, but were obtained illegally from Captain Calloway, Superintendent of the Navajo farms. Furthermore, the agent revealed that he had negotiated the purchase of government cattle from quartermaster officer, Captain Prince G. Morton. A subsequent investigation revealed seventy-five head of cattle with U.S. brands in the agent's herd grazing outside the limits of military control. Lorenzo Labadie had been caught red-handed in theft and fraud. On March 22 a court martial was convened to hear charges against the officers and the agent. Both Captains Calloway and Morton were found guilty and dismissed from service. As Labadie was a civilian, and thus not subject to the discipline of military courts, he was ordered to promptly leave the Bosque Redondo reservation.[7]

Dismissal from the army controlled preserve did not relieve Labadie of his duties. Following instructions from Superintendent Steck the agent moved his headquarters to Agua Negra — on the "frontiers of the reservation." This move might not have been made at all, however, for few if any Apaches visited there. Even if these Indians desired council with their agent the constant military surveilance around the forty-square mile reserve prevented them from straying too far. So too was unrest among the Apaches becoming more and more pronounced; and it was unlikely that Mescaleros would seek a solution to their problems with an agent who had never been able to offer help.

✕ ✕ ✕

The Bosque Redondo reservation had been initially set aside solely for the Mescaleros, and whatever other Apaches might be snared by the army. There upon the edge of the Llano Estacado these people would be slowly civilized — so it was hoped — by introducing them to agriculture, education and Christianity, as well as a semblance of organization and government. Men who possessed outstanding qualities of leadership and who apparently held the respect of their people were sought by the army as tribal leaders. Two men, Cadete and Ojo Blanco, were chosen as head chiefs; and entrusted with the responsibility of keeping careful count of their people, and of drawing rations to feed them.

In early spring of 1863, the Mescaleros, under the tutelage of Labadie and a half-dozen New Mexican laborers, commenced preparation for planting. An *acequia madre,* over a mile long, was dug, as well as lateral canals; and a section of land cleared and planted. For a while this experiment looked as if it might work. And practically everyone in New Mexico, including Michael Steck, awaited the outcome with high hopes.

However, the old adage "that there was never a shovel made to fit the hand of an Indian" was never more true — at least in the case of the Mescalero Apaches. For centuries their culture had been oriented to the chase and raid. They were essentially a Plains people, and possessed traits derived from close contact with other peoples dwelling throughout that hugh geographical area. Although they were Apachean in speech and genetic makeup, the Mescaleros utilized the travois and tipi, and their trade ties were with other Plains tribes. They were not sowers of seed. Out of more than 400 Mescaleros at Bosque Redondo only eighty-six submitted to the disgrace of tilling soil.

Every attempt the army made to settle these people in villages met with utter failure. Their nomadic life was indelibly stamped upon them. Unless retained by force of arms, they moved camp — never remaining in any one place for more than a week or ten days.[6] To the more perceptive these would have all been signs that the Mescalero experiment was doomed to failure even before the first Navajos arrived.

With internment of the Navajos at Bosque Redondo in late 1863, the problems of the Mescaleros were only compounded. The sudden tide of Navajo prisoners following Carson's winter campaign flooded the reservation, engulfing the Apaches. Much of the latter's cultivated lands were alloted to the new arrivals, who immediately demonstrated consummate skill in agricultural endeavors. The Fort Sumner reservation was now monopolized by a people whom the Mescaleros could never trust, and whom during times past, had considered as enemies.

Now a minority, surrounded by distasteful cousins, the Apaches manifested every desire for a separate reservation. All the army would grant, however, was permission for them to move about the forty-square mile reserve, establishing their camps wherever they pleased — and this only in an effort to forstall difficulties between the two tribes.[9]

By late spring 1864, Agent Lorenzo Labadie's reports constantly revealed the dreadful state of anxiety that his charges were living in; and which the army became aware of on the night of April 25,[10] when Ojo Blanco slipped away from the reservation with forty-two of his followers. In the months to come conditions between the Navajos and Mescaleros gradually became intolerable. Besides outnumbering the Apaches twenty to one, the Navajos were endowed with a capacity for not forgetting past grievances between the two tribes — and only a garrison of 400 soldiers prevented bloodshed. This potentially explosive situation finally reached a climax on the night of November 3, 1865. Under cloak of darkness, 335 Apaches deserted the reservation, and headed southward to their old haunts below Fort Stanton — leaving behind only nine enfeebled and aged members of the tribe. The army quickly transferred the lands which had been cultivated by Apaches to the Navajos; and they were planted next spring to corn, pumpkins and melons.[11]

Perhaps Carleton and his lesser officers could breathe a little easier now that Agent Labadie had been taken care of. The army, still in command of the situation at the reservation, no doubt felt greatly relieved when the last vestige of the Indian Office was gone. Decampment of the Mescaleros, however, was another matter. Their quiet desertion had been a crucial blow to Carleton's prestige and future plans. It had been demonstrated for all to see that the Athapascan-speakings peoples of New Mexico were not one big happy family. True, they were related linguistically, but there were enough other dissimilar traits as to make it impossible to settle Navajos and Apaches together on one reservation. This had been proven conclusively on that night of November 3, 1865.

X   X   X

A traveler approaching Bosque Redondo in the early months of 1865 would have been greatly surprised by what he saw. A few years before, there had been nothing but a desolate, uninhabited land. Approaching from the north, he would cross the *acequia madre*, which flowed eastward from the Pecos, toward the uplands, seven miles distant. A short way further, a broad avenue, sided by cottonwoods, would convey the visitor for nearly eight miles to the most important military garrison in the southwest — Fort Sumner.[12]

About this frontier post our traveler would, no doubt, witness scenes of intense activity as the labors of more than 8,000 Indians were being marshaled in another attempt to prepare the arable land of that reservation for planting. By the first week of January, 6,000 acres on the east side of the Pecos had been designated for a variety of crops. Under direction of a score of non-commissioned officers, Navajos

were put daily to work clearing and plowing the land, and repairing the old *acequias* and digging new ones.[13] Besides the usual corn, a large quantity of wheat would be sown as a safeguard against another disastrous grain failure. In addition, pumpkins, musk and water melons, and squash, as well as beans and peas, would also be planted.

So promising did the future agricultural yield look, that army personnel began to forget the many trials which during the past year nearly put an end to the Bosque Redondo reservation. Post commandant, Brigadier General Marcellus Crocker, was among the optimistic. If all went well during the planting season, and a full 6,000 acres could be harvested, he believed that the congressional appropriation for food could be abolished altogether. Playing safe, he calculated upon a rather low average acre-yield of 1,500 pounds of grain, which at 6,000 acres gave an estimated nine million pounds. This amount, Crocker figured, would give every Indian "a fraction less than three pounds . . . per day for 365 days." Added to the yield of the farms, Crocker hoped that produce from the gardens would add enough "to subsist the Indians now at Bosque Redondo, as well as any others that may come in."[14]

By spring a quadrangle of land embraced by the Pecos River on the west, the *acequia madre* on the north and east, extending south as far as Fort Sumner, had been planted. More than thirty plows, attended by Navajo labor, had furrowed 5,847 acres. Of this land, 1,000 acres were sown with wheat, which by mid-March had sprouted, and was reported "growing finely." Three thousand acres more were planted to corn, and the remaining land was devoted to lesser crops.[15]

Until crops reached maturity the Navajos would still be fed from army commissary stores. From January to June the Indians were subsisted on government issue to the tune of an average of $62,000 a month. To facilitate easy feeding of the many tribesmen, ration tickets, made of stout cardboard, were distributed to the Indians. These were presented every other day to commissary officers for food allotment. It was not long, however, before the army discovered an alarming number of tickets had been cleverly duplicated by skillful Navajos. Stamped metal slips were then substituted. But by Carleton's very orders, Navajos were being instructed in metal working and blacksmithing. Soon stamps and dies were being produced bearing marks of the government; and by end of March some 3,000 counterfeit metal tickets in excess of the authorized number, had been counted. Many of the forgeries were so well executed as to be virtually undistinguishable from the genuine. It was finally necessary to send to Washington for tickets of such intricate design as to be impossible to copy.[16]

The large number of fake ration tickets were embarrassing to the army. To overcome the difficulties of issuing food to Indians, and to eliminate fraud, a system of government for the Navajos was projected. Assistant Inspector-General of the Army, N. H. Davis, proposed an organization of the tribe along military lines. Already Navajos were living in bands — but each without recognized and clear-cut leadership. Davis therefore thought it would be best for each band to have one chief, and six sub-chiefs as assistants, who would be "clothed with the authorty for the preservation of good order, interior police, and regulation of their respective divisions." Over each "division," Davis recommended placing "a good and trusty overseer or agent" who would exercise special authority in managing the Indians. It would be this person's duty to recruit all able-bodied males for labor details, as well as keep close tab on the number of Indians constituting the band, so that adequate rations coud be drawn from the commissary.

Allotment of food would be issued to each band every sixth day — the overseer of each "division" drawing food in bulk. He would then re-issue it to families presenting tickets bearing the division number, and "such other marks as could not easily be counterfeited." With this system, Davis proposed to increase the Indians' work load, cut excessive number of forged ration tickets, and maintain better law enforcement. Carleton was ready to try anything that would decrease Navajo fraud, increase production of the farms, and quell the restlessness of the Indians. By late spring the plan was in full operation, much to the disgust of Navajos, who hated the cruel and militant overseers.[17]

By early summer the corn crop was almost ready for harvest — and appeared to be unblighted by disease or insect. On closer inspection, however, it was discovered that tiny larva were beginning to hatch from eggs laid in the moist silk of the growing ears. The silken strands leading to the points where kernels would develop had again been impregnated with eggs of the "army worm." The embryo kernels of corn were stunted in their growth. The disaster of the year previous was being repeated, and no reorganization of the tribe would forestall it.[18]

When the final harvest had been completed and the produce weighed and tallied, the results were heart-breakingly below expectations. The corn totaled 423,582 pounds; the wheat planted to sustain the Indians through just such an emergency as this, amounted to only 34,113 pounds. For lesser crops, 30,403 pounds of pumpkins and 3,500 pounds of beans were harvested. All this fell far short of the estimated nine million pounds of foodstuffs from the near 6,000 acres. Again Indians would be fed from army commissary supplies — supplies of such poor quality that they had been rejected by the army and transferred to Fort Sumner as fare for Indian palates.[19]

Since its founding, the Bosque Redondo reservation seemed cursed by disasters originating from natural causes. However, the human factor was also present — and to an alarming degree. One of Carleton's foremost reasons for locating Navajos and Apaches in the Pecos Valley was to erect a barrier to Comanche and Kiowa incursions into New Mexico. If there were any one group of people which could be labeled traditional enemies of the Diné, it would be those lords of the South Plains. Without exception, every account of Navajo-Commanche contact was of a hostile nature — and now Carleton had established these mortal enemies as neighbors.

Compared with Texas and the northern states of Mexico, New Mexico had little problem with Comanches. For decades an unrestrained commerce had existed between these Indians and the Mexican population of the territory. Thousands of head of cattle stolen from Texas ranches were driven into the territory by South Plains tribes, where a ready market was found. Unknowingly Carleton had contributed to this trade. The few licenses he had issued to New Mexicans to trade with Comanches were now being utilized by hundreds of itinerant traders — who not only dealt in livestock but also in liquor, arms and ammunition.[20]

These traders were generally opposed to the concentration of Apaches and Navajos — two tribes that had always been profitable sources of barter — upon the Bosque Redondo reservation. The strict army surveillance about the forty square miles made it practically impossible for wandering merchants to carry their wares to these Indians. Only by keeping Comanches and their cohorts, the Kiowas, stirred up against the Diné, could these unscrupulous men hope to eventually gain their ends.[21] Comanche raids upon Bosque Redondo increased in proportion to the number of traders operating among them. In January 1865 Carleton warned commanders of both Forts Bascom and Sumner to be on the lookout for raiding parties; and to inform stockmen in the vicinity of those posts to move their animals to the west side of the Pecos.[22] By spring Comanche raids were weekly occurrences. Some twenty Navajos, unlucky enough to have been caught upon the Staked Plain, were reported killed. The military was explicit in its warnings to tribesmen not to stray far from the sanctuary of Fort Sumner.[23]

Raids of Plains Indians began as forays conducted by small parties of not more than fifteen warriors, bent on pilfering livestock. As months passed, however, raids increased in daring and intensity. By 1866 parties of Comanches, numbering in the hundreds, were penetrating the confines of the Navajo reservation. On July 13 a war party of more than 100 Indians — and reputed to contain Mexicans — attacked Navajo herds. This group apparently paused long enough to inform New Mexican herders nearby of their strategy: "they did want cattle nor did they wish to kill Americans or Mexicans, but they would kill every Navajo they could."[24]

With unrelenting enemies prowling just outside their reservation, it was little wonder that Navajos lived in constant fear. Murmurings to return to redrock country daily grew louder. The receipts furnished by the commissary department at Fort Sumner revealed that 9,022 Indians drew rations during March 1865. From that time until year's end, monthly returns showed a sizeable decrease in Indian population.[25] Plagued by Comanche raiders, undernourished, ravaged by syphilis, gonorrhea and dysentery, the Navajos longed for their native country; and grasped at every opportunity that might bring freedom. Many squaws were being inveigled away by employees of contractors, who supplied the fort and reservation. Others were wandering to the settlements in search of food and other necessities of life. Carleton instructed the post commandant to tighten surveillance around the forty square mile area. Additional pickets were placed on all roads leading from the reserve, and ordered to search all wagon trains going and coming. Permanent guards were also situated around the post, from ten to forty miles distant; and a mounted patrol made its rounds daily — a distance of 125 miles — all in an effort to restrain Navajos. Only by a pass granted by the commanding officer would an Indian be permitted to leave Bosque Redondo; and it would be surrendered by the bearer upon return.[26] Even granting of a few passes, however, proved hazardous. Recent Comanche incursions were making many New Mexicans jumpy; and there was every possibility of trouble between them and Navajos from Bosque Redondo.

This possibility of conflict became a reality by March. Complaints of livestock losses were pouring into department headquarters in a steady stream — and many were attributed to Navajos leaving the Bosque. The letter of Miguel Des Marias, owner of La Turpentino Ranch near Los Conchas, is typical of the many received by the army. Marias complained that Navajos had been in the vicinity of his ranch for eight or ten days, and had slaughtered sheep belonging to him — to the number of sixty head. The rancher naively asked army authorities if they would "be so kind as to send and take these Indians back to their reservation at once. . . ."[27]

The army was at first reluctant to admit that Navajos were leaving Bosque Redondo — in fact, it was openly denied.[28] By May desertions had increased to such a point that their concealment and denial was impossible. Chief commissary officer at Fort Sumner, Captain H. B. Bristol, reported upon completion of the April 30 count, a loss of about 900 Navajos. These desertions were attributed to the poorer and ailing tribesmen, leaving either to find employment as herders for New Mexican sheepmen grazing in the vicinity of Alamo Gordo, or who were attempting to return to their old country, where they believed their health could be restored.[29]

By June more than a thousand Navajos had left, and many more were voicing a desire to return to their traditional homeland. Ganado Blanco and Barboncito had slipped away with their herds of horses and sheep.[30] The only Navajos remaining at the reservation were those too destitute of stock to carry them to freedom. Army garrisons and volunteer units throughout the territory were mobilized to intercept the Indians before they crossed the Rio Grande — for then capture would be impossible.

"Send an order for all the mounted men at Las Cruses, Fort Seldon and Fort McRae to march at once to Fort Craig; for Colonel Rigg, with Sanburn's company of cavalry and the company of infantry formerly commanded by Captain Haskell, to march at once to Los Pinos. Tell Colonel Rigg to say to General Montoya to raise one hundred well armed, well mounted men and go with Colonel Rigg or follow him as quickly as possible.

"Have Captain Shinn move at once with all the effective men of his command . . . to some point east of the mountains, where he can, by means of spies observe the plains towards the Bosque. Order Colonel Shaw to send fifty mounted men to join Captain Shinn at once by way of Los Pinos.

"Get Don Ambrosio Armijo to raise one hundred, picked, well mounted men, Americans and Mexicans, with Blas Lucero for guide, and to go with, or as soon as practicable join, Captain Shinn. Get General Clever to raise one hundred men, Mexicans and Americans, and proceed to Galisteo, or some point fifteen or twenty miles from there in the direction of Anton Chico, where, through his spies, he can get an idea as to the whereabouts of the Indians. . . ."[31]

During June there was every indication that a mass exodus was being contemplated by the remaining Indians. The garrison at Fort Sumner was kept under constant alert, and pickets about the reservation were strengthened. Carleton would use every means to discourage Indians from leaving; and he instructed the post commandant to

let the Navajos know that large parties of citizens are in pursuit of the Navajos who would not come in from their old country. Many of the latter have already been killed. Their crops will be destroyed and they will be extermi-

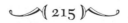

nated unless they come in. This information may put those who may have wished to leave the Bosque out of the notion.[32]

Navajos, however, continued to slip quietly away — and the garrison at Fort Sumner was powerless to stop them. The army could only cover up and smooth over the fact that discontent among the Indians was beyond all control. On June 25 Assistant Adjutant General, Benjamin C. Cutler, reported that "the Navajos who ran away from the reservation have returned with the exception of a small party not exceeding twenty-eight or thirty in number. . . . Many are said to have died from starvation and want of water, and those who could get back were glad to do so. . . ." Cutler further stated that at department headquarters in Santa Fe, a great many officers believed "these [runaway] Navajos had been tampered with by men, who for political purposes, have opposed the reservation and would be willing to see the interests of the country suffer, provided they could advance their own."[33]

Although Cutler may very well have been right in his assertions, there was no denying that the count of Navajos at Bosque Redondo was daily growing smaller. Even General Carleton finally acknowledged the futility of attempting to restrain them by force of arms. However, Carleton could not give up. He had committed himself too far in this "experiment" that was now collapsing around him. He would utilize every means at his command to keep Navajos on the reservation. On August 9 the general wrote again to the post commander:

"I regret exceedingly to learn that the Indians cannot be prevented from . . . leaving the reservation without passports. Again tell the Indians I will cause to be killed, every Indian I find off the reservation without a passport. A great many have been killed in the Navajo country. The troops are now fast coming in from the plains, and we will be sure to catch them. Tell them this!"[34]

✄   ✄   ✄

1. Special Orders No. 133 (dated December 20, 1864); Report of a Board of Officers convened at Fort Sumner (n.d.); *Superintendency Papers,* LR.

2. Carleton to Thomas, January 14, 1865; *Office of Adjutant General,* LR.

3. Steck to Dole, February 15, 1865; *Superintendency Papers,* LR.

4. *Condition of Tribes,* p. 173.

5. *Ibid.,* pp. 196-197.

6. Carson to Carleton, July 14, 1864; *Official Records* (Series I, Vol. XLI, Part II), p. 193.

7. For details relating to the fraudulent actions of Labadie and Morton see: Edgar to Crocker, March 27, 1865; Hosmer to Secretary of War, May 17, 1865; *Superintendency Papers,* LR. Also Carleton to Thomas, March 22, 1865; *Office of Adjutant General,* LR.

8. For an account of customs, behavior and crafts of both the Navajos and Mescaleros at Bosque Redondo see: Wallen's report to Assistant Adjutant General, April 26, 1864; *Department of New Mexico,* LR.

9. *Annual Report of Commissioner of Indian Affairs, 1866,* p. 140.

10. Labadie to Dole, May 1, 1864; *Superintendency Papers,* LR.

11. *Annual Report of Commissioner of Indian Affairs, 1866,* p. 150.

12. This description of the reservation was taken from: J. K. Graves, "The Navajos at the Bosque Redondo Reservation," (n.d.,) in *Superintendency Papers,* LR., 1866.

13. Report of Capt. F. McCabe, *Official Records* (Series I, Vol. XLVIII, Part I), pp. 525-527.

14. Crocker to Woolson, January 15, 1865; *ibid.,* p. 572.

15. Graves, "The Navajo Indians at Bosque Redondo . . .," *op. cit.;* Gwyther, "An Indian Reservation . . .," *Loc. cit.,* p. 127. Also Santa Fe *Gazette,* March 16, 1865.

16. Bristol to Taylor, May 9, 1865; *Official Records* (Series I, Vol. XLVIII, Part II); Report of McCabe, *op. cit;* Davis to Cutler, March 25, 1865; *ibid.* (Series I, Vol. XLVIII, Part I), p. 1259; and Gwyther, *ibid.,* p. 128.

18. Carleton to McCleave, July 18, 1865; *Office of Adjutant General,* LR.

19. During 1866 all food reported as "poor quality" was transferred to Fort Sumner by the commissary department for issuance to Indians. Despite this, cost of sustaining the Navajos was a staggering $748,307. McClure to Hunter, October 3, 1867; *Department of New Mexico,* LR.

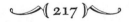

20. *Annual Report of Commissioner of Indian Affairs, 1866,* p. 146; and *Annual Report of Commissioner of Indian Affairs, 1867,* pp. 194-5.

21. *Ibid.,* 1866, p. 151.

22. E. W. Wood to E. H. Bergmann, January 6, 1865; *Official Records* (Series I, Vol. XLVIII, Part I), pp. 437-438.

23. Bergmann to McCleave, June 8, 1865; *ibid.* (Part II), p. 825.

24. This particular war party also ran off a dozen horses belonging to army pickets near Point of Rocks. For details consult Santa Fe *Gazette,* July 28, 1866.

25. J. K. Graves gives the following estimates of Indians at the reservation for the year 1865 (based on information furnished by Major Bristol): March: 9,022; April: 8,850; May: 8,324; June: 7,658; July: 8,180; August: 7,371; September: 7,554; October: 7,920; November: 6,815; December: 5,925. Report of J. K. Graves to Commissioner of Indian Affairs, December 31, 1865; *Superintendency Papers,* LR., 1866.

26. E. W. Wood to Crocker, January 5, 1865; *Official Records* (Series I, Vol. XLVIII, Part I), p. 427.

27. Marias to J. C. Edgar, March 1, 1865; *ibid.* (Part II), pp. 48-49.

28. On March 22, 1865, Lieutenant J. C. Edgar informed the post adjutant at Fort Sumner, "that the reports of Navajos [from Bosque Redondo] stealing stock were without foundation, and that they were first started by peons, who, it is quite likely, first sold the sheep and then, to save themselves . . ., laid it to the account of the unfortunate Navajos." *Official Records* (Series I, Vol. XLVIII, Part I), pp. 140-141.

29. Bristol to Taylor, May 9, 1865; *ibid.,* p. 378.

30. Ganado Blanco and Barboncito, and their followers, left the reservation on the night of June 14, and were reported heading for the Chuska Mountains — their former abode. McCleave to Carleton, June 15, 1865; *Department of New Mexico,* LR.

31. Carleton to W. H. Lewis, June 19, 1865; *ibid.*

32. Carleton to McCleave, June 17, 1865; *Official Records* (Series I, Vol. XLVIII, Part II), p. 915.

33. Cutler to W. H. Lewis, June 25, 1865; *Department of New Mexico,* LR.

34. *Condition of Tribes,* pp. 233-234.

XI

RETURN FROM "HWELTE"

WITH termination of the Civil War the nation could once again turn from problems of a strictly military nature to those facing the country as a whole. Turmoil stemming from maltreatment of the American Indians now pressed for attention. In Washington there was growing suspicion that many Indian wars were provoked by "aggressions of lawless white men;" that the number of red men were growing steadily less due to disease, "cruel treatment on the part of the whites — both by irresponsible persons and by government officials;" and by the ever increasing encroachments of the westward movement upon domain of the red man.

On March 3, 1865, a Joint Special Committee composed of members of both houses of Congress was appointed to inquire into these conditions. The work which this committee undertook was so immense — covering the problems of a continent — that holding of regular hearings, were in many cases, impossible. Instead, a circulating letter was sent to regular army officers, Indian superintendents and agents, inquiring into their knowledge of Indian affairs.

This Special Committee was split into three divisions; and its chairman, James R. Doolittle of Wisconsin, Vice President of the United States, Lafayette S. Foster, and Lewis W. Ross of Illinois, were assigned New Mexico, Utah, Colorado, Indian Territory and the state of Kansas.[1] This portion of the committee began its work at Fort Leavenworth on May 17; and by July 4, had extended its investigations to New Mexico. The short hearing in Santa Fe and a cursory inspection of the Bosque Redondo reservation revealed the depth of New Mexican Indian troubles. For the first time in the history of the territory, the real causes of the Navajo wars were being uncovered. The investigation revealed the fact that for generations, slave raids had been conducted against the Navajos, which only resulted in retaliation by the Diné. The horrors of the Navajo roundup and the tribe's subsequent imprisonment upon the Pecos River reservation were also looked into. Out of the mass of conflicting testimony and reports came one thread of truth — that the tribe was suffering from the ravages of disease and malnutrition; that their stock was nearly gone, as was their pitiful reserve of fuel.

The multiple reasons behind repeated crop failures at Bosque Redondo were analyzed. Doolittle and his colleagues saw that the soil there was impregnated with alkali, and the high mineral content of the Pecos induced dysentery among the Indians. But above all else, the committee saw that this "experiment" of James H. Carleton was doomed. No matter how hard the government endeavored to settle Navajos on a reservation, away from their old country, and instruct them in white man's ways, it would never succeed. Although Navajos had always been highly adaptive, they fought with tooth and nail those plans which would change basic traits of the tribe. They accepted only what ideas they could profitably use, and rejected all others.

To all outward appearances there were no immediate improvements brought by the Doolittle Committee. When once

back in Washington, the Committee began the tedious task of sifting through the mass of collected data. To make its investigation even more thorough, and thus give a clearer insight into problems facing Navajos at Bosque Redondo, the committee requested the Department of Interior to undertake an investigation of its own. Therefore in late 1865 the Office of Indian Affairs authorized Special Agent Julius K. Graves to investigate New Mexican affairs, prior to an anticipated takeover of the Fort Sumner reservation by civil authorities.

Upon reaching New Mexico in December 1865, Graves "found the Indian question the all absorbing topic of conversation." The main controversy revolved around the selection of Bosque Redondo as a permanent home for Navajos. The special agent soon found that feeling ran so high among the populace that political parties were being styled as "Bosque" or "anti-Bosque." Graves reported that the whole territory was politically split over the reservation: many favored it, others opposed the policy as being detrimental to the interests of New Mexico; and the entire matter seemed to drift off into a question of political expediency.[2]

Not knowing what to believe, the special agent journeyed to Bosque Redondo to investigate firsthand the source of all this conflict. On December 31 Navajo headmen were summoned to an interview with the agent. For six or seven hours the Indians poured out their woes. The Navajos conducted themselves in a dignified manner, paying deep attention to the entire proceeding, and taking a keen interest in everything this representative of the Indian Office had to say. Graves explained that he had been sent to their reservation to see that the Indians were all well fed and properly cared for. He earnestly told the assembled headmen that the only way he could find answers to his questions was for them, one by one, to tell him of their wishes and problems facing their people.

When their turn came to speak, the language of each headman was plain and practical, and their allusions and illustrations were truly eloquent and appropriate. In speaking, they expressed their sentiments as only Navajo orators are capable.

"This is the best place for us we know of outside of our country. We want to go back to that country. We have done wrong but we have learned better and if allowed to return to our mountain homes, we will behave ourselves well.

"If the government wants us to remain here we will do so and do the best we can — but we cannot be as contented as we would be in our old homes — we shall think of them — we all do think of them. There is something within us which does not speak but thinks — and though we remain silent, our faces speak to each other.

"Cage the badger and he will try to break from his prison and regain his native hole. Chain the eagle to the ground — he will strive to gain his freedom, and though he fails, he will lift his head and look up to the sky which is home — and we want to return to our mountains and plains, where we used to plant corn, wheat and beans."[3]

Although Special Agent Graves' report conceded that General Carleton's policy was having an "excellent effect," it suggested that the government should, once and for all, put an end to the quarrels among civil and military authorities in New Mexico. It must decide whether or not Navajos were going to be permanently retained at Bosque Redondo, and provide the necessary appropriations to adequately care for them. The existing jurisdiction — rationed by the army, and clothed by the $100,000 annually appropriated by Congress — only created animosities between the two branches of government. Graves felt that either the Navajos should be supported and educated by the military, or they should be turned over to civil authorities.[4]

Despite Graves' suggestions the controversy appeared as if it would never be resolved. Few men dared to attack Carleton and his death-like grip over the territory. Doctor Michael Steck had grown tired of matching wits, and resigned as Superintendent of Indian Affairs on May 1, 1865, as he stated — "for the good of the service."[5] Felipe Delgado filled the remainder of Steck's term until replaced by the appointment of A. Baldwin Norton, of Ohio, on February 17, 1866.[6]

Embracing the views of Steck, this new superintendent fought for removal of Navajos from Bosque Redondo. He had only to give that reservation a cusory inspection before prophesying that the whole experiment would prove a failure, for as he reported, "the soil is cold, and the alkali in the water destroys it."[7]

Since dismissal of Lorenzo Labadie there had not been a resident agent at Fort Sumner. The years 1865-66, however, marked the beginning of new management for the New Mexico Superintendency. When the Doolittle Committee arrived in the territory, it brought to the Navajos another agent. As an ex-military man and veteran of the Civil War in New Mexico, Colonel Theodore H. Dodd, was very acceptable to General Carleton; and ironically enough, he would soon prove to be a tireless administrator and a valuable friend to the Navajos.

Although Dodd obtained his appointment as Indian agent during the summer of 1865, it was not until May of the following year that he received his official commission from President Andrew Johnson.[8] While the Joint Committee was holding its investigations, Dodd was carefully examining the needs of his charges. On September 9 he submitted, in person, to the Department of the Interior in Washington, a comprehensive list of farming implements which he thought the tribe desperately needed for the next planting season.[9] Knowing that all previous crops had failed at Bosque Redondo, Dodd urged as early a planting as possible — to avoid "plant destruction by insects." He requested the Department of the Interior to purchase and ship immediately to Bosque Redondo the following tools, so that a wheat crop could be sown in February:

25	breaking-up plows	1000	handles for same
1	threshing machine	50	first class ox yokes
1	reaper	150	sets ox bows
1	doz. cradles	2	portable grist mills
200	pick axes	100	pitch forks
300	long handled shovels	5	farming mills
300	spades	2	sets blacksmith tools
50	strong rakes	2	doz. sheep shears
500	strong hoes	4	gross wool cards

In addition to the above list of agricultural implements, Dodd suggested purchase of the usual quantity of Indian goods, which included:

Blankets (red and blue)	Butcher knives
bayeta cloth	vermilion & indigo
buttons (bell)	brass wire
cotton (spools)	tin pans & cups
needles & thimbles	hickory shirts
calicos & plaids	coats
awls & awl handles	wool hats
mirrors	shoes
tacks	tacking & drilling[10]

Having obtained congressional approval for purchase of Indian goods, Agent Dodd proceeded from Washington to St. Louis, where he received a letter of credit from J. K. Graves with which he would be permitted to barter for the much needed supplies.[11] After assembling the implements, clothing, as well as fifty yoke of cattle to haul the supplies to New Mexico, Dodd left to take up his duties at Bosque Redondo.

Reaching his destination, Agent Theodore Dodd moved into the adobe quarters formerly used by Lorenzo Labadie.

However, the wretched two rooms constituting the agency, soon proved inadequate for both administrative and storage needs. But Dodd detailed Navajos to repair the old structure, and soon a new room, 20 by 60 feet, was added. With wood hauled from the Captain Mountains — a distance of 100 miles — a sixty square foot corral was also erected, as well as a fence enclosing ten acres adjoining the agency.[12]

Regardless of the new agent's boundless energy, tragedy struck the Navajos a third time. The 1866 crops failed miserably. The 2,500 depleted, alkali impregnated acres of the government farm produced little over 3,000 bushels of corn; and again the bulk of Indian food would have to come from army subsistence stores, which would amount to $582,513 for a nine months period.[13] Failure of the army superintended government farm convinced Dodd that other measures would have to be pursued, if a crop were going to be raised at all. He advocated reducing acreage of the military controlled farm to a mere 1,500 to 2,000 acres, and letting Navajos farm remaining land by their age-old, tried and proven techniques of planting. "Give an Indian a piece of land as his own," believed Dodd, "and implements to work it, and seeds to plant, and he will go to work with a will, and raise good crops."[14]

By now, however, Navajos had little incentive to cultivate the soil at Bosque Redondo. They had experienced one failure after another. The brackish water they drank brought dysentery; and the garrison infected them with syphilis and gonorrhea.[15] Balking at the twelve hour a day labor, Navajos had to be forced to work at bayonet point throughout the early months of 1867.

During March Dodd also had a good many Indians at work constructing a new *acequia*, which commenced near the issue house and ran along the Pecos, parallel to the adjacent hills. By April 1 this ditch was complete and ran for three miles, enabling Navajos to cultivate several hundred acres more.[16] However, the efforts of Dodd and his Navajos were wasted. That year would also prove to be as disastrous as all the others. The Pecos River shriveled to a mere trickle, and planting grounds parched and cracked under intense summer sun. Whatever crops survived were destroyed before harvest time by severe hail storms.[17]

Added to the multitude of problems threatening inevitable destruction to the reservation, was that of scarcity of fuel. Procurement of adequate quantities of wood had always been a headache to the military. The reservation, situated on the edge of a treeless expanse of prairie, quickly depleted fuel close at hand. Resources of cedar and mesquite retreated farther and farther from Bosque Redondo — until Navajos were traveling twelve to twenty miles for mesquite root, which they carried "upon their galled and lacerated backs." The garrison also suffered for want of wood. Fuel was being gathered by details sent as far as forty to fifty miles — and at a cost of over $75,000 per year. Timber and lumber for building purposes were transported from the Captain Mountains, as well as from the vicinity of Fort Union — a distance of over 100 miles by the shortest route.[18]

X X X

The plight of Navajos at Bosque Redondo could no longer be ignored. Try as it might, the army could not hide the fact that this reservation was little more than a concentration camp. Following the Doolittle Committee's return to Washington, the wheels of government began slowly to turn. Secretary of the Interior James Harlan, requested the Secretary of War to present reports of subsistence costs at the Bosque Redondo for study by the Joint Committee on Indian Affairs. The Department of Interior was at last waking up to its responsibilities. On December 16, 1865, Harlan informed the Secretary of War that his department "would cheerfully undertake the duty of supplying these Indians as soon as Congress shall provide the necessary means."[19]

Even before Harlan made this request, the army had taken steps toward assembling data so necessary for relinquishment of its control over the reservation. Two months previous, Carleton, though somewhat hesitantly, had issued orders authorizing preparation of an exact inventory of all equipment, livestock, and produce at the Navajo and Apache farms.[20] By December 27 this report was on its way to Secretary of War Stanton; and by January 31 it was before James Harlan. These inventories and receipts of issue revealed the tremendous costs at which Navajos were being sustained. For an eighteen month period (March 1, 1864 to October 1, 1865) $1,114,981.70 had been expended to feed the Indians alone.[21]

After carefully studying these papers, Harlan passed them on to Commissioner of Indian Affairs D. N. Cooley, for any consideration and recommendations which the latter might wish to make to the congressional committee. Harlan also requested Cooley to prepare an estimate of necessary appropriations for care of the Navajos during fiscal year 1866-67; and to report upon it to the Department of the Interior.[22]

In New Mexico, General James H. Carleton realized that a very definite move was now under way to place the Bosque Redondo reservation under exclusive control of the Department of the Interior. Such a move would signal the complete defeat of his "Indian policy." On February 11, 1866, Carleton wrote to the adjutant general of the army, pleading for continued army patronage of the reservation, and expressing fears of the consequences which might ensue if Navajos were placed under civil control:

> I beg to express the opinion that the whole of this matter of purchasing food etc., for the Indians, and of issuing the articles thus purchased to the Indians, as well as the direction of their labor, until they are more civilized be left in the hands of the War Department. I know and have so

written, that to do this will impose a burden upon the military not properly belonging to them . . ., but experience and observation compel me to say that if this matter passes out of the hands which hold the power there will be complications, embarrassment, misunderstanding, etc., which will result, I fear in great injury to, if not in the positive failure of the important measure of fixing forever the Navajo tribe of Indians upon a reservation.[23]

However, the matter was now out of General Carleton's hands. In fact, his career as commander of the Department of New Mexico was also fast approaching an end. During fall of 1865 New Mexican politicans were actively campaigning to obtain Carleton's removal. Expert in Machiavellistic art, the anti-Carleton faction maneuvered their fight into the Territorial Assembly of 1865-1866. Although it could do nothing directly to obtain the general's removal, the assembly could hope to accelerate it by resorting to the traditional New Mexican custom of adopting a memorial, professing to reflect the people's sentiments. As the Carleton controversy gained momentum, routine legislative matters became secondary. After much debate and possibly some bribery, the memorial was finally adopted on January 21, 1866, by a vote of 9 to 2 in the Council, and 20 to 4 in the House. The document was personally addressed to President Andrew Johnson, and urged "that a more capable officer be sent to command the troops immediately." The memorial stated that Carleton had failed in all attempts to subdue the Indians; and that the large military forces stationed throughout the territory were providing a lucrative business for army contractors and sutlers. The legislators also charged that Carleton, instead of pursuing Indian raiders as was his duty, had actually blamed depredations upon New Mexicans.

The legislative memorial did its job. On September 19, 1866, the Secretary of War directed the commander of the Department of the Missouri to relieve James H. Carleton from duty in New Mexico and order him to report to duty with his regiment (the Fourth Cavalry) in the Department of the Gulf. When word of the Secretary of War's action reached New Mexico, the Santa Fe *New Mexican* tersely heralded the commander's leaving:

> It thus appears that our territory will be relieved from the presence of this man Carleton, who has so long lorded it amongst us. For five years or more he has been in supreme command in New Mexico, and during that whole time, has accomplished nothing for which he is entitled to the thanks or gratitude of our people, or the confidence of the War Department.[24]

Close upon the heels of Carleton's transfer came the first official steps toward lifting the yoke of military suppression from the Navajos. On December 31 General U. S. Grant authorized issuance of Special Orders Number 651, directing the commander of the Department of the Missouri to give "immediate orders to turn over the control of the Navajo Indians . . . to such agent of the Indian Department as may be . . . designated to receive and take charge of them."[25] In accordance with General Grant's dictum another order was issued twelve days later which reiterated the instructions, and listed additional ones preparatory to relinquishment of military control. An "accurate detailed inventory," or census, would first be taken of all Navajo captives. The commander of the Department of New Mexico was instructed to give whatever military assistance to the Indian agent as may be deemed necessary — "but without going beyond the strict duties and administration of the military service, or interfering with . . . the Indian Department." Finally, authority was granted the Indian Department to make requisitions upon army subsistence and quartermaster departments for feeding the Navajos.[26]

Although orders authorizing transfer of the Navajo reservation to civil control had been made public, Superintendent A. Baldwin Norton had not received definite instructions from his superiors in Washington. The Bosque Redondo reservation was once again hopelessly snarled in government red tape. Superintendent Norton and Agent Dodd were completely and helplessly in the dark as to their duties. They could not assume the responsibility of caring for over 7,000 Indians until concrete instructions came through. To make matters worse, adequate appropriations for subsisting these Indians had not been passed by Congress for the fiscal year of 1867-68. Only the usual $100,000 had been approved — scarcely enough to feed 7,400 Navajos. Dodd saw only disaster in the congressional oversight. "The idea of trying to subsist them (7,400 Navajos) for one year for $100,000 is ridiculous. It cannot be done for less than $400,000," wrote the agent. "The government must either continue to feed them or turn them loose. . . . If turned loose to roam over the territory, they will again commence stealing from the flocks of their old enemies. . . . and another Navajo war will be the result, which will cost the government millions of money. . . ."[27]

While politicians and military officials dragged their heels in Washington, the Navajos continued to suffer upon their wretched reservation. Their sheep had dwindled to less than a thousand; and Comanches had driven off most of their horses and mules. The plight of the Navajos was desperate, and their discontented murmurings were loud. During July, Superintendent Norton journeyed to Fort Sumner to listen to their complaints. In council with Navajo leaders, he naively asked if they were satisfied with their reservation. As principal chief, Herrero eloquently confirmed what the superintendent already innately suspected.

"We want to have the herds we had before we left our old country. And, here we are hungry sometimes. We understand this was Comanche country, and their land. We are afraid our enemies will come here and steal our stock. We think the Comanches think this is their country and land, and they . . . have a right to come here and kill us and take our stock . . . The Comanches told me the land belongs to them. The water belonged to them. The hunting grounds belonged to them. The wood belonged to them. And I believe it now, because they (the Comanches) come here everyday and steal our stock. I think when our young men go out after wood, they won't come back again . . ., because our enemies are all around us.

"I am thinking more about my old country than ever before, because there I could secure myself from my enemies; here we have not that chance . . . We are all the time thinking of our old country, and we believe if the government will put us back, they could have us the same there as here.

"Notwithstanding the cold and heat we have worked and we will work, but poor as we are we would rather go back to our country. What does the government want us to do — more than we have done? Or more than we are doing?

"I think the world, the earth, and in the heavens we are all equal and we have all been born by the same mother — what we want is to be sent back to our own country. Even if we starve there, we will have no complaints to make."[28]

A week after these poetical words were uttered, the Department of the Interior finally acted. On July 24 the Commissioner of Indian Affairs informed Superintendent Norton that control of the Navajo Indians would be assumed as of September 1. This news was quickly relayed to Dodd, who at the same time was authorized to appraise the agricultural implements, working stock and Indian goods at the reservation. A contract for feeding the Navajos was awarded to a one Elizah Simerly, and would commence on date of transfer.[29] All seemed ready — providing the army was.

A. Baldwin Norton, however, was not sure that all was ready for assumption of control by the Department of the Interior. On August 21 he wrote to the new commander of the Department of New Mexico, General G. W. Getty, asking if the commander of Fort Sumner had been authorized to transfer the Navajos to Theodore Dodd. Norton was stunned when he learned from Getty that "no such order had been received or issued."[30]

Again the question of control over Bosque Redondo was being bantered around by both army and civil leaders; and the orders for relinquishment of control had been purposely held up. It had been eight months since the issuance of Special Orders Number 651. The slowness of the army was deliberate. The Department of War demanded one more investigation of the Navajo situation, and the task was assigned to Lieutenant R. McDonald, of the Fifth Cavalry. His report, completed on November 12, 1867, again revealed conditions as they actually were. Without mincing words, McDonald recommended Navajos be removed "to a suitable location, where wood, water and grass abound." When the report reached Washington, however, the debate focused upon the two words — "suitable location." Commander of the Department of the Missouri, General William Tecumseh Sherman, had suggested locating Navajos in Indian Territory, east of the 98th parallel; in fact, this latter proposal was under serious consideration when McDonald was carrying out his investigations. The Office of Indian Affairs had long known the views of its officials in New Mexico, as well as those of the Territorial Assembly. Both the Secretary of the Interior and the Commissioner of Indian Affairs looked favorably upon returning Navajos to their old country. By end of October 1867, the question had been resolved. The Indians would at last be transferred to civil control — and they would remain in New Mexico.

It had always been customary to count Navajos on the last day of each month, and it was therefore decided to turn them over to Agent Dodd on October 31 to prevent any alarm.[31] The civil control of the Bosque Redondo reservation would, however, be short-lived. Only one month passed before Agent Dodd recommended to the superintendent that "no more money be expended in building or permanent improvement upon the reservation, as . . . the government will be compelled to abandon the reservation at an early date." Dodd then suggested that a commission be appointed to carefully examine the Navajo's old country — "there to select land, with water, wood, and other resources for a permanent reservation."[32]

Dodd's suggestions were destined to come true — and very soon. The past year had been an exceedingly troublous one for Indian affairs. The Plains tribes were again at war. Both the army and the Office of Indian Affairs had endeavored to quell this turmoil through a series of military campaigns and treaty negotiations. A Peace Commission had been organized during summer of 1867, and was composed of Senators J. B. Henderson, John B. Sanborn and Samuel Tappan; Generals W. T. Sherman, Alfred H. Terry, William S. Harney and C. C. Auger; and the chairman of the commission was Commissioner of Indian Affairs N. G. Taylor. Together, these men attempted to revolutionize the Indian service, as well as iron out many of the squabbles existing between red and white men.

The Peace Commission bitterly criticized the existing administration of Indian Affairs. It saw rampant corruption within the service, and requested Congress to relieve all agents and special agents from duty by February 1, 1869 — "and replace them with new men of reputable character and integrity." A revision of intercourse laws was urged; and the commission concluded that the practice, which had so long prevailed, of appointing governors as *ex-officio* superintendents was detrimental to Indian affairs; and it was urged that no more legislators be permitted to fill these positions. State and territorial governing bodies would no longer be permitted to call upon militia during Indian uprisings, and all regulations governing Indian trade would be placed under stringent control. The military would be vested with authority to eject, by force, all traders and intruders found upon Indian lands. And finally, a treaty with the Navajos of New Mexico was urged.[33]

Lieutenant General William T. Sherman and Colonel Samuel F. Tappan were the peace commissioners appointed to negotiate this Navajo treaty. They arrived at Fort Sumner on May 28 and immediately commenced an investigation of the reservation. For two days they observed the miserable conditions at Bosque Redondo. During that time, Navajo headmen succeeded in convincing the commissioners that their people were unalterably opposed to being moved to any place other than their old country. The Navajos, starving, diseased and homesick, were willing to agree to anything, so long as they would be granted their one desire. By June 1, 1868 — three days after Sherman and Tappan arrived at Bosque Redondo — a treaty had been drafted and accepted by the Indians. The Diné would at once be allowed to leave this reservation and return to a new one — in their beloved redrock country.[34]

The Navajos at Bosque Redondo were destitute of all sustaining essentials. They had only 1,550 horses, 20 mules, 950 sheep and 1,025 goats.[35] These proud pastoral people, who were once credited with the possession of a quarter million sheep and sixty thousand horses, had lost everything. They had indeed been humbled. Sherman and Tappan could not let them return in this pitiful condition. They agreed, on behalf of the government, that the tribe should be alloted $150,000 for rehabilitation, and 15,000 sheep, and goats, as well as 500 cattle would be furnished. Every Indian would annually receive a token payment of five dollars; and those tribesmen planting crops were promised ten dollars.

Within two weeks of treaty signing, the Navajos were ready to return to the land of their forefathers. At dawn, on

June 18, 1868, a column, ten miles long, left Fort Sumner under escort of four companies of cavalry. The long line with its fifty wagons and a multitude of women and children moved slowly, covering only ten to twelve miles a day. Through Anton Chico and Cañon Blanco they marched; and on July 4 Tijeras Cañon, twelve miles east of Albuquerque, was reached. Next day the Navajos quietly, and without incident, passed through that town, and forded the Rio Grande on July 6. By end of the month the column had reached Fort Wingate.[36]

The pitiful remnants of the once "Lords of New Mexico" had returned to their picturesque domain, where they have remained ever since in comparative harmony with surrounding tribes and the white men — who still cast covetuous glances at their scenic and rich lands, as well as at their comely women.

⚔ ⚔ ⚔

1. The other portion of this Joint Committee consisted of Messrs. Nesmith and Higby, who were assigned the states of California, Oregon and Nevada, as well as the territories of Washington, Idaho and Montana. To Messrs. Windom and Hubbard, who constituted the other portion of the committee, went the state of Minnesota, and the territories of Nebraska, Dakota, and upper Montana.

2. Report of Special Agent J. K. Graves in *Annual Report of Commissioner of Indian Affairs, 1866*, p. 123.

3. Report of Graves' council Navajos (dated December 31, 1865); *Superintendency Papers*, LR.

4. *Annual Report of Commissioner of Indian Affairs, 1866*, p. 31.

5. Keleher, *Turmoil in New Mexico*, pp 506-7.

6. Commission of A. B. Norton (dated February 17, 1866); in *Superintendency Papers*, LR.

7. *Annual Report of Commission of Indian Affairs, 1867*, p. 190.

8. *Condition of Tribes, p. 233*. W. P. Clark to D. Cooley, May 18, 1866, *Superintendency Papers*, LR.

9. As usual, congressional appropriations were slow reaching New Mexico; and Carleton therefore advised Dodd, in early August, to go to Washington and personally see to the purchase of Indian goods. *Condition of Tribes*, p. 233.

10. Dodd to Department of Interior, September 9, 1865; *Superintendency Papers,* LR.

11. Graves to R. B. Van Valkenburgh, September 12, 1865; *ibid.*

12. *Annual Report of Commissioner of Indian Affairs, 1867,* p. 200.

13. Report of Lt. Robert McDonald, A.C.S., Fort Sumner (n.d.); *Department of New Mexico,* LR.

14. *Annual Report of Commissioner of Indian Affairs, 1867,* p. 202.

15. Medical officer, Capt. M. Hillary, reported that cases of syphilis far outnumbered those of all other diseases. He added that this "will always be the case as long as so many soldiers are around . . ., because the Indian women have not the slightest idea of virtue . . ." Although hospital facilities were available to the Indians, they preferred their own medicine men, for they feared the hospitals because death stalked there. As one headman remarked, "but few [Navajos] go there even if sick — the medicine kills them. They are afraid of it. We prefer our own medicine men. They don't kill if they cannot cure."
It was little wonder Navajos felt this way. When Captain Hillary assumed his duties in November 1865, he found the Indian hospital to consist of nine small rooms, measuring 15 by 16 feet; two rooms of which were occupied as surgery, kitchen, and two as attendant rooms, leaving five for sick wards. The building, reported Hillary, "is a regular tumble-down concern; even rain comes through the roof — in fact . . ., the place is only fit to keep pigs in." *Annual Report of Commissioner of Indian Affairs, 1866,* p. 150; also Norton to Taylor, September 21, 1867; *Superintendency Papers,* LR. For list of cases treated in Navajo hospital consult: National Archives, Records of War Department, *Office of Adjutant General,* Record Group 94, U.S. Army Hospital Department Registers, Vol. 50 and 52, Fort Stanton, N. M., 1862-67. Fort Sumner is included with those of Fort Stanton.

16. Dodd to Norton, April 2, 1867; *Superintency Papers,* LR.

17. *Annual Report of Commissioner of Indian Affairs, 1868,* p. 165.

18. *Ibid.,* 1867, pp. 190, 201.

19. Harlan to Doolittle, December 18, 1865; *Superintendency Papers,* LR.

20. Special Orders No. 5 (dated October 8, 1865); *Department of New Mexico,* LR.

21. For report of subsistence costs see: Report of Maj. C. H. DeForrest (dated 5, 1866); and A. B. Eaton to Stanton, December 27, 1865; and A. E. Shivas to Doolittle, December 28, 1865; all in *Superintendency Papers,* LR.

22. Harlan to Cooley, March 13, 1866; *ibid.,* LR.

23. Carleton to Thomas, February 11,1866; *Office of Adjutant General,* LR. Also *ibid.*

24. Santa Fe *New Mexican,* October 27, 1866.

25. Special Orders No. 651 (dated December 31, 1866); *Superintendency Papers,* LR.

26. Special Orders No. 10 (dated January 12, 1867); *ibid.*

27. Dodd to Norton, April 6, 1867; *ibid.*

28. Report of proceedings of a Council held with Navajos at Bosque Redondo (June 15, 1867) by A. B. Norton; in *ibid.*

29. Commissioner to Norton, July 24, 1867; Norton to Dodd, August 12, 1867; *Superintendency Records.*

30. Getty to Norton, August 22, 1867; *ibid.,* Miscelleaneous papers.

31. Getty to Norton, October 3, 1867; *Superintendency Papers,* LR.

32. Dodd to Norton, December 7, 1867; *ibid.*

33. Edward Dale, *The Indians of the Southwest* (Norman: 1951), pp. 43-44, 60-61.

34. See Kappler, *Laws & Treaties,* pp. 583-584; and Keleher, *Turmoil in New Mexico,* p. 464-468.

35. *Annual Report of Commissioner of Indian Affairs,* 1868, p. 165.

36. Dodd to Commissioner Webb, August 5, 1868; *Superintendency Papers;* also Getty to Capt. G. W. Bradley, May 31, 1868; *Department of New Mexico,* LR.

BIBLIOGRAPHY

ARCHIVAL COLLECTIONS

U. S. National Archives, War Records Division and Indian Affairs Records Division

Fort Canby Post Returns, 1864, Record Group 94.

Fort Craig Post Returns, 1864-68; Record Group 94.

Fort Defiance Post Returns, 1851-1861, Record Group 94.

Fort Fauntleroy Post Returns, 1860-61, Record Group 94.

Fort Lyon Post Returns, 1862, Record Group 94.

Records of the Office of Adjutant General, Record Group 94, Letters Received from Department of New Mexico, 1846-70.

Records of the Office of the Adjutant General, Record Group 94, U. S. Army Hospital Department Registers, Vols. 50 and 52, Fort Stanton and Fort Sumner, 1862-67.

Records of the Office of Quartermaster General, Record Group 92, Consolidated Correspondence File Relating to Fort Defiance.

Records of the Office of Quartermaster General, Record Group 92, Consolidated Correspondence File Relating to Fort Sumner.

Records of U. S. Army Commands, Department of New Mexico, Record Group 98, Letters Received, 1846-70.

New Mexico Superintendency of Indian Affairs Papers, Record Group 75, Letters Received, 1849-1880.
New Mexico Superintendency of Indian Affairs, Record Group 75, Letters Received, 1849-80.
U. S. National Archives, State Department Record Division State Department Territorial Papers, New Mexico, 1851-1860, Micro. Roll T-17.

OTHER ARCHIVAL COLLECTIONS

Haile, Berard. Collection of Ethnologic Notes pertaining to the Navajo Indians, University of Arizona, Special Collections Department, Tucson.

Hayden, Carl. Biographical Collection of Arizona Pioneers, Arizona Pioneers' Historical Society, Tucson.

Holliday Collection, Arizona Pioneers' Historical Society, Tucson.

Munk Collection, Southwest Museum, Highland Park, California.

Navajo Land Claims Files, Land Claims Office, Navajo Tribe, Window Rock, Arizona.

Pioneers' Biographical Collection, Arizona Pioneers' Historical Society, Tucson.

Ritch, William G. Collection, Huntington Library, San Marino, California.

Van Valkenburgh, Richard. Collection of Ethnological and Historical Notes, Arizona Pioneers' Historical Society, Tucson.

NEWSPAPERS

Albuquerque *Rio Abajo Weekly Press*, 1863-64.
Gallpu *Gazette*, August 18, 1939.
New Orleans *Picuyne*, June 19, 1850.
St. Louis *Republican*, 1846-48.
Salt Lake City *Valley Tan*, 1858-60.
Salt Lake City *Valley Tan*, 1858-1860.

San Francisco *Alta California,* 1850-70.
Santa Fe *Republican,* 1847-48.
Santa Fe *Weekly Gazette,* 1853-69.
Santa Fe *Weekly New Mexican,* 1849-71.
Tubac *Weekly Arizonan,* 1859.

DIRECTORIES, REPORTS, LETTERS, DIARIES, ETC.

Abel, Annie H. (comp. & ed.). *The Official Correspondence of James S. Calhoun While Indian Agent at Santa Fe and Superindentent of Indian Affairs in New Mexico.* Washing-Ton: 1915.

—————. (ed.). "Indian Affairs in New Mexico Under the Administration of William Carr Lane. From the Journal of John Ward," *New Mexico Historical Review.* April & July 1941.

Abert, J. W. *Report of Lt. J. W. Abert, of his Examination of New Mexico, in the Years 1846-47.* Washington: 1848.

Annual Report of Commissioners of Indian Affairs, 1849-70. Washington.

Appleton's Cyclopaedia of American Biography. New York: 1899-1900, 6 Vols.

Backus, Maj. Electus. "An Account of the Navajoes of New Mexico," *Indian Tribes of the United States,* edited by Henry Schoolcraft. Philadelphia: Lippincott, 1856, Vol. IV.

Bailey, L. R. *The Navajo Reconnaissance.* Los Angeles: Westernlore Press, 1964.

—————. *The A. B. Gray Report.* Los Angeles: Westernlore Press, 1963.

Bennett, James A. *Forts and Forays or A Dragoon in New Mexico,* 1850-56, edited by C. E. Brooks and F. D. Reeve. Albuquerque, University of New Mexico Press, 1948.

Bibo, Nathan. "Reminiscences of Early Days in New Mexico," Albuquerque *Evening Herald,* June 11, 1922.

Bloom, Lansing B. (ed). "The Rev. Hiram Walter Read, Baptist Missionary," *New Mexico Historical Review*. Vol. XVII, April 1942.

Brewerton, George D. "A Ride with Kit Carson Through the Great American Desert and the Rocky Mountains," *Harper's New Monthly Magazine*. August 1853.

Connelley, William E. *Doniphan's Expedition and the Conquest of New Mexico and California*. Topeka: 1907.

Cremony, John C. *Life Among the Apaches*. San Francisco: 1868.

Cullum, George W. *Biographical Register of the Officers and Graduates of the U. S. Military Academy*. Boston and New York: 1891, 2 Vols.

Davis, W. W. H. *El Gringo: Or New Mexico and Her People*. Santa Fe: Rydal Press, 1938.

Dictionary of American Biography. New York: 1928-44, 20 Vols.

Donaldson, Thomas. *Moqui Pueblo Indians of Arizona and Pueblo Indians of New Mexico*. Washington: Census Office, 1893.

Eaton, Lt. Col. J. H. "Description of the True State and Character of the New Mexican Tribes," *Indian Tribes of the United States*, edited by Henry R. Schoolcraft. Philadelphia: Lippincott, 1856, Vol. IV.

Edwards, Marcellus B. *Marching with the Army of the West 1846-48*, edited by Ralph P. Bieber. Glendale: Arthur H. Clark, 1936.

Emory, W. H. *Notes of a Military Reconnaissance, from Fort Leavenworth, in Missouri, to San Diego, in California . . .* New York: 1848.

Ferguson, Philip G. *Marching with the Army of the West*, edited by Ralph P. Bieder. Glendale: Arthur H. Clark, 1936.

Gibson, George R. *Journal of a Soldier Under Kearny and Doniphan,* edited by Ralph P. Bieber. Glendale: Arthur H. Clark, 1935.

Gregory, Herbert E. *The Navajo Country, a Geographic and Hydrographic Reconnaissance of Parts of Arizona, New Mexico and Utah.* Washington: 1916.

Greiner, John. "Private Letters of a Government Official in the Southwest," *The Journal of American History.* Vol. III, 1919.

Gwyther, George. "An Indian Reservation," *Overland Monthly.* Vol. X, January 1873.

Heitman, F. B. *Historical Register of the United States Army.* Washington: 1890, 3 Vols.

Hodge, Frederick W. *Handbook of American Indians North of Mexico.* New York: Pageant Books, 1960, 2 Vols.

Hughes, John T. *Doniphan's Expedition; Containing an Account of the Conquest of New Mexico.* Cincinnati: 1847.

Jones, Daniel W. *Forty Years Among the Indians.* Los Angeles: Westernlore Press, 1960.

Kappler, Charles J. (comp. & ed). *Indian Affairs; Laws and Treaties.* Washington: 1904, 3 Vols.

Letterman, Jonathan. "Sketch of the Navajo Tribe of Indians," *Smithsonian Report, 1855.* Washington: 1855.

Lindgren, Raymond E. (ed). "A Diary of Kit Carson's Navaho Campaign, 1863-1864," *New Mexico Historical Review.* Vol. XXI, July 1946.

Meline, James F. *Two Thousand Miles on Horseback.* New York: American News Co., 1873.

Mansfield, Joseph. *Report to the Secretary of War on Military Posts in Texas and New Mexico Territory* ... Washington: 1853.

Marino, C. C. "The Seboyetanos and the Navahos," *New Mexico Historical Review.* Vol. XXIX, January 1954.

Palmer, William R. "Pahute Indian Government & Laws," *UtahHistorical Quarterly.* April 1929.

"Reminiscences of Fort Defiance, New Mexico, 1860," *Journal of the Military Service Institution of the U. S.* Vol. IV, 1883.

Robinson, Jacob S. *A Journal of the Santa Fe Expedition Under Colonel Doniphan.* Princeton: Princeton University Press, 1932.

Royce, Charles C. (comp.). "Indian Land Cessions in the United States," *18the Annual Report of the Bureau of American Ethnology.* Washington: 1897, Part II.

Simpson, James H. *Journal of a Military Reconnaissance, from Santa Fe to the Navajo Country.* Philadelphia: Lippincott, Grambo & Co., 1852.

Sitgreaves, Capt. L. *Report of an Expedition Down the Zuñi and Colorado Rivers.* Washington: Armstrong, 1853.

U. S. Army. *Revised Regulations, 1863.* Washington: 1863.

U. S. *Congressional Globe.* Washington: 1866-67, Appendix, 238.

U. S., 29th Congress, 2nd Session, *House Executive Document.* No. 19.

U. S. 31st Congress 1st Session, *House Executive Document,* Vol. XVII.

U. S. 32nd Congress, 2nd Session, *House Executive Document.* Vol. I, Part II.

U. S. 33rd Congress, 1st Session, *House Executive Document.* Vol. I.

U. S. 34th Congress, 3rd Session, *House Executive Document.* Vol. I, Parts II and III.

U. S. 35th Congress, 1st Session, *House Executive Document.* Vol. XIII.

U. S. 35th Congress, 2nd Session, *House Executive Document.* Vol. II, Part II.

U. S. 38th Congress, 1st Session, *House Executive Document.* No. 70.

U. S. 40th Congress, 2nd Session, *House Executive Documents.* Vol. XIX.

U. S. 40th Congress, 2nd Session, *House Executive Documents.* Nos. 97, 185, 248 and 308.

U. S. Joint Special Committee on Indian Affairs. *Condition of the Tribes.* Washington: 1867.

U. S. 30th Congress, 1st Session, *Senate Executive Document.* Vol. I.

U. S. 31st Congress, 1st Session, *Senate Executive Document.* Vols. I and II.

U. S. 31st Congress, 2nd Sesssion, *Senate Executive Document.* No. 26.

U. S. 32nd Congress, 1st Session, *Senate Executive Document.* Vol. I.

U. S. 33rd Congress, 2nd Session, *Senate Executive Document.* No. 78.

U. S. 36th Congress, 1st Session, *Senate Executive Document.* Vol. II, Part II.

U. S. 36th Congress, 2nd Session, *Senate Executive Document.* Vol. I.

U. S. 40th Congress, 1st Session, *Senate Executive Document.* Vol. XII.

War of the Rebellion: Official Records of the Union and Confederate Armies. Washington: 1891-96.

White, W. J. H. *Medical Topography and Disease of Fort Defiance.* Washington: 1856.

BOOKS, MONOGRAPHS, ARTICLES, ETC.

Amsden, Charles. "The Navaho Exile at Bosque Redondo," *New Mexico Historical Review.* Vol. VIII, January 1933.

Arrott, James W. *A Brief History of Fort Union.* Las Vegas: Highlands University, 1962.

Bailey, L. R. "Thomas Varker Keam: Tusayan Trader," *Arizoniana.* Vol. II, Winter 1961.

——————. "The Captive Wars: Slave Taking as a Source of the Navajo Wars, 1846-68," *The Brand Book.* Los Angeles: Corral of Westerners, 1963.

Bancroft, Hubert H. *History of Arizona and New Mexico.* San Francisco: The History Co., 1890.

Bender, A. B. "Frontier Defense in the Territory of New Mexico, 1846-53," *New Mexico Historical Review.* Vol. IX, July and October1934.

Boyce, George A. and Fryer, E. R. *Dineh and Government in Kaibeto District.* Window Rock: 1939.

Dale, Edward E. *The Indians of the Southwest.* Norman: University of Oklahoma, 1949.

Dunn, J. P. *Massacres of the Mountains: A History of the Indian Wars of the Far West.* New York: Harpers, 1886.

Franciscan Fathers. *An Ethnologic Dictionary of the Navaho Language.* Saint Michaeils: 1910.

Haile, Berard. "Navaho Chantways and Ceremonials," *American Anthropologist.* October-December 1938.

Hill, W. W. "Navaho Warfare," *Yale University Publications in Anthropology.* New Haven, 1936, No. V.

—————. "Some Aspects of Navajo Political Structure," *Plateau.* Vol. XIII, No. 2.

—————. *The Agricultural and Hunting Methods of the Navajo Indians.* New Haven: Yale University Press, 1938.

Hunt, Aurora. *Major General James H. Carleton.* Glendale: Arthur H. Clark Co., 1958.

Keleher, William A. *Turmoil in New Mexico.* Santa Fe: Rydal Press, 1951.

Kerby, Robert L. *The Confederate Invasion of New Mexico and Arizona.* Los Angeles: Westernlore Press, 1958.

Kluchohn, Clyde and Dorothea Leighton. *The Navaho.* Cambridge: Harvard University Press, 1946.

Lipps, Oscar H. *The Navajos.* Cedar Rapids: Torch Press, 1909. Luomala, Katharine. *Navaho Life of Yesterday and Today.* Berkeley: Department of Interior, 1938.

McNitt, Frank. *The Indian Traders.* Norman: University of Oklahoma Press, 1962.

Mangiante, Rosal. *History of Fort Defiance, 1851-1900*. Unpublished Master's thesis, University of Arizona, Tucson, 1950.

Reeve, Frank C. "Federal Indian Policy in New Mexico, 1858-80," *New Mexico Historical Review*. Vol. XII, July 1937.

————. "The Federal Indian Policy in New Mexico," *New Mexico Historical Review*. Vol. XIII, January 1938.

————. "The Indian Policy in New Mexico," *New Mexico Historical Review*. Vol. XIII, July 1938.

————. "The Government and the Navaho, 1846-58," *New Mexico Historical Review*. Vol. XIV, January 1939.

————. "A Navaho Struggle for Land," *New Mexico Historical Review*. Vol. XXI, January 1946.

————. "Early Navaho Geography," *New Mexico Historical Review*. Vol. XXXI, October 1956.

Reichard, Gladys A. *Social Life of the Navajo Indians*. New York: Columbia University Press, 1929.

Rister, C. C. "Harmful Practices of Indian Traders of the Southwest, 1865-1876," *New Mexico Historical Review*. Vol. VI, July 1931.

Sabin, Edwin L. *Kit Carson Days, 1809-68: Adventures in the Path of Empire*. New York: 1935.

Sapir, Edward and Hoijer, Harry (eds.). *Navaho Texts*. Iowa City: Linquistic Society of America, 1942.

Tschopik, Harry, Jr. "Taboo as a Possible Factor in the Obsolescence of Navajo Pottery and Basketry," *American Anthropologist*. April-June 1938.

————. "Navaho Basketry: A Study of Cultural Change," *American Anthropologist*. July-September 1940.

Twitchell, Ralph E. *The Leading Facts of New Mexican History*. Cedar Rapids: Torch Press, 1912, 2 Vols.

Underhill, Ruth. *Here Come the Navaho!* Washington, Indian Service, 1953.

Van Valkenburgh, Richard. *Diné Bikéyah*. Window Rock: Department of Interior, 1941.

————. "Navajo Naataani," *The Kiva*. Vol. XIII, January 1948.

Waldrip, William I. "New Mexico During the Civil War," *New Mexico Historical Review*. Vol. XXVIII, July 1953.

————. "New Mexico During the Civil War," *New Mexico Historical Review*. Vol. XXVIII, October 1953.

Wallace, Edward S. *The Great Reconnaissance*. Boston: Little, Brown and Co., 1955.

Weber, Anselm. *The Navajo Indians; A Statement of Facts*. St. Michaels, 1914.

Widdison, Jerold G. "Historical Geography of the Middle Rio Puerco," *New Mexico Historical Review*. Vol. XXXIV, October 1959.

Woodward, Arthur. "Sidelights on Fifty Years of Apache Warfare," *Arizoniana*. Vol. II, Fall 1961.

————. *A Brief History of Navajo Silversmithing*. Flagstaff: Museum of Northern Arizona, 1946.

INDEX

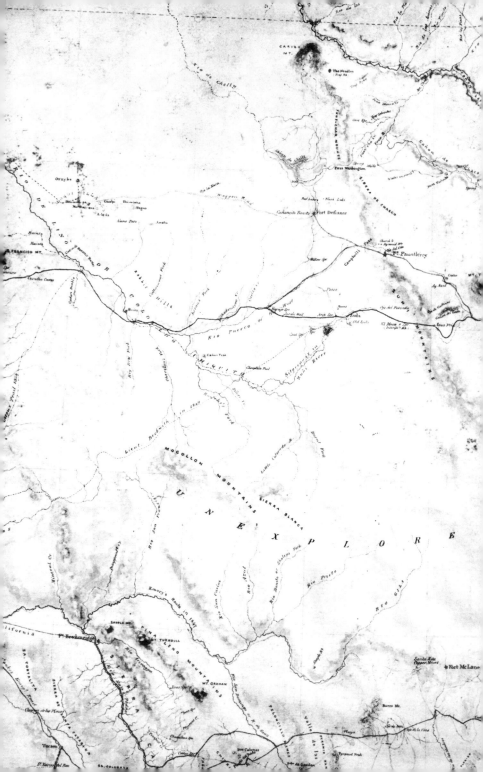